W9-BJV-150

Fidel *and* Religion

Castro Talks on Revolution and Religion with Frei Betto

*Translated by The Cuban Center for
Translation and Interpretation
Introduction by Harvey Cox*

A TOUCHSTONE BOOK
Published by Simon & Schuster Inc.
NEW YORK LONDON TORONTO SYDNEY TOKYO

First Touchstone Edition, 1988

Published by Simon & Schuster Inc.
Simon & Schuster Building
Rockefeller Center
1230 Avenue of the Americas
New York, New York 10020

Originally published in Cuba by the
Oficina de Publicaciones del Consejo de
Estado under the title *Fidel y la Religión*.

TOUCHSTONE and colophon are registered trademarks
of Simon & Schuster Inc.

Designed by Karolina Harris

Manufactured in the United States of America

10 9 8 7 6 5 4 3 2 1
10 9 8 7 6 5 4 3 2 1 Pbk.

Library of Congress Cataloging in Publication Data

Castro, Fidel, date.
    Fidel and religion.
    Translation of: *Fidel y la religión*, the Spanish edition of *Fidel e a religião*.
    1.Castro, Fidel, 1927–   —Interviews.
    2. Castro, Fidel, 1927–   —Religion.
    3. Church and state—Cuba. 4. Cuba—Church history.
    5. Heads of state—Cuba—Interviews. I. Betto,
    Frei, 1944–   II. Title.
    F1788.22.C3A5   1987   972.91'064'0924   87-4489

ISBN 0-671-64114-X
ISBN 0-671-66237-6 Pbk.

To Leonardo Boff—
priest; doctor; and, above all,
prophet.

To the memory of Friar Mateus Rocha,
who taught me the liberating dimension
of Christian faith and, as Provincial
of the Brazilian Dominicans, stimulated
this mission.

To all Latin American Christians
who, in the midst of lack of understanding
and in the blessedness of the thirst for justice,
are preparing, in the manner
of John the Baptist,
for the coming of the Lord in socialism.

Contents

Fidel *and* Religion

Introduction
by Harvey Cox

FIDEL CASTRO has never been noted for his diffidence. During the twenty-eight years the Comandante has ruled Cuba, he has entertained, instructed, informed and admonished his people with what must now add up to millions of words. Castro considers himself to be—among other things—a teacher of the Cuban masses. Indeed, had he not become the political leader of his homeland, he might have become a professor or a practicing lawyer. In either case, his vigorous style of presentation would have stood him in good stead. As it turned out, however, Fidel now seizes upon almost any opportunity to expound and declaim. He can turn any occasion into a bully pulpit. His audience may be a group of farmers gathered to harvest sugarcane, or a visiting delegation of journalists—or a gaggle of young men lounging around a makeshift basketball court. No matter what the forum, the Great Communicator of Cuba loses no opportunity to share his experience and ideas with those who will listen. And people do listen. Even his severest critics rarely suggest that Castro is boring. He may be accused of being long-winded or histrionic, but no one has ever claimed he is dull.

In this volume we are invited into a series of conversations Fidel carried on with a Brazilian priest, Frei Betto, on what is billed as "religion," but turns out in fact to be Christianity, mostly Catholic Christianity at that, since this is the religion he knows about or at least has thought a great deal about. Some might describe these discourses as "interviews," but the extensive questions and comments of the priest sometimes make the exchange read more like a conversation than a question-and-answer session. Apparently religion is a subject about which Mr. Castro is not the least reluctant to speak. He did not need to be prodded or stimulated. In fact, his willingness to talk about it at such length to Frei Betto makes one wonder why such a book has not appeared years ago. Between puffs on his sweet-smelling small cigars he seems to savor the subject much more than might be expected from a self-designated atheist. (Incidentally, I have been told that shortly after he completed these interviews Mr. Castro gave up smoking completely and has not had a cigar for more than a year, and that he has backed an effort to persuade young Cubans never to take up the filthy weed.)

In the course of the conversations, parts of which occurred in the wee hours of the morning, Castro muses about a wide variety of subjects, not just religion in the narrow sense. But this is just as well. Religion never exists in a vacuum, and therefore the portrait the Comandante paints of growing up in the Cuba of the thirties and forties (he was born August 13, 1926) grounds his comments in a colorful social and cultural setting. He reminisces about his boyhood on a small farm in Birán, in what was then called Oriente Province, where there was no church and no opportunity for religious instruction, and where the cattle, pigs and chickens were sheltered under the Galician-style stilted house. He fondly recollects his father, a Spanish soldier sent to Cuba to quell the rebellion of 1895, who liked the country so much he returned and settled there. The elder Castro started as an employee of United Fruit, but quickly became an independent entrepreneur and eventually a modestly wealthy man. But Castro's fondest memories are reserved for his mother, apparently a woman of simple but genuine piety who filled the house with images of Mary, Christ and the saints, and who prayed the rosary and the Lord's Prayer every day.

Later young Fidel was sent to an elementary school run by the Christian Brothers; then to a Jesuit junior high, the School of Our Lady of Sorrows in Santiago de Cuba; and following that to an elite Jesuit high school in Havana, the Colegio de Belén. Even today he admires his teachers for instilling certain virtues in him—the spirit of sacrifice, adventure, effort—and he describes the Jesuits as "...untouched by the profit motive" They were, he says, "austere, strict, self-sacrificing and hardworking...If they had been men who earned salaries and all that, the tuition wouldn't have been just 30 pesos." One wonders whether Castro's stern denunciation of the middlemen who appeared in Cuba after the legalization of free peasant markets in 1980 may be rooted in this early religious training. The values of the Revolution, he said, could never be based on money. They had to be built "on concepts, on ideas, on principles, and on certain moral values that people treasure."

But young Fidel was not fully satisfied with his Jesuit education. He criticizes the elitist composition of the student body and the reward-and-punishment view of morality he was taught. He wishes he'd been given a more reason-oriented approach to faith rather than the emphasis on willpower he associates with the Jesuits. It is amusing but not surprising that even as a young boy this man who loves to talk disliked intensely the silences the students had to maintain during school-sponsored religious retreats. He also hated the sermons on the fires of hell he had to sit through during these retreats, homilies that must have been similar to the one James Joyce re-creates in *A Portrait of the Artist as a Young Man*. Still, Castro concedes that his religious education did pique his fascination for philosophy and ethical theory, an interest this book demonstrates is still alive and well. Also, in a side remark that may stoke the slumbering fires in the breasts of those who still prefer to blame the Jesuits for all that has gone wrong in the Church recently, the Comandante says, "Undoubtedly, my teachers... clearly influenced me with their strict organization, their discipline and their values. They contributed to my development and influenced my sense of justice...."

Perhaps it is just as well that these sentences were not published a few years ago when Opus Dei and its supporters in the Catholic Church were blaming the Jesuits for corrupting the youth of South America—and elsewhere—with revolutionary ideas. But Castro also recalls that politically all his Jesuit teachers—he says without exception—were right-wing reactionaries and supporters of Franco. What the young Fidel apparently picked up from the warriors of Loyola's militia was their style, not their content.

Still, many people will wonder why any of this qualifies Castro to soliloquize for so long about religion, or—more pointedly—why anyone should be interested in what he has to say about it. Isn't he, after all, not just an atheist (as were Freud and Sartre, both of whom had some interesting things to say on the subject) but also a self-declared Marxist-Leninist? Is he not the Communist leader of a Communist country, and aren't Communists not just atheists but vehemently antireligious? Why indeed should anyone care what Castro has to say about a subject that, however dear it may be to the hearts of many Americans, is not something most care to learn anything about from him?

The answer is not entirely obvious. And an additional complicating fact is that this book appears at what is paradoxically both the best of times and the worst of times for such a disquisition by such a person. It is the best of times because in recent years the relationship of religion to politics in Latin America and more particularly the relationship of Christianity to revolutionary movements have loomed more prominently in the attention of the American public. There are a number of reasons for this, all signaled by events that have found their way into our newspapers and onto our television screens.

For example, just a few years ago Pope John Paul II made a widely publicized trip to Central America. During his pilgrimage he stopped in Guatemala and El Salvador, where dozens of priests and nuns and lay workers, including four American women, have been killed in the last decade by government and paramilitary groups that sometimes boasted they had killed these religious workers because they were either "Communists" or were working with them. While the pope was in El Salvador, he briefly visited the tomb of Archbishop Oscar Romero, who was shot through the heart while saying Mass, probably by an anti-Communist gunman who thought the archbishop had become too sympathetic with the guerrilla movement. In these countries the pope underlined the Church's teachings on human rights.

Later, when the Holy Father visited Nicaragua, he shook a fatherly finger at Father Ernesto Cardenal, the Minister of Cultural Affairs in the Sandinista government, and warned him that he should *"arreglar"* his relationship with the Church. The word *"arreglar"* can mean "arrange," "fix up," "repair" or "put in order." Presumably the pope had all these meanings in mind. His finger-shaking furthermore was probably directed not just to Father Cardenal, but to the so-called "People's Church" in Nicaragua, which had emerged from the Christian Base Communities movement even before the Revolution. In fact many members of these grassroots congregations took an active part in the overthrow of the Somoza regime and have continued to be supporters of the revolutionary process in their country. A popular slogan these groups promulgate and which one sees on walls and placards all over Nicaragua today states "Between Christianity and Revolution there is no contradiction."

What does the pope think of this idea? In its most recent pronouncement on Liberation Theology, the Vatican reaffirms the standing Catholic teaching that armed rebellion is indeed morally justified in case of prolonged and obdurate tyranny. But still the pope seems nervous about the Latin American branch of his realm. We all need more light on the subject, and people are listening. And when people listen, Fidel Castro is always more than willing to instruct.

Understandably many American television viewers and newspaper readers have been puzzled by the contradictory stories they hear about the Church's involvement with political conflict in Central America. Whereas in some places Church leaders were being killed by right-wing governments, in other places they were holding public office in what the Reagan Administration called Communist governments. In some countries, according to the President, the guerrillas were all terrorists, whereas in other countries they were freedom fighters who were the "moral equivalent of our founding fathers." People were confused. Archbishop Romero and the American churchwomen who were killed in El Salvador were no doubt victims of the right wing. But in Nicaragua the cardinal archbishop of Managua has become the principal domestic political critic of the Sandinista government while, on the other side, the Franciscans, the Jesuits and the Maryknollers support it, and the other five bishops are divided. Wasn't there a time when the phrase "Christian revolutionary" was a pure oxymoron? What ever happened to the good old days when God and Satan, good and evil, religion and atheism, faced each other in unambiguous and unequivocal goods and evils? It is a good time for this book to appear because the noise and confusion and suffering in Latin America, in which in one way or another revolutionaries and

Christians are involved, have succeeded at least in capturing the attention of the American public.

It is also the worst of times. The relationship between the United States and Cuba, which has been volatile and abrasive ever since the defeat of the Batista regime in 1959, has fallen once again on evil days. In 1982 the U.S. State Department imposed new travel and currency restrictions that made it much more difficult for Americans to visit Cuba. In 1985 the United States enraged Castro (though apparently not all Cubans) by beaming toward Havana a radio station carrying anti-Castro messages and named after José Martí (1853–1895), the Cuban patriot. Castro retaliated by canceling an emigration agreement. In August of 1986 the State Department announced even more severe embargoes on Cuba, designed—it said—to stop up some of the gaps in the economic boycott that has continued since the early months of the Castro period. At the same time Amnesty International indicated that despite its reluctance to talk about it, Cuba does in fact hold a number of political prisoners. In recent months many Americans have either read or heard about a book by Armando Valladares, *Against All Hope*, in which the writer describes his long years of suffering and deprivation in a Cuban jail cell as a prisoner of conscience. Meanwhile, through a bizarre chain of events, Cuban troops guard American oil installations in Angola against a guerrilla force that the American President and many of his advisers say they would like to support at least with money if not with direct military weaponry. But the worst may still be to come. Some of President Reagan's supporters are openly criticizing their hero today for being too soft on Castro. In Cuba itself the Catholic hierarchy is at one and the same time more open to "dialogue" with the government than any other hierarchy in a Communist country and more uncritically pro-Vatican than most of the other hierarchies in South America. No wonder people are perplexed. If the picture of the relationship between religion and politics and Church and revolution in Latin America as a whole seems perplexing, the role of Cuba in all of this seems downright convoluted.

This is also not a particularly good time for Cuba. Any revolution going on 30 years of age is bound to have lost some of its initial pizzazz. Visitors to Cuba testify that its health-care standards are higher than those of almost any other country in Latin America, that their unemployment is low and there is equal access to education, and that illiteracy has been virtually eliminated. But even Cuba's best friends admit they detect an element of weariness among the Cubans they meet, a weariness, however, that is always mixed with gratitude for what the Revolution has done for ordinary people and a continuing hope that someday, somehow, relations with the United States will improve. It is also evident that in the imaginations of many young Latin Americans Nicaragua has stolen some of Cuba's thunder as the new David standing tall against the Yankee Goliath. Even in Cuba, Nicaragua has become a source of inspiration. Indeed one recent visitor to Cuba told me he did not think this book would have been published had it not been for the extraordinary influence Nicaraguan Christians have had on the Cubans who have gone there as doctors and teachers. Meeting people who are both Catholics and revolutionaries apparently convinced many Cubans that the classical versions of Leninist atheism don't hold water anymore. A few have even joined the Catholic Church in Nicaragua. There is no doubt whatever that Castro himself has also been influenced not just by Nicaraguan Christians but also by the courage and revolutionary spirit of ordinary believers in Guatemala, El Salvador and other parts of Latin America.

In the midst of this admixture of good times and bad times there now appears this surprising book based on 23 hours of conversation between the Cuban president and Frei Betto, a Dominican priest and a man Castro respects in part because he was imprisoned and tortured during the military rule in his native Brazil. Although the fact may puzzle Americans, this book has already caused a near sensation in other parts of the world. It has been widely read in Brazil, Argentina, and elsewhere in Latin America. In Cuba itself *Fidel y la Religión* sold more than 200,000 copies in a few days and within a few months had been bought by a million Cubans, one-tenth of the entire population. Thousands of people stood in line one day in Santiago de Cuba to buy copies personally signed by Frei Betto. A German translation has recently been released, but even before it appeared, the Catholic Church in Switzerland ran an hour-long television program on the book. In increasingly conservative France the book has been widely read and discussed. The Cuban publisher reports that editions are being prepared in Hungary, The German Democratic Republic, Bulgaria, Czechoslovakia, the U.S.S.R., Vietnam; also in Italy, Spain, and other countries, even Australia. It has already been published in Poland and editions are underway in Hindi and English in India, in Tagalog, in Japanese, etc. One can imagine why it is being pondered with considerable interest in Rome and Moscow, but why in so many other places? No one knows for sure. The reader must judge this for him- or herself. Still, anyone will have to agree that the loquacious Fidel's sermon, whatever else one may say about it, is keeping the folks in the pews awake.

Surely among those who will read this book in one of its translations with consummate interest will be the leaders and ideologists of the various Communist regimes and parties around the world. For obvious reasons, of which Poland is only one example, they are upset and worried about the current rebirth of religion in a world that was supposed to be headed irrevocably away from such archaic obscurantism. But Castro is widely known and respected among these people. What he has to say in this book about religion will—from their point of view—seem shocking and unorthodox and maybe even (to use a term that in the present context could sound somewhat ironic) "heretical." Why? Simply stated: Castro does *not* believe that religion is always an "opiate of the people." This is not news for anyone who is already familiar with his views on the subject, but here he puts it bluntly and he puts it in print. For the Comandante, religion can be either an opiate or a stimulant. He says, "From a political point of view, I think one can be a Marxist without ceasing to be a Christian and can work together with a Marxist Communist to transform the world. What is important in both cases is a question of sincere revolutionaries disposed to abolish the exploitation of man by man and to struggle for the just distribution of social riches." Again, this is not an utterly new sentiment. Italian Communists have been saying the same thing for years. So have out-of-power Marxist intellectuals in both Eastern Europe (Milan Machoveč) and Western Europe (Roger Garaudy). But here a Communist head of state says it in print in his own country. That is surely a first.

Sometimes the way Castro speaks about religion sounds almost regretful, as though he would like to have become a religious person earlier in life, but somehow missed. "The name of Jesus Christ was one of the most familiar names for me," he says. "Practically from the time I first had use of reason. . . . Yet I really didn't acquire a religious faith. All my effort, my attention, my life was concentrated on the development of a *political* faith. Yet never did I see a contradiction between the ideas I upheld and the idea of that symbol, of that extraordinary figure who had been so familiar to me..."

Hard-line Communist ideologists around the world may shake their heads over this. What is happening to Fidel? Is he getting soft as he approaches old age? Was he never a true-blue Leninist in the first place? Is he just playing a crafty game on a continent where, if the pope does not have many divisions, the Catholic Church still wields enormous cultural influence and moral power? None of these answers is correct, but each of them may have a tiny grain of truth. First, of course Castro *is* aging. He has just turned sixty and has been in power for nearly three decades. He is presumably an older and wiser man than he was when he and his handful of comrades stormed the Moncada military barracks nearly 35 years ago in the first armed attempt to overthrow the Batista dictatorship. Anyone entering the last decade before the scriptural threescore years and ten is bound to become a little more reflective, and as the Comandante combs through his memories of earlier religious influences one can almost hear him at times trying to see his life within the big picture and get it all together.

As for being a simon-pure Leninist, it is difficult to find anybody who incarnates this paradigm anywhere in the world today. Even Secretary Mikhail Gorbachev in addressing the plenary session of the Communist Party Congress in the USSR in 1985 felt safe cracking a joke during his five-hour speech about omitting a reference to the "timeless principles of Lenin." It is probably also safe to say that although Marxism—in one of its dozen intellectual expressions—remains a potent influence in many places in the world today, Leninism has few real advocates. This is important to keep in mind when one is discussing religion because it was Lenin and not Marx himself who made atheism into a metaphysical tenet rather than a political issue. On the issue of religion, whatever Fidel Castro may call himself, from the earliest days he was not a Leninist, at least not in this respect. In 1961, for example, shortly after he came to power, he expelled several priests, some of them Spaniards associated with the Opus Dei movement, but others native Cubans. In a speech which was published in Cuba at the time, Castro accused these priests of spending their time among the rich and the privileged instead of working with the poor, where, he said, Christ himself would have wanted them to work. "The doctrine of Christ," he said, "found an echo among slaves and humble people. It was persecuted by the aristocracy and the dominant classes... [But] these gentlemen [the expelled foreign priests] separated themselves from... the exploited masses... in order to carry religion on a silver platter to the great exploiters." (*Obra Revolucionaria #8*, Imprenta Nacional de Cuba, March 4, 1961.) At that time Castro was calling himself a Leninist, but any self-respecting Leninist would have been glad the priests were not corrupting the poor. Castro said similar things in Chile in 1971 during the Allende government; in Nicaragua, when he visited in 1980 to celebrate the first anniversary of the Sandinista victory; and once when he spoke to the Caribbean Council of Churches meeting in Jamaica in 1977. But now he has said it systematically. And at home.

But what about the possibility that *Fidel and Religion* is a clever gambit by a wily and resourceful tactician who knows that he needs to have Christians on his side—at least temporarily—in order to get what he wants? No one knows for sure, but on the other hand, Castro is no fool. It would be idle to suggest that his thinking about the role of religion on the Latin American continent, and in the revolutionary process that is sweeping that hemisphere, has not been influenced by the visible institutional Church that has become such an important actor on that stage. It is that actor and that stage we must look at briefly now in order to put Fidel's book into its proper context.

It is hard to put one's finger immediately on just when the big change took place in the Latin American Church. Some people date it back to the Second Vatican Council. They point to the historic convocation of that epochal meeting by Pope John XXIII and to the words he used, calling on the Church "to become once again a church of the poor." Some say the beginning was the experience the various Third World bishops, including the Latin American bishops, had at that council—meeting each other, often for the first time, and determining that they would take initiatives in applying the Gospel to their own continent in a new and vigorous way. Some trace the ideas that eventually emerged in Latin American Liberation Theology back to the Young Christian Workers movements in the France of the 1930s, to the worker-priest experiment just after the Second World War, and to the ideas carried to Latin America by dedicated young missionaries from Europe and the United States during those same years.

What do the Latin Americans themselves say about this? Gustavo Gutiérrez of Peru, who is sometimes thought of as the father of Liberation Theology, believes that the change had to occur because Latin America is a continent in which the people are—as he puts it—"both oppressed and Christian." Gutiérrez believes that this explosive combination of the experience of disenfranchisement and an exposure to the Gospel of Jesus catalyzed the fundamental change that took place in the Church. Still others believe that the continent-wide conversion that has shaken the Catholic Church would simply not have happened had it not been for the phenomenal growth of the so-called Christian Base Communities movement. Ironically these CEBs (Comunidades Eclesiales de Base) were originally started by the bishops, to parry the growth of Protestant missions and to fight back against the spread of Socialist trade-union movements.

Which of these was the principal cause of the change? Probably all these factors and more entered into the mix. Nevertheless almost everyone agrees that the Magna Carta of the newly reborn Church of Latin America was written at the historic conference of the continent's bishops at Medellín, Colombia, in 1968. It was there that the Latin American bishops spoke openly about "the international imperialism of money" and where they commended the base community movements for their work among the poor and the marginal people of their countries. But most importantly it was there that the bishops coined the phrase that has become the In Hoc Signes of Liberation Theology when they declared that the Church should have a "preferential option for the poor."

But what—exactly—does this hotly disputed slogan mean? It means, in short, that a church which had for centuries made its alliance with the rich and powerful, which had trained and educated the children of the elite (including the youthful Fidel Castro), was now in effect changing sides. It was putting itself and its resources at the disposal of the vast majority of Latin Americans who were then and continue now to be poor and dispossessed.

Often church bodies make high-sounding declarations, and nothing happens. The Medellín Conference, however, was an exception. Inspired and instructed by its message, many hundreds of Catholic Church workers—priests, nuns and lay people—literally moved the site of their work and their homes from the suburbs to the slums. Some religious orders closed their elite schools and initiated educational programs in the shanty towns. Perhaps the thing that has impressed me most as I have traveled extensively in Latin America in recent years has been that virtually every theologian I have met there lives in what in the United States would be considered decidedly substandard housing in parts of the city we would view as unsafe, and among people who are not only poor but often hungry and sometimes desperate.

When the Church began to align itself with the poor, it began to experience persecution. By now the stories of the martyrs among Latin American Catholics have been told so many times they sound almost trite. Still it is remarkable to recognize that in a tradition where the blood of the martyrs is believed to be the seed of the Church, many martyrdoms have actually taken place and a newly revived Church is actually flowering in Latin America. Some even describe it as a resurrection. The Brazilian theologian Leonardo Boff calles it an *ecclesiogenesis*, the birth of a newly sanctified Church freshly blessed by the Spirit of God, finding a home in the hearts of the despised and neglected of that vast continent.

When the Catholic bishops of Latin America met again in Puebla, Mexico, in 1979, they represented a church that had become deeply divided. The base communities, the preferential option for the poor, the excitement for Liberation Theology, had so stirred their various lands that stiff opposition had begun to appear, not just in society, but also in the Church itself. John Paul II came to Puebla in the very first foreign visit of his pontificate. His message to the bishops, however, was ambiguous. At times he seemed to be calling the Church to an active role in the struggle for social justice. At other times he seemed to be warning church workers, especially priests and nuns, not to be "social workers," but to stick closely to their specifically religious calling. The pope appeared ambivalent. A few years later, in 1985, when Cardinal Joseph Ratzinger, the Prefect of the Congregation for the Doctrine of the Faith, silenced Father Leonardo Boff, the silencing caused an enormous uproar throughout Latin America. Many of the bishops of Brazil felt their authority had been challenged, that their pastoral program had been undermined, and that the heavy hand of Rome was throttling the nascent life of their Church. In less than a year Rome decided to lift the silence and it was rumored that the pope had intervened to support Boff. Whether that is true or not, we do know that just after the silence was ended His Holiness wrote a special personal letter to the Brazilian bishops commending the base communities and telling them that the theological work being carried on under their auspices "promised a possible renewal for Catholic theology throughout the world."

As this book appears, the future of Liberation Theology seems bright. Leonardo Boff, one of the movement's principal spokesmen, has been freed from his silence. The discussion has begun in earnest; the door is open for the churches of Latin America to make a significant contribution to the worldwide Catholic Church and indeed to all the Christian churches. This happens just at the moment Christianity has become a global rather than a European movement. Sometime in the 1970s the tipping point was reached. There are now more Christians in Africa, Asia and Latin America than there are in the United States and Europe. Someone pointed out recently that with every passing day there are 4,000 fewer Christians in Europe and 40,000 new Christians in the Third World. Whatever one may think of Fidel Castro from the point of view of North American political or religious values, he is still something of a hero to many people in the Third World and served from 1979 to 1983 as chairman of the Organization of Non-Aligned States, in which capacity he addressed the U.N. General Assembly in October 1979. He was listened to with considerable interest at the September 1986 meeting of the nonaligned nations in Zimbabwe. Whether what he says about religion is of particular interest to us or not, it is of considerable interest to them. And because it is of interest to them, it should also be of interest to us.

But what difference, if any, will all these words make for the Christian people of Cuba themselves? Few people deny that for years believers have lived under vexing and unfair restrictions. Now some of them have greeted this book as a *milagro*, a miracle, perhaps because it seemed to have come without expectation and with no natural explanation. As we have already seen, however, this is not quite the case. The book did not appear *ex nihilo*. Fidel, after all, had met with a delegation of U.S. Catholic bishops in 1985 and had made a very public visit to a Methodist church during Jesse Jackson's visit to Havana the year before. Also, it remains to be seen how much the book will actually help the Christians of Cuba. One Cuban Catholic wryly observed that at Cuba's Third Communist Party Congress in February 1986 Castro devoted all of three short phrases to Christianity. In two he saluted some of the Christian Democratic parties of Latin America and in one he commended Liberation Theology. Again, this is hardly vintage Leninism, but neither does it say much to Cuban Christians who live in a country ruled by one party where there is no Liberation Theology.

Still, one also has to understand Fidel's decision to encourage his sympathetic thoughts on religion to be published in Cuba in the light of some remarkable changes that have taken place recently within the Catholic Church in Cuba itself. When Castro's bearded rebels marched into Havana in 1959, the vast majority of Catholic priests in Cuba were foreigners—mostly Spaniards and (here Castro is correct) mainly very conservative. Although the Church extended some charitable care to the poor and aged, it concentrated most of its resources—schools, hospitals and parishes—in the more privileged areas of the cities. The bulwark of the Church's support was middle-class urban women. There was very little religious outreach into the countryside, where 70 percent of the people lived. Castro believes that the conflict that soon arose between the Church and the new revolutionary regime was rooted in this socioeconomic pattern. The Revolution drew its support largely from the impoverished rural areas. The Church's base was elsewhere. The clash, he believes, was more one of class than of religion.

In any case, in 1954, three years before the Revolution began, only 17 percent of the people of Cuba reported attending a Christian church of any denomination. This was an unusually low figure for a Latin American country. But in 1976, 15 years after Castro's government declared itself to be Marxist-Leninist and atheist, and after a large number of people most closely tied to the churches had left, only 2 percent of the people identified themselves as Christians. Monsignor Carlos Manuel de Céspedes, secretary-general of the Cuban bishops' council, says that today, although many people want a Catholic funeral, there are only about 100,000 genuine "practicing Catholics" in a total population of 10 million. His estimate may be low since many more people consider themselves to be Catholic in a less rigorous sense. The remainder of the Christian population of Cuba consists of various evangelical groups, including Baptists and Pentecostalists. There are only 36 Catholic seminarians now preparing for the priesthood. But despite this statistically grim profile, leaders of all the churches insist there has been a change for the better recently. Archbishop Jaime Ortega, of Havana, recently told Stanislas Maillard, an editor of the French journal *L'Actualité Religieuse*, "For three or four years there has been a current, a consistent tendency on the government's part to ease the tensions, to do away with discriminations." Apparently *Fidel and Religion* signals a favorable change in the government's attitude toward religion. Visitors report that church members who still experience discrimination in trying to enroll in universities or get particular jobs almost always have their complaints dealt with quickly and favorably. Maillard believes this softening has taken place because, in effect, the Catholic Church in Cuba decided in about 1980 to try to live *within* a society in which an avowedly atheistic government says it is "building socialism," and to do so as constructively as possible— contributing to the health of the society wherever it can—while at the same time maintaining its Christian identity.

Some of the theological groundwork for this move toward a dialogue between Christians and Marxists in Cuba was prepared by a key article published in 1981 by Professor René David of San Carlos Seminary in Havana. It was entitled "For a Theology and a Pastoral Policy of Reconciliation." The article begins by suggesting that most Latin American Liberation Theology, in which landlessness, hunger and fatalism are cited as the principal enemies, does not apply in Cuba where private ownership of the means of production has already been abolished. The author also candidly points out that Cuba does not yet offer "all the desirable conditions of freedom" nor has it "achieved the difficult balance between equality and liberty necessary for a more authentic fraternity." Given all this, David goes on however to decry the atmosphere of "confrontation, misunderstanding and condemnation on both sides which is prolonged in mutual mistrust." He objects to "harassment against the faith" by the government but also faults Catholics for their refusal to contribute to society. The central kernel of the article reads as follows:

> To put Christianity and Communism in opposition in general terms is to condemn oneself never to see the values in Communism as well as its faults and to close the door to reconciliation—when in reality the Christian faith is not and should not be a contradiction of

Communism but of its "atheistic faith" and its consequences for human rights and the achievement of a society which does not discriminate; while Communism should not be a contradiction of the Christian faith but of its distortions and their socio-political effects. . . .

If Communists do not make atheism a dogma, a pseudo-religion, we might suppose that the Church could be reconciled with them. . . . That would permit a Christian to be politically Communist and a Communist to be religiously Christian. But reconciliation does not signify identity; the faith is the faith and a political ideology is a political ideology. . . .

Where will it all lead? If Castro can toss Christians their own Master's teaching, "by their fruits ye shall know them," it is not perhaps wholly inappropriate to toss the same dictum to the Comandante. He resented being force-fed Christian doctrine by the Jesuits in his youth. Will the Cuban schools now allow open inquiry about religion and Christianity as alternatives to atheism? What do the Comandante's newly published and unorthodox views on this subject say to the people who are imprisoned or banished for publishing other kinds of heresy? Castro applauds the active role Christians are taking in Latin American society today. But what would happen in Cuba if base communities of ordinary people not controlled by either a church hierarchy or a state bureaucracy began to appear? It is sad but true that in most countries today where Communist governments are in power, the political leaders seem to prefer a strictly controlled hierarchical church just as corporate managers often prefer to rely on union chiefs to discipline workers. If Castro likes Liberation Theology, will his government allow for the growth of the vigorous, critical and independent base communities out of which Liberation Theology has arisen in the rest of Latin America?

Finally, one cannot help wondering about Fidel himself. Despite attempts by the CIA and others to kill him—once, it is said, by poisoning his cigar—he has reached the edge of old age, and as a man who keeps on thinking, he undoubtedly carries with him some profound questions that remain unanswered. If he sometimes regrets he never developed a religious faith as a boy, does he think it is too late now? He has already defied Communist orthodoxy on this touchy subject at the philosophical level. What about the existential level? Castro is a man who has tasted pain and disappointment as well as fame and power. After the failed attempt to storm the Moncada barracks he spent 19 months in solitary confinement. But now what? St. Augustine began his famous *Confessions* by saying that our hearts are restless until they find their rest in God. Fidel Castro, a man hated and despised by many, loved and admired by many, is a man with a restless heart. He does not open very much of that heart in this book. But he opens it a little. And that is a start.

Note to the Cuban Edition

SOME TRUTHS are hidden in the tangled skein woven in the course of millennia of obscurantism. In the early years of the Revolution, Fidel Castro said, "We were wedded to lies and forced to live with them; this is why it seems that the world is overwhelmed when we hear the truth."

The heavy veil thrown over the possibilities of promoting close political ties between Christians and Communists is drawn back in this interview that Fidel granted to Frei Betto, a Brazilian Dominican friar. Readers are presented here with an "amazing" happening to be read and studied, and, if we stick strictly to the definition given in the dictionary, we might say that those who study this talk in depth will find "an extremely outstanding or unusual event, thing or accomplishment" —that is, a *miracle*.

A practicing Catholic with deep Christian faith and a Communist leader well known for his firm principles held an extensive dialogue, and, when the exchange was over, each felt surer of his own convictions and more interested in establishing closer, deeper relations in the practical political struggle. Moreover, each based his arguments—and this may be the most interesting aspect for researchers—on the original sources of Christianity and Marxism. Neither of them ceded any of his principles, and each understood the other deeply on such important topics as morality, contemporary economic and political problems, and the need for Christians and Communists to unite in the struggle for a better world.

28

This isn't, however, a unity conceived of only as a tactic of struggle. It isn't just a happenstance occurrence or a political alliance. It *is*, of course, by definition, but the tie that is established here on the ethical or moral plane concerning man's role—whether he be a Christian or a Communist—in defense of the poor has the nature of a lasting, permanent, strategic alliance. It is a proposition with a solid moral, political and social basis. This, in itself, is a tremendous achievement in the history of human thought. The ethical-moral note appears in these lines to bear the human feeling that unites fighters for freedom and in defense of the poor and exploited.

How did this miracle come about? Social theoreticians, philosophers, theologians and a whole range of intellectuals in different countries should ask themselves this question. Moreover, Christians will surely feel obliged by their beliefs to ask it of themselves, as will Marxist-Leninists. The Cuban people, to whom this edition is dedicated, have made a revolution, know Fidel Castro well and know what this dialogue is about.

The reactionaries' beloved dogma of the impossibility of understanding between Christians and Communists comes tumbling down when you have a deep understanding of both doctrines. Marxism-Leninism is essentially antidogmatic. It is guided by the principle formulated by Lenin that the first and foremost point of view of the theory of knowledge should be the point of view of life and practice—a principle that Fidel has applied in the modern world with exceptional skill.

The point of view of practice is presented in this book. It sets forth the possibility of and need for deep human understanding among all who honestly struggle for the people, no matter what their ideas about God and religion may be.

To appreciate once more the consequences of Fidel's thinking, it is good to emphasize that he is setting forth ideas that he has held throughout his revolutionary life, expressed here with ever-greater breadth and depth, in their full conceptual maturity and richness. We should recall his 1971 talk with Catholics in Chile, his 1977 meeting with ministers in Jamaica and that phrase of his in the first few years of the Revolution: "He who betrays the poor betrays Christ."

This book brings out important roots of Fidel Castro's ethical training, how he was influenced by his elementary and secondary school education in the best Catholic schools in Cuba. This training, of course, included the tradition that has been handed down to us from the last century and that was summed up in the historically important moral messages of Félix Varela, José de la Luz y Caballero and especially José Martí. This ethical element may well be one of the most important aspects of the dialogue.

Thus, a deep exchange of ideas—not only at the tactical and political but also at the strategic and moral level—has been initiated between forces that, up until very recently, seemed to be unable to understand each other. It took place in Latin America because this is a region in tumult, where an acute economic, political and social crisis is reflected in all of the people's spheres of cultural and spiritual life as a harbinger of the inexorable changes that will take place, one way or another; because the Cuban Revolution has already ushered in a stage of great renovation for socialism that has reached the region's essence and roots; because of the unquestionable contribution that the Nicaraguan Revolution and the processes that are taking place in El Salvador and other countries have made and are making to this topic; and because part of the Catholic Church and other Latin American and Caribbean Christian currents are stating a topic that has very old roots in a new way: what the role and mission of believers is with regard to social and political problems.

Two of the most important historic wellsprings of man's thinking and emotions—Christianity and Marxism, which the enemies of human progress have always presented as irreconcilable—have found new and surprising paths of understanding here. This is a question on which all who are sincerely concerned about the future of mankind will surely wish to meditate.

ARMANDO HART
CUBAN MINISTER OF CULTURE

Paths to a Meeting

I planned this work in 1979. I had proposed the idea of a book to be called "Faith in Socialism" to Enio Silveira, my beloved editor and brother in God. In order to carry it out, I would have to travel in the Socialist countries so as to get in contact with the Christian communities living under a regime classified as materialist and atheist. Many tasks forced me to set the idea aside; moreover, it would have proved too expensive.

Immediately after the triumph of the Sandinista Revolution, the pastoral center in Nicaragua invited me to offer advisory services at meetings and training sessions, especially for the farmers. I went to that country two or three times a year to preach in spiritual retreats, give introductory Bible study courses and help the Christian communities in articulating their life of faith with political commitment. I completed a program sponsored by the Center for Agrarian Promotion and Education (CEPA) that consisted of seven pastoral meetings with the farmers in the mountains of Diriamba, in El Crucero. Those trips enabled me to get to know the priests who served the people's regime of Nicaragua. On July 19, 1980, I took part as an official guest in the celebration of the first anniversary of the Revolution. That same evening, Father Miguel D'Escoto, the Minister of Foreign Affairs, took me to the home of Sergio Ramírez, now Vice President of the Republic. That was the first time I talked with Fidel Castro, whom I had seen that morning at the people's rally at which he had spoken.

I remembered the impact that his statements to the priests he had met with in Chile in November 1971 had made on me. I'd read them as a political prisoner in São Paulo, serving a four-year sentence "for reasons of national security." On that occasion, he had said, "In a revolution, there are moral factors which are decisive. Our countries are too poor to give men great material wealth, but they *can* give them a sense of equality, of human dignity." He said that, on his protocol visit to Cardinal Silva Henríquez, of Santiago, he'd spoken to him "about our peoples' objective need to free themselves and of the need for Christians and revolutionaries to unite for this purpose." He said that it wasn't Cuba's exclusive interest, since it didn't face that sort of problem, but, within the Latin American context, it was "an interest and a duty of all revolutionaries and Christians—many of whom are low-income men and women of the people—to close ranks in a liberation process that is inevitable." The cardinal gave the Cuban leader a Bible and asked if the gift annoyed him. "Why should it?" Fidel answered. "This is a great book. I read it, studied it as a boy, and I'll brush up on many things I'm interested in." One of the priests asked him what he thought about the presence of priests in politics. "How, for example, can any spiritual guide of a human collective ignore its material problems, its human problems, its vital problems? Can it be that those material, human problems are independent of the historical process? Are they independent of social phenomena? We've experienced all that. I always go back to the time of primitive slavery. That's also the time when Christianity emerged." He observed that Christians had "gone from a stage in which they were persecuted to others in which they were the persecutors" and that the Inquisition "was a period of obscurantism, when men were burned." Now, Christianity could be "a real rather than a utopian doctrine, not a spiritual consolation for those who suffer. Classes might disappear, and a Communist society might arise. Where is the contradiction with Christianity? Rather than a contradiction, there would be a revival of early Christianity, with its fairer, more human, more moral values." Addressing the Chilean clergy, Fidel recalled the time he attended a Catholic school. "What was happening to the Catholic religion? A great slackening. It was merely formal and had no substance. Nearly all education was permeated with this. I studied with the Jesuits. They were strict, disciplined, rigorous, intelligent and strong-willed men. I've always said this. But I also experienced the irrationality of that kind of education. Just between us, I tell you there's great coincidence between Christianity's objectives and the ones we Communists seek, between the Christian teachings of humility, austerity, selflessness and loving thy neighbor and what we might call the content of a revolutionary's life and behavior. For, what are we teaching the people? To kill? To steal? To be selfish? To exploit others? Just the opposite. Responding to different motivations, we advocate attitudes and behavior that are quite similar. We are living at a time when politics has entered a near-religious sphere with regard to man and his behavior. I also believe that we have come to a time when religion can enter the political sphere with regard to man and his material needs. We could endorse nearly all of the Commandments: Thou shalt not kill. Thou shalt not steal. . . ." After criticizing capitalism, Fidel said, "There are 10,000 times more coincidences between Christianity and communism than between Christianity and capitalism . . . not to create those divisions among men. Let's respect convictions, beliefs and explanations. Everyone is entitled to his own positions, his own beliefs. We must work in the sphere of these human problems that interest us all and constitute a duty for all." In regard to the Cuban nuns who work in hospitals, he stressed that "the things they do are the things we want Communists to do. When they take care of people with leprosy, tuberculosis and other communicable diseases, they are doing what we want Communists to do. A person who is devoted to an idea, to work and who sacrifices himself for others is doing what we want Communists to do. I say this in all frankness."

There, in Sergio Ramírez' library, I remembered that talk between the revolutionary from the Sierra Maestra and the Chilean priests—I'm consulting it now—and it served as a basis for our exchange of ideas on the religious question in Cuba and the rest of Latin America. On that occasion, in Chile, one of the participants asked Castro if his crisis of faith had taken place before or during the Revolution. He answered that faith had never been inculcated in him. "I could say that I never had it. It was a mechanical, not a rational thing." Recalling his experiences in the guerrilla war, he commented, "No churches had ever been built in the mountains, but a Presbyterian missionary went there, and the members of some so-called sects did too, and they got some followers. They used to tell us, 'Don't eat animal fat.' And they wouldn't eat it; they wouldn't eat it! There wasn't any vegetable oil, and they went without lard for a whole month. That was their precept, and they abided by it. All of those small groups were much more consistent. I've heard that U.S. Catholics too are much more practical in terms of religion—not socially, because when they went and organized the Bay of Pigs ivasion and the war in Vietnam and other things of that sort, they weren't being consistent. I'd say that the wealthy classes distorted religion and made it serve them. What is a priest? Is he a landowner? Is he an industrialist? I always used to read the discussions between the Communist and Don Camillo—the famous priest in Italian literature. I'd say that was one of the first attempts to dispel that atmosphere. . . ." In connection with Cuba, a priest asked him to what extent Christians had been an obstacle to or a driving force in the Revolution. "No one can say that the Christians were an obstacle. Some Christians participated in the struggle at the end; there were even some martyrs. Three or four students from the Colegio de Belén were murdered in northern Pinar del Río. There were some priests, such as Father Sardiñas, who joined our ranks on their own. An obstacle? What happened at the beginning was a class problem. It didn't have anything to do with religion. It was the religion of the landowners and the wealthy. When the socioeconomic conflict erupted, they tried to pit religion against the Revolution. That was what happened, the cause of the conflicts. The Spanish clergy was quite reactionary." At the end of the long talk with the Chilean priests, Fidel Castro emphasized that the alliance between Christians and Marxists wasn't just a matter of tactics. "We wanted to be strategic allies, which means permanent allies."

The First Secretary of the Communist Party of Cuba returned to the topic of religion during his visit to Jamaica in October 1977, nearly six years after his trip to Allende's Chile. This time, he was addressing a mainly Protestant audience. He reaffirmed that "at no time has the Cuban Revolution been inspired by anti-religious feelings. We based ourselves on the deep conviction that there needn't be any contradiction between a social revolution and the people's religious beliefs. All the people—including those with religious beliefs—participated in our struggle." He said that the Revolution had been particularly careful not to present itself to the Cubans and other peoples as an enemy of religion. "Because, if that had occurred, we would have been doing the reaction a favor, cooperating with the exploiters—not only the ones in Cuba but the exploiters in all the rest of Latin America, as well." He said that he'd often been asked, "Why must the ideas of social justice clash with religious beliefs? Why must they clash with Christianity?" He replied by saying, "I'm rather well versed in Christian principles and in Christ's teachings. I believe that Christ was a great revolutionary. That's what I believe. His entire doctrine was devoted to the humble, the poor; His doctrine was devoted to fighting against abuse, injustice and the degradation of human beings. I'd say there's a lot in common between the spirit and essence of His teachings and socialism." He also went back to the theme of the alliance between Christians and revolutionaries, saying, "There are no contradictions between the aims of religion and those of socialism. There aren't any. I was saying that we should form an alliance, but not a tactical one." Then, recalling his trip to Chile, he added, "They asked me if it was to be a tactical or a strategic alliance. I said it should be a strategic alliance between religion and socialism, between religion and revolution."

Recalling those statements, I talked to Fidel about the evolution of the Christian Base Communities and about how the long-suffering believers' faith, meditation on the Word of God and participation in the Sacraments gave them the energy they needed to struggle for a better life. I felt that Latin America was divided not into Christians and Marxists but into revolutionaries and allies of the forces of oppression. Many Communist parties had made the mistake of professing an academic atheism, which estranged them from the faithful poor. No alliance could be maintained on the basis of theoretical principles and bookish discussions. Liberating practice was the ground on which Christian militants and Marxist militants would meet or not—since, just as there are many Christians who defend the interests of capital, there are also many who claim to be Communists who never divorce themselves from the bourgeoisie. Moreover, as a man of the Church, I was particularly interested in the Catholic Church in Cuba. What we said with regard to this specific topic is contained in the interview that is published here.

Many of the topics that were discussed in the Managua talks

are dealt with again in this interview. I have retained the impression, that, as an individual, Fidel is a frank, sensitive person, someone you can ask any kind of question and even disagree with. Even though he says that he never had any real religious faith, he wasn't totally immune to his training in Catholic schools, which was preceded by his coming from a Christian family. Five days after our dialogue in Sergio Ramírez' home, during a meeting I attended with some Nicaraguan priests and nuns, Fidel repeated the basic ideas he had defended in Chile and stressed in Jamaica. This group of Christians embodied an advance that Fidel himself hadn't foreseen. The Sandinista Revolution was the work of a traditionally religious people and had the blessing of the episcopate. It was the first time in history that Christians, motivated by their own faith, had participated actively in an insurrectional process with the support of their pastors. The Nicaraguan clergy insisted that this wasn't a strategic alliance. There was unity between Christians and Marxists, among all the people. For his part, the Commander of the Cuban Revolution said that he had the "impression that the Bible has very revolutionary content; I believe that the teachings of Christ are very revolutionary and completely coincide with the aims of Socialists, of Marxist-Leninists." Self-critically, he admitted that "there are many doctrinaire Marxists. I think that being doctrinaire on this matter complicates the issue. I believe that both you and we should think about the kingdom of this world and avoid conflicts over matters related to the kingdom of the next world. There are still some doctrinaires around, and it's not easy for us, but our relations with the Church are gradually improving, in spite of many factors, such as this principle of antagonism. Of course, we've gone from a state of antagonism to one of absolutely normal relations. In Cuba, no churches are closed, and we've even suggested cooperating with the churches—in terms of materials, construction and resources—that is, giving the churches material cooperation, just as we do with other social institutions. Our country doesn't have to become a model of what I was saying, but everything seems to indicate that it will. This is even more the case in Nicaragua and El Salvador. Thus, the things I've said are beginning to be implemented in practice and historic reality. I think the churches will be much more influential in those countries than they were in Cuba, because the churches have been very important factors in the struggle for the people's liberation, national independence and social justice."

Before leaving, the Cuban leader invited me to visit his country. I was able to do so for the first time in September 1981, as a member of the large Brazilian delegation that attended the First Meeting of Intellectuals for Peoples' Sovereignty in Our America. Apart from the meeting, the American Study Center (CEA) and what is now the Office of Religious Affairs (OAR), headed by Dr. Carneado, invited me to give a series of talks on religion and the Church in Latin America. Before I left Cuba, they proposed that I return to continue the dialogue that had been begun. I had the impression that, in connection with theological and pastoral matters, both the Communist Party of Cuba and the Catholic Church were still influenced by the conflicts that had arisen between them at the beginning of the Revolution and, as a result, were kept from having a more open vision—one more in keeping with the great advances that the Latin American Church had made since the Second Vatican Council (1962–1965). I said I would be glad to accept the invitation if I would be able to serve the Cuban Catholic community as well. There was no opposition, and I attended the meeting of the Episcopal Conference of Cuba at El Cobre in February 1983 as a special guest. It was held at the Sanctuary of Our Lady of Charity, the national patron saint, and the bishops supported my pastoral activity in the country.

When I gave editor Caio Graco Prado the manuscript of my book *O que é comunidade eclesiale de base* (What Are the Christian Base Communities?), which was published by the Primeiros Passos collection, and told him about my trips to Cuba, he suggested the idea of an interview with Commander Fidel Castro on religious topics. Between September 1981 and this interview, I've been to the island 12 times, thanks to the support of Canadian— and, later, German—Catholics, who gave me the tickets, except for the times I came to attend some cultural event sponsored by the Cuban government. On one of those trips, I drew up a draft for the interview and the book but got no reply.

In February 1985, I returned as a member of the jury of the Casa de las Américas Literary Awards Contest. I was then invited to a private audience with Fidel Castro. It was the first time we talked in Cuba. Once again, we took up the subject we'd discussed in Managua, enriched by the discussion of Liberation Theology. The interest that this awakened in the Cuban leader led us to continue the dialogue during the next few days. We devoted nine hours to the religious question in Cuba and the rest of Latin America. I took up the draft of this interview again, and he accepted it for a later date. Editor Caio Graco Prado spared no efforts or resources to see it carried through. I returned to the island in May. Commander Fidel Castro and I spent 23 hours talking about religion, the transcript of which follows below. I would like to express my special thanks to Chomi Miyar for his invaluable cooperation in recording and transcribing the tapes and to Minister of Culture Armando Hart, who encouraged the dialogue.

FREI BETTO, *Havana, May 29, 1985*

Publisher's Note

Fidel and Religion is presented in this English-language edition exactly
as Fidel Castro and Frei Betto gave it to the publisher.

I
Chronicle of a Visit

One

F RIDAY, May 10, 1985. Chadli Bendjedid, President of Algeria, arrived in Cuba on an official visit. That same night, Fidel Castró gave a reception for him at the Palace of the Revolution. The guests included a small group of Brazilians who had arrived on the island the day before: journalist Joelmir Beting; Antonio Carlos Vieira Christo, my father; Maria Stella Libanio Christo, my mother; and I. It was the first time the others had ever been in Cuba. I had been there on other occasions, either in the service of the Church or as a participant in cultural events, and returned now with just one purpose: to interview Fidel.

Sergio Cervantes, our host, a black who looks Brazilian, told us that we should wear ties at the reception. I hadn't had a tie around my neck in 17 years. I didn't even own a suit. When I had visited Mafalda and Erico Veríssimo, the author of *O Tempo e o Vento*, in Pôrto Alegre in 1975, Erico had told me that he had burned all his ties many years ago. I had done the same thing, mentally. And, in Havana, all of a sudden, I vacillated. Should I break with protocol and show up in one of the two pairs of jeans that I'd brought? Should I refuse the invitation in protest over Socialist formalities? What the hell kind of a custom was this, when, in the National Congress in Brasília and in the Palace of the Revolution in Cuba, a strip of cloth wrapped around the neck was considered a sign of being well dressed? I racked my brains, a thousand imaginary protests chasing one another through my head; finally, I wavered and accepted the loan of a suit and tie from Jorge Ferreira, a Cuban friend. They fit me perfectly, and there I went, all wrapped up, putting up with Joelmir's teasing.

The Palace of the Revolution, which is located in the square of the same name, behind a monument to José Martí, is a solemn building from Batista's time reminiscent of the fascist architecture of the first Getulio Vargas Administration in Brazil. The never-ending staircase looked like the Maracaná amphitheater. At the door, protected by an honor guard, we presented our invitiations. We stayed in the entranceway until the Cuban and Algerian anthems had been played. In the immense hall of marble and stone, decorated with live plants, stained-glass windows and abstract murals, the guests listened to the speeches in Spanish and Arabic that preceded Fidel's presenting Chadli Bendjedid with the José Martí Medal, the most important one in the country. Members of the diplomatic corps and Cuban leaders—members of the Political Bureau and of the Central Committee and Ministers—were present, in addition to the visiting delegation. When the laudatory formalities were over, trays of *mojitos*, daiquiris and juice were passed among the informal groups. I went over to Minister of Culture Armando Hart, a man who doesn't separate reason from emotion—a rare quality. We expressed our sorrow over the fact that Alí Gómez García, a 33-year-old Venezuelan, had been killed in battle the day before while defending Nicaragua against Reagan's mercenaries. Last February I was part of the jury that awarded the prize for Spanish-language testimony to *Falsas, maliciosas y escandalosas reflexiones de un ñángara* (False, Malicious and Scandalous Reflections of a *Ñángara*), the text Alí had sent to the Casa del las Américas Literary Awards Contest. Raúl Castro, Fidel's youngest brother and Minister of the Revolutionary Armed Forces, walked over, and Hart introduced us. On learning that I was religious, he said, "I spent so many years in boarding school that I attended enough Mass to last me the rest of my life. I was taught by the Christian Brothers and the Jesuits. Just think: I'd studied in Santiago de Cuba, yet, when I took part in the attack on the Moncada Garrison, in 1953, I realized that I didn't really know the city. I haven't stayed in the Church, but I've kept the principles of Christ. I don't renounce those principles. They give me the hope of salvation, and the Revolution carries them out: it sends the rich away empty-handed and gives bread to the hungry. Everyone can be saved here; there are no rich, and Christ said it's easier for a camel to go through the eye of a needle. . . ."

Raúl said this in a very good-natured way. You could see that he was an affable person. Nevertheless, outside Cuba he's reputed to be tough. Imperialism's caprices: with its powerful communications media it paints caricatures of its enemies in our minds. It paints Raúl as a sectarian and John Kennedy as a handsome boy. But the one who planned, organized, sponsored and financed the Bay of Pigs invasion in 1961, in flagrant disregard for the Cuban people's sovereignty, was Jacqueline's young, smiling, democratic, Catholic husband. In his personal relations, Raúl is relaxed and talks with a smile, which is a rare thing among capitalist politicians, who are always so circumspect. And how could the husband of a woman as sweet as Vilma Espín be tough?

It seemed it would be impossible to greet Fidel, who is always surrounded by guests, photographers and TV people. Then they invited us into a small, less ceremonious room. We were in the entranceway when the Commander, in dress uniform, came in with Chadli Bendjedid. When they saw us, they came over. His shyness was evident. Yes, a man of that size, who yells what he thinks in Uncle Sam's face and makes four-hour speeches, was practically apologetic about who he is. I introduced him to Joelmir Beting and to my parents.

"You've made two revolutions. The first was the Cuban Revolution, and the second was getting my father to leave Brazil for the first time—and on an airplane too!"

"Don't worry; I'll get him to return by train," Fidel said.

In February, I'd been with the Commander at the home of Chomi Miyar, his personal secretary, doctor and photographer and had given him my shrimp *bobó* recipe, but Cuba has no *dendé*[1]-oil in which to cook the seasonings. I couldn't find someone to take him the *dendé* until March.

"I made your shrimp recipe," he said. "It came out good, but I can't say great, 'cause there wasn't any *dendé*. The famous oil didn't arrive till later. Plus, I made some changes, and I want to discuss them with you."

Dona Stella saw her chance and commented that she and I had our differences over the shrimp *bobó*. Despite the fact that,

[1] A kind of Brazilian coconut.

somewhat Oedipally, I consider her the best cook in the world—thanks to which I am alive and healthy—the *bobó* recipe that appears in her *Quentes e Frios* (Hot and Cold) isn't the one I learned at Victoria. The Capixabas'[2] secret is to beat the boiled yucca in the water the shrimp were boiled in. This tones down the yucca flavor and brings out the flavor of the shrimp.

We were involved in the middle of a culinary discussion when Fidel excused himself politely to go over to the Algerian President, who was waiting for him. We went over to a corner and, when the Algerian leader had made himself comfortable, the Commander came back to us. He wanted to know how long we would be in Cuba. He said he was sorry Joelmir would have to leave the next Wednesday, so as to arrive in Brazil on Thursday and fly to the Federal Republic of Germany on Friday. Fidel was going to be busy with Chadli Bendjedid until Monday and, on Tuesday, he would be participating in the fortieth anniversary celebration of the Allied victory in World War II. Thoughtful, holding a small cigar, with his right thumb rubbing his lips—almost lost among the white hairs of his beard—shaking his head as if to say no, he made up his mind right away: "Look: Joelmir isn't the one who wants to talk to me. I want to talk to him. We can meet Monday night and at some time on Tuesday. I have to find some time."

After posing for a picture with my parents, he asked them, "What do you think of the reception? Receptions always have good food, but I never get a chance to eat, because I'm busy taking care of the guests and then doing some exercises."

He turned to Cervantes and asked about our itinerary on the island.

Our friend gave him a general rundown: a visit to the Hemingway Museum, the Centro Habana hospital, Alamar, etc.

Fidel replied, "Tourist places. The hospital is good, but they need to know our country better. Go to the Isle of Youth and see how more than 10,000 foreign scholarship students from Africa and other continents are studying there. Go to Cienfuegos and see the nuclear power plant that's under construction. Visit a small rural community and find out how ready it is for military defense. I'll put my plane at your disposal. It's not comfortable, but it's safe."

[2] Inhabitants of Espírito Santo Province, on the eastern coast of Brazil.

He called Chomi, his secretary, and asked him to write down the itinerary he'd proposed. We told him that we had visited the Central Planning Board that morning, where we had been received by Comrade Alfredo Ham. He had explained that the Board drew up annual, five-year and longer-range plans running through the year 2000. Thus, Cuba's social and economic investments are planned and have few surprises. A factory in Holguín turns out more than 600 sugarcane harvesters every year, which are used in harvesting more than 55 percent of Cuba's sugarcane. Joelmir asked if planning was done from the top down. Alfredo replied that nothing was final until approved by the Council of Ministers and the National Assembly of People's Power, whose members are elected every five years. In addition, Cuba can plan its development process with a certain margin of security because it is free of capitalist market speculation. Eighty-five percent of its trade is with the other Socialist countries and is protected by agreements with the Council for Mutual Economic Assistance, of which Cuba is a member and in which it is given the same preferential measures as Vietnam and Mongolia.

Cuba's third five-year plan will begin in 1986. In the first few years of the Revolution, sugar, tobacco, rum and coffee were exported. Now, its most important exports are sugar, citrus fruits, nickel and fish. For a ten-year period, from 1971 to 1981, there was no change either in the prices of the staples on the domestic market or in the Cuban workers' minimum wages. The 1981 wage reform set a minimum wage of 85 pesos. (A Cuban peso is equal to U.S. $1.13.) The average monthly wage is 185 pesos. The maximum wage is 600 pesos—that is, less than ten times the minimum wage. Rent, which is paid to the state, is less than 10 percent of the renter's wage, no matter what the size of the property. The consumption of staples is controlled by means of ration books that regulate the supply, so Cuba's 10 million inhabitants are not subjected to the tragedy of hunger, which scourges most of Latin America's and the rest of the world's population. Surplus production is sold at a higher price on the parallel market, which is official. In the ration book, a kilogram of beef costs $1.35; a quart of milk, 25 centavos.

In 1981, the year of the last census, 52 percent of the population was under 30 years of age. In the first few years of the Revolution, demographic growth was higher than 2 percent per year, which is considered very high in this country. Now, it is 0.9 percent. In 1959, fewer than 2,000 students were graduated from the universities; 28,000 were graduated in 1984. Cuba now has 20,500 doctors, one for every 488 Cubans. The gradual reduction of disease has allowed Cuba to provide medical care in 28 other countries.

Alfredo Ham told us that per capita consumption and services for the population had increased by 2.5–3 percent per year. Inflation—which can't be estimated using capitalist criteria, because there isn't any financial speculation—is regulated by the state so the real value of workers' wages isn't affected; it comes to about 3 percent per year. Every year, real income grows more than inflation. The country is in a position to absorb the entire work force, and the low unemployment that does exist—approximately 6 percent of the economically active population—is due to the fact that, since family budgets are relatively high, some people can afford to remain unemployed until they can get the jobs they want—such as the case of a young university graduate or intermediate-level technician who wants a specific job in a certain place and doesn't want another job, even though often he would be paid as much as an engineer. Average daily calorie intake is between 3,000 and 3,500, much higher than the average minimum of 2,240 established by FAO. The Gross Domestic Product is more than $24 billion, with industry responsible for 50 percent of it.

Two

O N the evening of Monday, May 13, Fidel Castro received the small group of Brazilians in his office at the Palace of the Revolution. The worktable was surrounded by shelves full of books, cassettes and a transistor radio. On the table were papers; a glass jar full of candy; and a round box containing short, thin cigars—the Commander's favorites. An enormous picture—of Camilo Cienfuegos's face painted in soft lines—hung over some leather armchairs and a marble table from the Isle of Youth. Beyond them was a large meeting table with four chairs on each side and two at each end. There was another huge oil painting, of young students doing agricultural work. The office was large, comfortable and air-conditioned but not luxurious. Fidel, wearing an olive-green uniform, invited us to sit at the table. He was especially interested in talking with Joelmir Beting, who had to go back to Brazil before the rest of us. He asked about Joelmir's work, how he apportioned his time, how much time he had for study and how he managed to keep so much economic information in his head. He also asked about our trip to the Isle of Youth and Cienfuegos, commenting, "The Cienfuegos nuclear power plant is being built with all the requirements for absolute safety—to withstand tidal waves, earthquakes, even a passenger jet crash."

My mother praised Cuban cooking, especially the seafood. Fidel, who is also a chef, agreed. "The best thing is not to boil either shrimp or lobster, because boiling water reduces the substance and the taste and toughens the flesh. I prefer to bake or broil them. Five minutes of broiling is enough for shrimp. The lobster takes eleven minutes to bake or six minutes on a skewer over hot coals. Baste only with butter, garlic and lemon. Good food is simple food. I think that international chefs squander resources; in a consommé, many of the ingredients are wasted by including the eggshells; only the white should be used, so the leftover meat and vegetables can be used in a pie or something. One very famous chef is Cuban. Not long ago, he was preparing fish with rum and some other things for a visiting delegation. The only thing I liked was the turtle consommé—but, as I said, there was waste."

Turning to Joelmir Beting, he asked, "What's your daily work schedule like?"

"An hour and a half of radio programs every morning, half an hour of television in the evenings, and I write a daily column of economic commentary that's published in 28 Brazilian newspapers."

Fidel addressed him again: "How do you find the time to read and keep up with things? I spend an hour and a half every day reading the wire services, the dispatches from almost all the agencies. I receive them typed, in a folder, with a table of contents. The dispatches are in order, by topic: everything related to Cuba, then sugar—which is our basic export—U.S. politics, etc. If I read that a new pharmaceutical product has been discovered or a very useful new piece of medical equipment has been developed in some country, I immediately send for information about it. I don't wait for the specialized medical journals that take from six months to a year to publish the information. This week I found out that a new device had been developed in France to destroy kidney stones by means of ultrasound. It's much more economical than the one produced in the F.R.G. Two days later, a comrade left for Paris to get the information. We've also asked for information about a new pharmaceutical product that was discovered in the United States that halts infarction. Public health is one of the sectors I follow closely with great interest, as are scientific research in Cuba and abroad and national and international economic matters. Unfortunately, I don't have enough time to gather and analyze all the information I'm interested in. I wanted to be more up-to-date for this conversation with you, and I sent for all the important international economic news items from the last two months. I got four volumes of 200 pages each! It's not easy to keep up with the dynamics of events, the adventures of the U.S. dollar and the consequences of the United States' nefarious economic policy on the world economy."

Joelmir Beting said, "The dollar is a currency of intervention —armed intervention in our countries—rather than a reference currency. The rise of the dollar reflects the ruin of the U.S. economy. The ruble is tied to gold. The ruble has backing; the dollar doesn't. This is why the Soviet Union has been adversely affected by the increased value of the dollar since Nixon—over the phone —suspended the U.S. currency's gold backing. In a way, the currency that is buying the world today is counterfeit. The number of dollars circulating outside the United States is a mystery."

Fidel leafed through the folder containing the transcript of Monday's international dispatches. He commented that the folder wasn't very thick because politicians and journalists weren't used to working over the weekend.

"No one understands the computer man has in his head," he said. "I often wonder why so many people go into politics. It's a hard job. It's only worthwhile if it's done as a function of something useful, if some problem can really be solved. In conversations such as this one, with visitors, I try to learn. I try to find out what's going on in the rest of the world—especially Latin America."

"As Commander in Chief, you are responsible both for the administration of Cuba and for its international relations," Joelmir Beting observed. "Might two Commanders be necessary?"

"Everything here is decentralized and follows well-drawn-up plans. Moreover, there's a central group that facilitates the administration. It used to be a Roman circus, with each agency, each Ministry, struggling with the Planning Board, squabbling over appropriations. Now everyone is responsible for everything. The Ministry of Education also participates in the main decisions having to do with the plan, as do the Ministry of Public Health and the other service and economic agencies. Decisions are made quickly, without bureaucracy. Decisions can be made without talking to me, except when there's something very important or when it has to do with an area that I follow closely, such as health."

"Or special projects, such as the nuclear power plant?"

"I realized that that project was lagging behind. It was a matter of supervision methods. The team responsible for the project held quarterly assessment meetings. I found out, for example, that the workers' food, transportation and other living conditions weren't getting all the attention they required. Together with some of my staff, I went to the site and asked about the living conditions, the quality of the shoes and other work clothes, the transportation that took the workers to visit their families, the material supplies for the project, the lack of construction equipment and other aspects. What interests me is taking care of the men. A worker will feel more interested in the project if he has decent conditions and sees that his work is appreciated and that there is constant concern about his human and material problems. I saw that they were taken to their home provinces in trucks. I asked, 'How many buses are needed—30? We're going to try to get them. We'll use the ones we have in reserve.' I made some suggestions. I even gave them the idea of building a campsite near the project so their families could visit them and rest with them near the job site. Of course, the agencies responsible for the project needed resources and more direct support; they got it."

Fidel lit his small cigar with a chrome-plated cigarette lighter. He ran his slender fingers over his beard and continued: "I work directly with a team of 20 comrades, 10 of whom are women. They form a coordination and support group. Each one tries to find out what's going on in the country's main production and service centers by maintaining contact with them. Without clashing with the Ministries, this team makes decisionmaking more dynamic. It is composed of people, not departments. When I visited the nuclear power plant and found out about the quarterly meetings, I pointed out that the development of the project couldn't wait even one month, much less three. The meetings were an inventory of difficulties that had to be solved quickly. Now, representatives of the job site must report to the team office every day on how the work's progressing, what difficulties they have, etc. One of the team members who is specialized in this task visits the site systematically. The problems can't wait; they must be solved immediately. We do the same thing with other important, decisive projects."

"In Cienfuegos," Joelmir Beting interrupted, "I realized that knowing that the Commander is keeping an eye on the work is a great incentive."

"No office in the world has fewer people than mine. How many people do you work with?" Fidel asked Chomi, Secretary of the Council of State and former president of the University of Havana, who works closely with him.

"Six," he replied.

The Brazilian journalist asked, "Which agency assigns priorities for resources?"

"It used to be the Central Planning Board. Now it's more decentralized. People's Power, for instance, administers the schools, hospitals, transportation, trade and practically all local services. In a province such as Santiago de Cuba, People's Power selects the hospital director. Logically, this is done in consultation with the Ministry of Public Health, which provides the professional cadres and is in charge of the work methodology in the hospital."

"Is this decentralization something new?"

"No. We've always shared functions and responsibilities here."

"Is that the Cuban model?"

"There is a lot that is Cuban in the model. The electoral system, for example, is completely Cuban. Each election district—consisting of around 1,500 people—elects a delegate to People's Power. The voters nominate and elect the candidates without any intervention by the Party. They are the ones who nominate the candidates—from two to eight of them in each district. The Party isn't involved; it simply guarantees that the established standards and procedures are observed. On election day—they're held every two and a half years—whoever gets more than 50 percent of the vote is elected; if no one does, then there's a runoff election. Those elected are delegates to the Municipal Assembly and elect the members of the Municipal Executive Committee. Immediately after this, these delegates, together with the Party and the mass organizations, draw up a slate of delegates to the Provincial Assembly and the 500 members of the National Assembly. More than half of the members of the National Assembly are elected at the grassroots level of People's Power. Meetings are held periodically in each election district. In them, in the presence of the delegates who were elected, the voters discuss the delegates' work and, if they decide to, can revoke their mandate."

"When I visited a hospital, I noticed that the mothers had the right to accompany their sick children," Joelmir Beting observed.

"For a sick child," Fidel Castro explained, "the best nurse in the world is his mother. Before, they weren't allowed in, and they stayed at the hospital door, anxiously awaiting news about their children. The concept was that since the mothers hadn't had medical training, they might interfere with the medical treatment. Many years ago, we adopted another system that has had excellent results. In any pediatric hospital, the mother has the right to accompany her child; she's provided with the appropriate clothes to wear while in the hospital and is given meals free of charge. In the latest congress of the Federation of Cuban Women (FMC), which was held last March, the mothers asked for fathers to be given the same right. Frequently, a mother is busy with her other children and can't be at the hospital with the one who's sick. That petition is already being studied. We're even studying the possibility—also because the women have requested this—of having a son, a brother or the father of any other hospitalized patient accompany him. So far, only women have been allowed to do this, but they feel that this puts all the family burden on them, thereby limiting their possibilities for fulfilling their duties at work and obstructing their social advancement. Nowadays, women constitute 53 percent of the technical work force."

"Does the new five-year plan for 1986–1990 contain innovations in its methodology?"

"Yes. It's more rational. The emphasis is on the economic aspects—mainly on export products. For example, even though a certain province may want to build a new sports stadium or a theater, building a factory that will help to increase exports has priority. The stadium and the theater will be built when it's possible, but never at the expense of a priority economic objective. No aspect of the plan is a result of disputes among state agencies; rather, a global, rationalized policy is followed and accepted by all agencies. Thus, for example, we avoid struggles between the Ministry of Education and the Central Planning Board. The plan sets the standard for planning; it establishes priority sectors and organizes the distribution of resources. The fact that, during the past 26 years, we have built almost all the social projects we need in the fields of education, health, culture and sports allows us to assign most of our investments to economic projects without sacrificing social development. Growth in social services will be mainly in terms of quality and not so much in new installations, although some new facilities will also be built."

Calmly and clearly, Joelmir Beting asked, "Is there social projection in Cuba?"

"Yes, in its essential aspects," the President of the Council of Ministers replied.

"Are there deficiencies in the health sector?"

"As I said, we're investing to improve quality; this is the case, for example, with the building of pediatric hospitals. We have created family doctors, each of whom looks after a group of families directly in the neighborhood. They aren't the doctors who cure diseases; rather, they protect health by giving the families orientations regarding preventive measures. On the Isle of Youth, which you visited, there are junior high schools with students of 22 different nationalities. In the beginning, we were afraid they would bring in diseases that had already been eradicated here or even ones that were unknown here. We've been completely successful in confronting this possibility and have proved that all of the diseases that are scourges in Africa or other continents can be controlled by medical science and modern medicines. All foreign students are given medical examinations before they come from their countries, but if a sick person does slip through, he is never sent back home. Rather, he is looked after and cured in Cuba. Fortunately, the vectors for most of those diseases don't exist in Cuba. Our Institute of Tropical Medicine has made great progress in this field, which also serves to protect Cubans working in other Third World countries. Nutrition on the Isle of Youth is higher on the average than in the rest of the schools. Thanks to these initiatives, as I said, we've never had to send a student back to his country of origin for health reasons. Those students are very strong and healthy."

"Having achieved quantity, you are investing in quality."

"The Revolution has created the material base. Some sectors still have deficiencies and require large investments; this is the case with housing, though we are making progress. More than 70,000 housing units are being built each year."

"What about transportation?"

"During the first ten years of the Revolution, we didn't import any cars. Both the economic and trade blockade to which we were subjected and our own priorities channeled resources to other sectors, such as health and education. Whatever automobiles we import mustn't adversely affect social needs. About 10,000 are coming in every year now, and specialists, technicians and outstanding workers have priority."

"What about public transportation?"

"We import the motors and some other parts and build the rest of the buses here. Now we're working on the production of motors. Two out of every three automobiles that are imported are assigned to workers directly linked to production and services; they are sold almost at cost, to be paid for in installments over periods of up to seven years, at minimal interest. The workers' assembly in each work center decides who deserves them. Some of the imported cars are, of course, used for car rental services and for state administration."

"Does private property still exist in rural areas?"

"Yes. We still have nearly 100,000 independent farmers. They plant coffee, potatoes, tobacco, vegetables, a little sugarcane and some other products. So far, more than half of the independent farmers—there used to be 200,000 of them—have joined production cooperatives and have been very successful. Their incomes are high. Joining a cooperative is entirely voluntary. This movement is progressing on very solid foundations. It frees the state from mobilizing manpower to help them with the harvest, as used to be the case. Moreover, cooperatives bring improvements in the farmers' lives. They make it easier to provide them with schools, new housing, safe drinking water, electricity, etc. More than 85 percent of the homes in Cuba are supplied with electricity. Credits and prices are fixed by the government at levels that encourage production. Production surpluses bring even higher prices and are sent to the parallel market. The farmers don't pay taxes, and, like all other Cubans, their families are entitled to free health care and education. Members of cooperatives have annual incomes that range from $3,000 to $6,000—more than those of individual farmers, whose production costs on their isolated plots are higher and whose work is more difficult to mechanize. Ever since the beginning of the Revolution, we've been creating credit and service cooperatives. The services cover everything in the field of work implements, such as tractors, silos, trucks and cane harvesters. Now the production cooperatives own that equipment."

"May farmers contract manpower?"

"Yes, in accord with the laws of the land that protect the workers. Nowadays, thanks to progressive mechanization, it takes only 70,000 cane cutters to bring in a harvest of more than 70 million tons of sugarcane. Fifteen years ago, 350,000 were needed. Most of this manpower is supplied by the agricultural workers themselves. For many years now, we've had to mobilize very few volunteers, and we haven't had to mobilize any soldiers or high school students for these tasks. Unemployment isn't a problem in Cuba; to the contrary, most of our provinces have a labor shortage."

"Don't students participate in productive activities any more?" I asked.

"In the schools in the countryside, they do. We have about 600 schools of that type and about 300,000 students in them. They've been a tremendous success. In the cities, the junior and senior high school students may go voluntarily to the countryside for 30 days each year. More than 95 percent of them do. They help to harvest vegetables, pick citrus fruit, and bring in the tobacco and other crops. If a society universalizes the right to study, it should also universalize the right to work. Otherwise, you might create a nation of intellectuals who are divorced from physical work and material production. One example of that work-study combination is the schools on the Isle of Youth. Much of what has been done there was based on my own experience. I spent 12 years in boarding schools. I could go home only once every three months. We weren't allowed out of the school, even on Sundays. There was no coeducation. Now we have boys and girls in the same schools on the Isle of Youth. They are out in the open, with no walls around them; they can leave the school every day for their productive, sports or cultural activities. They don't just study, as we did in my time; that was tedious—sometimes unbearable—and produced much lower academic results. In any case, the main purpose of having the student work is pedagogical, not productive. We now have a million junior and senior high school students. Ninety-two percent of all the young people between the ages of 6 and 16 attend school. Enrollment in the middle level is already equal to that in the elementary level, where practically all of the children between 6 and 12 are enrolled."

I made a brief comment: "By eradicating economic antagonisms, socialism does away with the social classes. This is an objective phenomenon, but it doesn't necessarily reduce social differences from the subjective angle. Those who do nothing but intellectual work may feel superior to those who do direct work."

Fidel said, "Yes; that's why it's important for everyone to do manual labor. In addition to thinking, people also have to know how to do things. 'Doing is the best way of saying,' Martí said. That's why the students from the cities go to the countryside for 30 days. They used to go for 42 days, but now there are too many students and not enough places to send them. The ones who go do so voluntarily. But, as I said, 95 percent of them go. More than 600,000 workers are employed in education and health—in a country with a population of 10 million. It's as if 8 million people were employed in those activities in Brazil. Most of them are women. That is, six out of every 100 citizens are employed in health or education."

"Is there an oversupply of doctors in Cuba or a shortage of patients?" Joelmir Beting asked.

"Before answering, I'd like to add that we have a total of 3 million workers. There's a teacher for every 12 students, more or less. There are 30,000 students in the schools that specialize in training elementary school teachers. Fifteen years ago, 70 percent of our elementary school teachers had no degrees; now, they are all graduates. We have created a reserve of elementary school teachers. Ten thousand of them aren't teaching; they are being paid their salaries while receiving further training in the university. A Cuban elementary school teacher has studied for nine years at the elementary level and four at the secondary level and now has the opportunity to study for six years at the university level when he begins to work. He does this through independent study courses for part of the time and full-time study with pay for two years, winding up with a B.A. in elementary education. Our plan is to have all the elementary school teachers get university degrees. We already have 20,500 doctors and will graduate 50,000 more in the next 15 years. We already know where each of them is going to work. We also plan to introduce a sabbatical year for doctors: one year of full-time study for every seven years of work. There will never be too many doctors if there is an ambitious health program and adequate planning of services and of technical cadre training."

"Is bureaucracy a congenital disease of socialism?" the Brazilian journalist asked a little ironically.

"Bureaucracy is an evil of both socialism and capitalism. Since we can use our human resources better, I think we're going to win this battle. As I see it, the most irrational feature of capitalism is the existence of unemployment. Capitalism develops technology and underutilizes its human resources. It may be that socialism doesn't yet make the best possible use of human resources, but it doesn't subject human beings to the humiliation of unemployment, and we are making steady progress in increasing efficiency and work productivity."

It was already past 1:00 A.M. Fidel rose and began to walk back and forth, thinking out loud about how he was going to arrange things the next day—Joelmir Beting's last in Cuba—so he could continue talking with his Brazilian visitor. They agreed to have one interview in the afternoon and another in the evening.

Three

T UESDAY, May 14, 1985. At 4:00 P.M., Fidel Castro met Joelmir Beting and me in his office on the third floor of the Palace of the Revolution. The President of the Council of State led us through the halls to a suite of rooms where his Coordination and Support Team works. He introduced us to nearly the entire group, explaining the responsibilities of each. The Brazilian journalist asked about imports of oil, the main raw material for the island's energy system.

"We generate a part of our electricity from bagasse during the harvest season," Fidel answered. "All the sugar mills are run on sugarcane bagasse. Our country produces 20 million tons of bagasse—the equivalent of more than 4 million tons of oil. We use all of the bagasse. We have five factories that make wood from bagasse, and several factories use it to make paper. We aren't going to produce alcohol to fuel cars for recreational purposes. We use molasses as an animal feed and in the production of proteins. In addition, it's the raw material for making rum and domestic and industrial alcohol."

"What about must?" the commentator of the Bandeirantes TV network asked.

"It's being used a lot for animal feed. The must is washed, dried in the sun and given to the animals. Ten factories are producing feed from molasses. Up to 50 percent protein is obtained through a special fermentation process. It is used as poultry, hog and cattle feed. We trade a ton of this animal feed to the German Democratic Republic for a ton of powdered milk."

"I've heard that, because of an environmental protection law, every automobile in the United States will use yucca alcohol as fuel starting in 1986," Joelmir Beting said, "and it'll cost 45 cents a liter. Brazil would be in a position to ship alcohol to U.S. ports at 30 cents a liter, but the legislation of that country keeps it out, defending local industry. Brazil produces 2,500 liters of alcohol from every hectare of sugarcane—enough to meet a car's needs for a year."

Fidel said, "Just imagine how many hectares of sugarcane are needed for so many cars! It's sad to think that all that land is used to feed cars, not people."

Joelmir Beting explained, "It takes 4 million hectares of sugarcane to produce 10 billion liters of alcohol a year; this means a saving of $600 million a year for the country."

"Cuba produces more than 8 million tons of sugar a year in an area of 1.8 million hectares. We want to extend that area by 200,000 hectares."

"Brazil imports wheat," Joelmir said. "It's spending $1.2 billion a year—twice as much as it saves by producing alcohol—on wheat. If Brazil planted a million hectares to wheat, we'd save more than we're saving now by planting 4 million hectares to sugarcane for producing alcohol. A policy promoting the planting of wheat—which we don't have—would be more profitable than the policy of producing alcohol. Unfortunately, fuel for machines is more important to the Brazilian government than energy for men."

"Here in Cuba, we invest first in human energy."

Later on, Fidel explained, "We're building 157 new facilities in the field of public health. We have more than 20,000 medical students. Every year, more than 5,500 young people chosen on the basis of their sense of vocation and school record enter medical school."

The Commander in Chief invited us to enter a small lounge beside his office. Two people were working there, surrounded by IBM minicomputers. These memory banks of the Cuban government contain duly computed data, including the names of the country's 500 best doctors, by specialty. At Fidel's request, the comrade operating the machines touched the keys. The information appeared in different colors: Havana now has a population of

1,902,173. The Cuban capital has 7,856 doctors, 10,481 nurses and 11,136 health technicians; it has a doctor for every 242 inhabitants and a nurse for every 181. There are 20,403 doctors in the country as a whole, for a population of 9,952,699. There are 1,880 pediatricians—one for every 1,500 children.

After leaving the computer room, Fidel Castro invited us to go into a room where all the Ministers in the economic field were meeting. He introduced us and exchanged some information on the preparations for the third five-year plan. It was almost 6:00 P.M. when we left the Palace of the Revolution. In a few minutes, the Commander was due to attend a solemn celebration of the fortieth anniversary of the Allied victory in World War II, in the Soviet Embassy's new building.

Four

T HAT same night, at 10:30, Fidel Castro met us again in his office. Joelmir Beting would have to leave Cuba the next morning, and it was his last chance for talking during this trip. Eight Ministers in the economic field and Carlos Rafael Rodríguez, Vice President of the Council of State, were also there. Next to the wall, facing a rectangular meeting table, was a blackboard and chalk that our host placed at the disposal of the Brazilian journalist. In preparation for this talk, Joelmir Beting had read Fidel Castro's most recent interviews on the Third World's—especially Latin America's—foreign debt, including the interview given to the Mexican daily *Excelsior*, in which the Cuban leader had stated that the debt was unpayable.

"The political solution of the foreign debt," the journalist, who is a specialist on economic matters, said, "requires changes in U.S. and European bank legislation, changes in the creditor bloc. The participation of parliaments is vital. This is why," he told the group, "Fidel should send his suggestions to the parliaments. Cuba should issue a document on the foreign debt. The problem won't be solved unless there are government-to-government negotiations, not government-to-creditor-bank negotiations. At present, the understanding is between Brasília and Wall Street, not Brasília and Washington. In this way, the U.S. government washes its hands of the matter and takes part only through the IMF, which is really a bank auditor. The IMF should be a government-to-government forum. The dollar has stopped being a reference currency and become a means for intervening in world economic relations. In fact, the dollar is counterfeit currency, because it isn't backed by the U.S. economy; it isn't backed by the U.S. GNP. It's as if the United States were buying the world with counterfeit money. It's an unheard-of situation in capitalism. The last person to challenge this situation was General de Gaulle, and nothing came of it."

Fidel put his cup of tea down on the saucer and said, "Latin America borrowed devaluated dollars and now has to repay its debt with dollars that are worth more."

"That's financial piracy, to put it mildly," Joelmir said. "The proposal for a new economic order should link trade with debt— something that the big seven of the capitalist world now meeting in Bonn won't accept. The Third World must be protected from the monopoly the rich countries hold on technology. Brazil has just passed market reserve laws in the field of data processing."

"What does that mean?" Fidel asked.

"That no foreign industry may build minicomputer or personal computer factories in Brazil. They have to be set up with national capital."

"When was that?"

"Last September."

"Why was it done?"

"To protect technological innovations and the domestic market for national industries."

The Brazilian guest wrote the number 12 on the blackboard and added, "Brazil has to pay $12 billion in interest this year. It might capitalize half of the debt as 'new money' and send the rest. Instead of paying it all, it should turn this capitalization into risk capital for the multinationals. For instance, an automobile plant is going to be opened in Brazil. Instead of making a direct investment, the corporation is using a part of the capitalized interest. So, as soon as General Motors opens its automobile plant in Brazil, a part of the Brazilian debt is transferred to GM."

"So half the money that Brazil should pay isn't paid. It's used as a transnational investment in Brazil. Is that right?" Fidel asked.

"Yes."

"Did you hear what Alfonsín said in Chicago? That the interest which Argentina has to pay on the debt should be reinvested there. Is that the same thing?"

"Yes, but there's a real problem: the United States sets the interest rate. Banks establish an interest rate that is the rate of return on capital. Once that's turned into risk capital, it's Brazil—not the banks—that sets the profit remittance rate."

"How much profit remittance does Brazil allow at present?"

"Fiat, of Italy, made a $680 million investment in Brazil, not as a direct investment but rather as a loan from the main Italian office to the Brazilian branch, through a bank. It was a triangular operation. On that debt, Fiat sends the branch's interest to the main office and pays Brazil only 12.6 percent tax on the income."

"It pays 12.6 percent on the remittance of interest?" the Cuban leader asked.

"Yes. If Fiat remitted profits instead of interest, it would have to pay a 35.7 percent tax to Brazil. For remittance of profits and direct risk capital, a 35.7 percent tax has to be paid. Only 12 percent is paid on debt interest. Therefore, Fiat will turn debt into capital only if Brazil changes its fiscal laws so as to favor capital rather than the debt."

"It's trying to pay the lowest possible taxes," Fidel said.

"That's right. There won't be interest capitalization unless there's a reduction in the taxes on direct capital, because returns on direct investment are taxed at 35 percent, while the tax on returns on loans is 12 percent."

"Brazil doesn't limit return capital? It taxes it?"

"That's right."

"How much profit would there be on $680 million?"

"From 5 to 8 percent a year."

"That's low," Fidel Castro observed. "It won't stimulate investment."

"It's low because it costs the main office a lot to finance the branch. Fiat has to pay interest to the main office, and it transfers that cost to the Brazilian economy."

"Under present conditions, how much profit is there? On an investment of almost $600 million, what return does the main office get if there's been a direct investment, without the presence of the bank?"

"In the case of Fiat, it amounts to 8 percent of total sales."

"Of total sales!" our host exclaimed. "What does that amount to in terms of the $680 million? Less than 10 percent?"

"Less than 10 percent; 8 percent, liquid."

"With such low returns on capital invested, what incentive can the transnationals have for investing in Brazil?"

"They want to take over the market in the first stage. There's idle capacity at the world level, and Brazil is an important market in Latin America, which can be a springboard for the rest of the region. Brazil has very liberal laws on foreign capital. Financial costs are a camouflaged, clandestine profit, because returns on capital take the form of debt payments. For the main office, it's the same capital coming back. The main office is the branch's creditor. It's a recent invention that international capitalism came up with in Brazil. In Brazil, the transnationals owe their main offices $18 billion, all told, through the banks."

"Isn't that included in the foreign debt?" Fidel asked, lighting a small cigar.

"Yes. It amounts to a fifth of the debt."

"Because, supposedly, that money was lent?"

"Yes, it was lent by the main office to the branch, through the banks."

"What would be the profit on $600 million in South Korea?"

"Three times as much."

"Why did they invest so much over there? For that reason? Why did the transnationals invest so much in Taiwan and South Korea?"

"Because they're some sort of tax-free zone."

"They must be making more than 20 percent on what they invested."

"More," Joelmir Beting affirmed.

"More than 20 percent?"

"Yes, after a maturity period."

"And in Brazil it's a lot less?"

"A lot less."

"Then why have they invested so much in Brazil in the last few years? What motivated them?"

"They did it for the market potential. It's the scale of the market. Brazil is some kind of *Belindia*: Belgium plus India. It's an island of contrasts. In Brazil, we have 32 million consumers with the per capita income of Belgium. It's a big market. Every year, a million cars are manufactured. It's the seventh-largest automobile market in the world."

"Luxury cars," I stressed.

"Television sets and household appliances are manufactured too. There are 32 million consumers in a population of 133 million."

"The consumers don't amount to 25 percent of the total population," the Commander remarked. "I've been told that 10 percent of the population gets more than 50 percent of the national income. That is, a fourth of all Brazilians constitute an important mass market. How many are out of that market?"

"All the rest."

"A hundred million?"

"Yes, one hundred million people are literally out."

"Of those hundred million people, how many live in extreme poverty?"

"Thirty million live in a state of absolute poverty, and 40 million in relative poverty; that makes 70 million. The 32 million who are on the borderline constitute a market following the international pattern. Between the 70 million poor and the 32 million consumers, there's a working class that basically survives. The 70 million poor are really 70 million political prisoners of the system. This state of absolute poverty is equal to the worst there is in India in terms of hunger, disease and permanent unemployment. There are 18 million children under ten years old who don't have any homes or relatives. They're abandoned, like street dogs, and may be found all over Brazil."

"Sixty-four million Brazilians are under 19 years old," I added.

"Do those homeless children come from the 30 million workers' families?" Fidel asked, puzzled.

"No. They come from the 70 million people," the economics journalist explained.

"So that's where the 18 million abandoned children come from?"

"Yes, from 'India.' But the 32 million 'Belgians' constitute a larger mass market than there is in Argentina, Uruguay and Mexico. It's the biggest market in Latin America."

"Where are the Brazilian doctors and engineers?"

"In the 32 million."

"And the teachers?"

"In the 32 million too."

"How much does an elementary school teacher earn?"

"About $80."

"It may be that there are elementary school teachers among the 40 million living in relative poverty," the Cuban President commented.

"During the last five years of the great foreign debt crisis, there was a 27 percent drop in the 32 million Brazilians' purchasing power."

"For the 32 million? What about the 30 million workers?"

"A drop of 12 percent."

I gave another statistic: "Twelve million people are unemployed in Brazil right now."

Fidel concluded, "It can't be said that there are great incentives for the transnationals to invest in Brazil right now."

"That's right, because of the difficult problem of the foreign debt, the change of government and the possibility of great international confusion."

"Do you have information on the transnationals' investments all over the world? I think they must come to about $600 billion."

"No, it's $930 billion."

"Nine hundred and thirty billion?"

"Yes, that's the Third World's foreign debt."

Fidel said, "No, I'm asking about direct investments, not the debt."

"They amounted to $640 billion in 1982."

"Seventy-five percent of that is in the industralized countries."

"Yes," Joelmir Beting agreed.

"So that means around $150 billion in the Third World."

"Approximately."

There was a break for coffee, which was immediately followed by a long, exclusive interview that Fidel Castro gave the Brazilian journalist concerning the Cuban proposal regarding an analysis of the poor countries' foreign debts. I was present at the interview but didn't take any notes, for the publication of that material is the interviewer's responsibility, but he has allowed me to transcribe here the first part of his talk with the Cuban leader.

It was 5:30 A.M. Our host rose and said, "I still have to do my exercises and eat something. I haven't had a bite in 15 hours."

He walked through a doorway and invited us to follow him.

We went into a private elevator that took us to the garage in the basement of the Palace of the Revolution. We got into the Commander's Mercedes-Benz and drove through the streets of Havana, which were still dark in this presummer period. Another Mercedes, with guards, followed ours. A little later, the cars parked in front of the house where we were staying. Fidel Castro got out, said a warm good-bye to Joelmir Beting, who had to be at the airport in two hours, and shook my hand as well. In the living room, still feeling the excitement of the long meeting, Joelmir and I had some whiskey and some Cuban cheese. Outdoors, the blushing night withdrew before the discreet arrival of the day.

Five

FOLLOWING Joelmir Beting's return to Brazil, I waited for the time I would be called to interview the Commander. It was a long wait, as all anxious waits are. My parents and I spent the days going around Havana: visiting the Federation of Cuban Women, where Vilma Espín greeted us warmly; a nursery school; and the national office of the Committees for the Defense of the Revolution (CDRs). We strolled through the downtown part of the city, had ice cream at Coppelia—the best ice-cream parlor in the world, where only fresh products are used—and went shopping in the international hotels' shopping centers—dollar stores that are only for tourists. While paying a call on Jaime Ortega, Archbishop of Havana, my mother was given a beautiful picture in color of an effigy of Our Lady of Charity, Cuba's patron saint—a mulatto, as so many Latin American Marys are. Moreover, like our own Lady of the Apparition, the effigy was found in the ocean by poor fishermen, in 1607.

I had no hopes of interviewing Fidel Castro over the weekend. On Saturday afternoon, my parents went off to Varadero, which is considered the most beautiful beach in Cuba. I couldn't go, because I was scheduled to give a public talk on Jesus' spirituality that evening at the Dominican convent. Around 70 people attended, including several Communist friends: Brazilian Hélio Dutra and his wife, Ela; Marta Harnecker, of Chile, the author of several books on the fundamentals of Marxism; and Jorge Timossi, from the Casa de las Américas. Two very dear friends were also there: Cintio Vitier, one of the best Cuban poets, and Fina, his wife. Among the priests, the congenial Father Carlos Manuel de Céspedes, Vicar General of Havana and Secretary of the Cuban Episcopal Conference, was outstanding. Young and adult lay people, monks, nuns and seminarians also attended. I gave the talk in the conference room of the convent; it brought to mind the lingering presence of the Dominican friars in Cuba; of Bartolomé de las Casas, defender of the Indians; and of those who founded the University of Havana in 1728. Now, there are only five Dominican friars on the entire island, two of whom are at the Vedado convent.

When we speak of spirituality, the word reminds us of spiritual retreats, quiet and secluded places, saintly people and photographs of sunsets by the sea or ponds like mirrors. Spiritual life sounds like something opposed to carnal, material life; something that entails a retreat from the world, from everyday life; a unique privilege for those poor mortals who don't benefit from the haven offered by contemplative monasteries. There are countless "spiritualities" within the Church: the Dominican, the Franciscan, the Jesuit, the Marian; those offered by workshops on Christianity; etc. Theologically, what does it mean to "adopt spirituality"? It means adopting *a way of following Jesus*. We can follow Him the way Francis of Assisi or Theresa de Avila or Thomas a Kempis or Teilhard de Chardin did. Despite the fact that, among the Latin American low-income classes, several native, devotional and pilgrim spiritualities sprang up around black- and brown-skinned Marys— such as Our Ladies of Charity, of Guadalupe and of the Apparition—at the institutional level of the Church, the spiritualities imported from Europe prevailed; the theology was also imported. Religious schools taught a European, bourgeois way of following Jesus that contradicted not only our reality—which was characterized by flagrant social contradictions—but also the Gospel's own prescriptions. Rome's difficulties in understanding Liberation Theology are the result of its inability to accept a theology other than the one prepared in Europe, within the Church. Can there be different theological approaches within one and the same Church? When I lived in the hills of Santa María, in Victoria, a worker who lived next door asked me for a book on "the life of Jesus." I gave him a copy of the New Testament. Every time I saw him, I would ask, "Tell me, Seu Antonio, have you read the life of Jesus?" One day he told me, "Betto, I've read all the Gospels and learned a lot, yet I must tell you something: I found that the stories about Jesus are too repetitious." This is a good example, showing that, in the Gospels themselves, there are four different theologies: Matthew's, Mark's, Luke's and John's. Theology is the reflection of faith within a given reality. Luke wrote his evangelical account with pagans in mind, whereas Matthew wrote for the Jews. Who writes theology within the Church? All Christians do. Theology is the fruit of the reflection that the Christian community—immersed in a reality— makes of its faith. Thus, each Christian theologizes, just as each housewife economizes at the market. Not every housewife is an economist, just as not every Christian is a theologian. Theologians are those who have a good command of the scientific bases of theology and who, at that same time, grasp the reflection of faith given by the community and formulate it systematically.

After Vatican II, the Latin American Church started to formulate its own theology. It stopped importing it from Europe. Prior to this, every seminarian had had to speak some French in order to study the works on theology of Father Congar, De Lubac, Guardini or Rahner. This new Latin American theology, which came into being in the Christian Base Communities in the region and was the result of the challenge posed by the liberation process of the oppressed, has been systematized by such men as Gustavo Gutiérrez and Leonardo Boff. It differs from Europe's Liberal Theology in its methodology. Theology is faith's answer to the challenges posed by reality. What were the most important events in Europe during this century? Undoubtedly, World Wars I and II. They gave rise, in European culture, to disturbing questions regarding self, the value of the human being and the purpose of life. All of the philosophical work of Husserl, Heidegger, Sartre and Karl Jaspers, the literary work of Albert Camus and Thomas Mann, and Buñuel's and Fellini's films try to answer those questions. Theology is no exception. In its attempts to relate to European reality, it seeks the mediation of personalist philosophy, whose axis is the human being. Now, then, what is the aspect that has characterized Latin America in this century? It is the collective, majority existence of millions of hungry people. It is the nonperson. And theology has discovered that the mediation of philosophy doesn't suffice for understanding the political and structural reasons for the massive existence of the nonperson. It is necessary to resort to the social sciences—even to Marxism. This relationship gave rise to the methodology of Liberation Theology, which corresponds to the liberating, evangelical experience of the Christian faith in Latin America. To fear Marxism is like fearing mathematics because you suspect it was influenced by Pythagoras. Today, no one can honestly talk about social contradictions and not pay some tribute to the concepts systematized by Marx. It doesn't matter whether or not they are Marxist concepts; what's important is that they scientifically convey the reality they express. Even Pope John Paul II borrowed from Marx when he spoke of class tensions and social inequalities in his encyclical on human work, *Laborem Exercens*. Before fearing Marxism because it declares itself to be atheist, we should ask ourselves what kind of fair society we have built in this world that declares itself to be Christian.

Spirituality refers not only to our spiritual life. It refers to man as a whole, in his spiritual and bodily unity. No such division between matter and spirit exists for the Hebrews. St. Paul even mentions "spiritual body," which sounds contradictory. In the Bible, spiritual knowledge is experimental knowledge. Actually, you only know what you experience. The spirit-body division comes to us by way of Greek philosophy, which made inroads on Christian theology starting in the fourth century. The Greeks thought that the more we negated physical, corporal and material reality, the more spiritual we were. In the Gospels, the totality of the human being is what brings life to the spirit. Thus, spirituality isn't the way you *feel* the presence of God. Nor is it the way you *believe*. Jesus said, "Not every one that saith unto me, Lord, Lord, shall enter into the kingdom of heaven; but he that doeth the will of my Father which is in heaven." Thus, spirituality is a *way of living*, life according to the spirit. José Martí, outstanding hero and forerunner of Cuba's liberation, said that "doing is the best way of saying." For Christians, living is the best way of believing. Faith without deeds is worthless; as James stated, "What doth it profit, my brethren, though a man say he hath faith, and have not works? can faith save him? If a brother or sister be naked, and destitute of daily food, And one of you say unto them, Depart in peace, be ye warmed and filled; notwithstanding ye give them not those things which are needful to the body; what doth it profit? Even so faith, if it hath not works, is dead, being alone" (2:14–17).

Our way of life is the result of what we believe. Our way of being in the Church is a reflection of our concept of God. In order to know a church, the best question to ask is, "What do your faithful think about God?" It is a mistake to think that all believers believe in the same God. I often ask myself if there is any similarity between the God I believe in and the one in whom Reagan believes. We forget that, in the Old Testament, the prophets were worried by idolatry, the gods created in accord with human interests. There is still much idolatry. In the name of God, the Spaniards and Portuguese invaded Latin America and massacred millions of Indians. In the name of God, multitudes of slaves were brought from Africa to work the land. In the name of God, bourgeois rule was established in this part of the world. Could it be that the name spoken by conquistadores, slave owners and capitalist oppressors is that of the God of the poor, of whom Jesus spoke? I remember the tragedy of Albert Schweitzer, who was a musician, doctor and theologian. Influenced by Protestant research works on the authenticity of Jesus, he concluded that the young man from Nazareth hadn't expected to die so soon and that, therefore, the conspiracy woven around Him had taken Him by surprise. Now, then, a god is never wrong. If Jesus couldn't anticipate the time of His death, it was because He wasn't God, Schweitzer concluded. A few years ago, an English minister by the name of Robinson published a book that became a best seller: *Honest to God*, which was translated in Brazil as *A Different God*. The author states that we must be honest with God and confess that we do not know Him. What we know are sketches, such as the God invoked in official documents, at critical moments in life and in political speeches.

How do you know a person: by what you think about him or by what he reveals? If true knowledge is derived from revelation, we can best know God in Jesus Christ, His historic presence. Even though medieval theology defines God as omniscient, omnipresent, omnipotent, etc., what we find when we open the Gospels is a fragile being who lives among the poor; cries over the death of a friend; feels hunger; argues with the Apostles; is enraged by the Pharisees; insults Herod; is aware of temptation; and, when in agony, goes through a crisis of faith when He feels abandoned by His Father. Perhaps Albert Schweitzer wouldn't have lost faith in the divinity of Jesus if he had recognized that divinity is not expressed by the fact that Jesus had some kind of a computer in His head enabling Him to foresee everything. According to the New Testament, God's main attribute is love. In his first epistle, John the Apostle is quite clear: "Beloved, let us love one another: for love is of God; and every one that loveth is born of God, and knoweth God. He that loveth not knoweth not God, for God is love" (4:7–8). For the Greeks, who influenced the medieval definition of God, love can never be an attribute of a god; to the contrary, it is a lack, to the extent to which it implies a relation with the loved object. In this sense, Jesus is God because He loved only as God loves, and, therefore, He did not sin. He was a man centered not upon Himself but upon His Father and the people. This concept of loving God led to the founding of a Church based on fraternity, on a community of interests, rather than authoritarianism. It is a concept which enables Christians to discover the presence of God in all those who, though lacking faith, are capable of attitudes of love. God is present even in those who lack faith, and He has identified historically with all those who most need our love: the oppressed. "For I was an hungred, and ye gave me meat: I was thirsty, and ye gave me drink..." Jesus said in Matthew 25. Love is necessarily a liberator.

Once you have clarified this question of a loving God, a God calling for justice and defending the rights of the poor, it is easier to speak of Jesus' spirituality. If we consider the Gospel accounts, we can clearly see that Jesus' spirituality wasn't one of withdrawal from the world, of moving away from everyday life in order to better serve God, of denying earthly realities. In John 17:15, Jesus asked His Father to keep His disciples from evil without taking them out of the world. Jesus' entire existence was one of immersion in the ideological conflict, in the arena where different concepts and options for or against the oppressed were discussed. Nor was Jesus' spirituality that of moralism. That is the spirituality of the Pharisees, who turn their moral virtues into a sort of conquest of sanctity. Many Christians have been trained along these lines to lose strength in their faith because they don't manage to adjust to the pharisaical moralism they seek. God seems to live on the top of a mountain, and spirituality is taught as a manual for mountain climbing to be used by Christians interested in scaling its steep slopes. Since we are of a fragile nature, we begin our climb over and over again.... It is the constant repetition of the Sisyphus legend, rolling the stone uphill. Now, then, one of the best examples of Jesus' nonmoralism is the story of His encounter with the Samaritan woman. From the point of view of the morals prevailing in those times, she was an outcast—for being a woman, a Samaritan and a concubine. It was to that woman, however, that Jesus first revealed the messianic nature of His mission.

An interesting dialogue took place between them: "The woman saith unto him, Sir, give me this water, that I thirst not, neither come hither to draw. Jesus saith unto her, Go, call thy husband, and come hither. The woman answered and said, I have no husband. Jesus said unto her, Thou hast well said, I have no husband: For thou hast had five husbands; and he whom thou now hast is not thy husband: in that saidst thou truly. The woman saith unto him, Sir, I perceive that thou art a prophet. Our fathers worshipped in this mountain;

and ye say, that in Jerusalem is the place where men ought to worship. Jesus saith unto her, Woman, believe me, the hour cometh,
when ye shall neither in this mountain, nor yet at Jerusalem, worship the Father. ... But the hour cometh, and now is, when the true
worshippers shall worship the Father in spirit and in truth..." (John
4:15–23).

At no time did Jesus recriminate her for having had six men in
her life. He was interested in verifying that she was real. She didn't
lie, didn't take a pharisaical position; therefore, she was able to adore
"in spirit and in truth," in a subjective opening to God and in an
objective commitment to the truth. Thus, Jesus showed that Christian life wasn't a movement of man toward God; before that, there is
God's love directed toward man. God loves us irremediably. It only
remains for us to know if we are more or less open to that love, for
every love relationship demands reciprocity and entails absolute
freedom. Christian morality, then, doesn't stem from our pharisaical
intention of being sinless; it is a consequence of our love relationship
with God, as love imposes fidelity in a couple. The parable of the
Prodigal Son is a good example of the gratuitousness of the Father's
love. "But when he was yet a great way off, his father saw him, and
had compassion, and ran, and fell on his neck, and kissed him"
(Luke 15:20). The father's pardon and happiness is expressed over
the mere fact of the son's return, even before the latter explains the
reason for his absence and apologizes. So is God's love for us.

We see that Jesus' spirituality was *life in the spirit, within the
historical conflict, in a communion of love with the Father and the people.*
This spirituality was the result of His opening to the Father's gift
and of His liberating commitment to the life aspirations of the oppressed. For Jesus, the world wasn't divided between the pure and
the impure, as the Pharisees wished; it was divided between those
who favored Life and those who supported Death. Everything that
generates more life—from a gesture of love to social revolution—is
in line with God's scheme of things, in line with the construction
of the Kingdom, for life is the greatest gift given to us by God.
Whoever is born is born in God, to enter the sphere of life. At the
same time, Jesus' spirituality contradicted that of the Pharisees,
which consisted of rites, duties, asceticisms and the observance of
discipline. Fidelity is the center of life for the Pharisees; the Father
was the center of life for Jesus. The Pharisees measured spirituality
by the praxis of cultural rules; Jesus measured it by the filial opening to God's love and compassion. For the Pharisees, sanctity is a
human conquest; for Jesus, it was a gift of the Father for those
who opened up to His Grace. Jesus' spiritual vigor stemmed from

His intimacy with God, whom He familiarly called *Abba*—that is, Father (Mark 14:36). Like all of us who believe, Jesus had faith, and He spent hours in prayer to nourish it. Luke recorded those hours in which Jesus allowed His spirit to be replenished by the Father's Spirit: "And he withdrew himself into the wilderness, and prayed" (5:16); "And it came to pass in those days, that He went out into a mountain to pray, and continued all night in prayer to God" (6:12); and "And it came to pass, as he was alone praying" (9:18). In that communion with the Father, He found strength for struggling for the scheme of Life, challenging the forces of Death, represented particularly by the Pharisees, against whom the Gospels present two violent manifestos (Matthew 23 and Luke 11:37–54). And, in this sense, all who struggle for Life are included in God's scheme, even if they lack faith. "Then shall the righteous answer him, saying, Lord, when saw we thee an hungred, and fed thee? or thirsty, and gave thee drink? When saw we thee a stranger, and took thee in? or naked, and clothed thee?... And the King shall answer and say unto them, Verily I say unto you, Inasmuch as ye have done it unto one of the least of these my brethren, ye have done it unto me" (Matthew 25:37–40).

It is your fellow man, and especially the one who lacks life and needs justice, in whom God wishes to be served and loved. They are the ones with whom Jesus identified. Therefore, there is no contradiction between the struggle for justice and the fulfillment of God's will. One demands the other. All who work along the line of God's scheme for Life are considered Jesus' brothers and sisters (Mark 3:31–35). This is the best way to follow Jesus, especially in Latin America's present situation. I prefer to say that Jesus had a *spirituality of the conflict*—that is, a vigor in His commitment to the poor and to the Father who granted Him immense internal peace. True peace is not obtained by erecting walls; it is the result of trust in God. Courage is not the opposite of fear; faith is. That faith gave Jesus the necessary will for carrying out the scheme of Life, even by sacrificing His own life in confrontation with the forces of Death, such as oppression, injustice and religion made sclerotic by rules and rites.

After the talk, few questions were asked. The audience seemed inhibited. It was late, and I went with Jorge Timossi and Marcela to have some rum at Marta Harnecker's house.

Six

O N the afternoon of Sunday, May 19, 1985, I gave the second talk at our Cuban convent. There were fewer people, around 50 of them. My subject was the scheme of Life in Jesus.

Jesus' way of fulfilling God's will was through a commitment to the scheme of Life. This is made very clear in this account of St. Mark's:

> And it came to pass, that he went through the corn fields on the sabbath day; and his disciples began, as they went, to pluck the ears of corn. And the Pharisees said unto him, Behold, why do they on the sabbath day that which is not lawful? And he said unto them, Have ye never read what David did, when he had need, and was an hungred, he, and they that were with him? How he went into the house of God in the days of A-bí-a-thar the high priest, and did eat the shewbread, which is not lawful to eat but for the priests, and gave also to them which were with him? And he said unto them, The sabbath was made for man, and not man for the sabbath: Therefore the Son of man is Lord also of the sabbath" (Mark 2:23–28).

The account shows a conflict between Jesus' group and that of the Pharisees. Jesus and His disciples picked the ears of corn, which the law of God forbade on the sabbath, which was considered a holy day, when no work was allowed. Jesus knew this, but, as usual, He didn't apologize. Instead, he referred to the testimony of David, whom the Pharisees respected greatly and who had apparently behaved much worse than Jesus and His disciples, respecting neither the sabbath nor the very house of God, the temple. He didn't pick mere ears of corn; he took the shewbreads —the Host, as we would say today—ate some and gave some to his comrades. Jesus knew that David's behavior also went against the religious rules. What strong reason led Jesus not only to justify David's behavior but to behave in the same manner? The answer is in verse 25: "Have ye never read what David did, when he had need, and was an hungred, he, and they that were with him?" That is, man's material need, the basic foundation of life, was the most sacred thing for Jesus. Idolatry deprives human beings of sacredness, transferring it to liturgical observances and to the material of the cult, such as the temple. For Jesus, it was impossible to speak of spiritual life apart from the material conditions of existence. There is nothing more sacred than man, the image and likeness of God. The hunger of that man was an offense to the Creator Himself. A religion that cares for the supposed sacredness of its objects but turns its back on those who are the real temples of the Spirit is worthless. In São Bernardo do Campo, a city where I work with workers, whenever there are strikes and the government takes over the union, the priests of the local parish open their doors so the metalworkers can hold their meetings. Other priests are shocked and believe that this is a profanation of the temple. They don't understand that, to Jesus' way of thinking, there is nothing more sacred than the right to life. And a strike, a union meeting, is a collective effort to obtain better living conditions. Hence, Jesus' conclusion in Mark's account: "The sabbath was made for man, and not man for the sabbath." The most sacred thing that can exist—such as the sabbath—should be at the service of human life, not the other way around. A church that places its patrimonial interests ahead of the demands of justice, life and the people among whom it is inserted is certainly a church that considers man less important than the sabbath and, like the Pharisees, reverses evangelical priorities.

In His practice, Jesus didn't separate spiritual needs from the material demands of human life. This is made very clear in the parable of the multiplication of the loaves (Mark 6:34–44). A multitude, "five thousand men," had just heard Jesus' sermon. His disciples came to Him and suggested, "This is a desert place, and now the time is far passed: Send them away, that they may go into the country round about, and into the villages, and buy themselves bread: for they have nothing to eat." The people's hunger wouldn't be a problem to one who preached spiritual life, but Jesus reacted: "Give ye them to eat." You can't send a hungry crowd away. This too is a problem you should confront. It is interesting to observe that the disciples used the verb *to buy*, and the Teacher, *to give*. Yet the disciples didn't understand Jesus' proposal: "Shall we go and buy two hundred pennyworth of bread, and give them to eat?" There were some who thought that money was enough to meet the people's needs. It was the *bolo*[3] theory: first have it grow, accumulate a lot of capital and then distribute it among everyone. Jesus replied, "How many loaves have ye? go and see." He didn't ask how much money His disciples had; rather, He asked how many goods, how many loaves, they had. Wanting to meet the needs of the collective's life through income distribution, as social-democratic countries seek to do, is very different from meeting its needs through the distribution of goods, as is done in Cuba. In order to amass so many resources, countries such as Sweden—where even the workers have a high standard of living—need to keep the transnational corporations exploiting the Third World countries. In order to socialize its few assets and eradicate poverty, Cuba didn't need to exploit any other country. Mark went on to say that the Apostles checked that there were five loaves and two fishes. "And they sat down in ranks, by hundreds, and by fifties." People organize themselves to solve their problems. Jesus took the loaves and the fishes, "looked up to heaven, and blessed, and brake the loaves" for his disciples to distribute. Throughout the Gospels, the distribution of bread symbolizes the Father's kindness and the establishment of fraternity. Food is associated with life's abundance; it appears in the marriage in Cana and the meeting of the resurrected with the disciples at Emmaus. "And they did all eat, and were filled. And they took up twelve baskets full of the fragments, and of the fishes." If, at the end, twelve baskets of fragments are left, how many extra baskets were there in the crowd? And what did they have? Now, wherever a crowd is gathered, salesmen come up with sandwiches, soft drinks and candy. In Jesus' time, food was carried in baskets. Moreover, five loaves plus two fish is equal to seven, and seven in the Bible means "many," just as our number eight, on its side, symbolizes the infinite. Thus, it is said that our sins will be forgiven not only seven but seventy and seven times. Therefore, there were many fish and many loaves. Does it mean there was no miracle? Miracle,

---

[3] The cake theory of the economic policy of the Brazilian military regime. It defended the principle that you must let the cake grow before distributing it among the people—which never occurred under the military.

yes; not magic. Magic would be the spectacular action of taking five loaves in one hand and two fish in the other, covering them with a cloth, saying "Abracadabra" and showing a bakery on one side and a fish shop on the other. What is the miracle? It is God's power to alter the natural course of things. That power acts mainly on the human heart. That day, those who had goods shared them with those who had none; there was enough to satisfy everyone, and some was left over. At the same time, this account is the prefiguration of eschatological reserve. The twelve baskets with food are related to the twelve tribes of Israel, protagonists in God's scheme in history, and to the group of twelve Apostles, pillars of the Church.

The source of Jesus' spirituality, of the force that impelled Him to struggle determinedly for the scheme of Life, was His intimacy with the Father, which was nurtured through prayer. The Gospels refer to Jesus' prayers and transmit His teachings in this regard. They teach us the Our Father and encourage prayers of petition and of praise. However, the texts speak of the great amount of time that Jesus spent praying. As I see it, this is one of the critical points of Christian spirituality in the West and of the superficiality of our faith. We don't pray deeply. We ask, praise and meditate, but that's merely the threshold of the life of prayer. Only farther on can we attain the mystic vigor that inspired Jesus. During this learning period, the best thing is to refer to the experiences of the Christians who lived intensely in intimacy with God and described the route they took.

St. Augustine said that God was more intimate for us than we were for ourselves. Thus, the deepest prayer is the one that springs from the silence of the senses and of the mind and swells the heart for the Spirit to manifest itself. St. Paul said, "Likewise the Spirit also helpeth our infirmities: for we know not what we should pray for as we ought: but the Spirit itself maketh interces- sion for us with groanings which cannot be uttered. And he that searcheth the hearts knoweth what is the mind of the Spirit, be- cause he maketh intercession for the saints according to the will of God" (Romans 8:26–27). This letting the Spirit pray within us re- quires gratitude in the relation with God, as happens in the rela- tions of a couple. We then attain moments of inner silence in which we experience that unutterable Presence that fertilizes our faith. From thence springs Christian life rooted in theological expe- rience. At that level, we go beyond Christian life as mere sociologi- cal conditioning, as a kind of ideology of faith that, in principle, is opposed to an ideology of atheism. We are all born atheists. As

Vatican II says in *Gaudium et Spes*, atheism is also present in the lack of testimony of Christians. I don't think it should cause us as much concern as the idolatry that exists in various expressions of faith that have nothing to do with the God heralded by and embodied in Jesus, as in the case of those who call on God in defense of capital, colonialism, social and racial discrimination, and repression against the workers. The dialogue between Christians and Marxists should be held not at the level of truths of faith but rather at the level of the praxis of liberation, of the demands of justice, of selfless service to the life of the community. That is the level of love, the fundamental criterion of our realization and our salvation. St. Paul even says that though we have the faith to move mountains, if we don't have charity, it serves no purpose: we would be as sounding brass or a tinkling cymbal (I Corinthians 13:1–13). In the praxis of liberation, those who struggle in the name of God for the scheme of Life will be separated from those who join the party of Death. That praxis brings together Christians and atheists who are committed to building a society of fraternity in which the bounty of life will be shared equally. However, the possible opening of those atheists to the call of faith will undoubtedly depend on the testimony and coherence of the Christians, so the gift of God, as a seed, may find tilled soil.

There were few questions. One of the young people complained that the lecture hadn't been well advertised. A man replied, saying that a lot of announcements had been made. Perhaps this approach to Christianity was unheard of for an audience such as that one. The blockade that the United States imposed against Cuba also, in a way, isolated the Christians on the island. Many remained on imperialism's side against the socialism and communism that were established, which proclaimed themselves to be atheist. Nevertheless, in recent years, new winds have been blowing in the Cuban Church. In mobilizing all of its forces to review its pastoral practice and establish new lines in its evangelizing activity, the Cuban Church is now experiencing a new Pentecost.

Seven

ONDAY, May 20, 1985. The island awoke and was startled by a new imperialist act of aggression: Radio Martí had just begun broadcasting on shortwave from the United States. The fact that an anti-Cuban radio station used the name of the most venerated national hero and inspirer of the Revolution hurt the people's feelings. For 14 hours every day, the radio station broadcasts news and commentary from the Voice of America, music, and speeches hailing Reagan's policy and attacking the Cuban government.

The Cuban government reacted immediately. On the morning of that same day, *Granma*, the official organ of the Central Committee of the Communist Party, carried an article called "Information for the People" on its front page. Signed by the government, it announced that the agreement on migratory matters that had been signed by delegations from the two countries in New York on December 14 was thereby suspended, as were visits to Cuba by Cuban citizens living in the United States—"except those authorized for purely humanitarian reasons"—and that measures regarding the communications between the two countries would be adopted. These included a decision that "the government of Cuba reserves the right to transmit medium-wave radio broadcasts to the United States to make fully known the Cuban view on the problems concerning the United States and its international policy."

I wondered whether or not it would be possible to interview

the man who, once again, was the center of attention because of his fearless confrontation of the U.S. government's acts of aggression. In any case, I stayed at home, waiting for his office to phone me. Nobody called, and the day dragged slowly by, weighing on the harsh agony of my silent anxiety. The graphic symbols in the books I tried to read failed to break through the blockade of imaginings that flooded my mind.

At 10:30 P.M. on Tuesday, May 21, 1985, the phone rang. It was the Commander's office, telling me not to go out. At midnight, a small Alfa Romeo driven by a member of the Ministry of the Interior picked me up and took off like a jet, going first along 5th Avenue and then along Paseo, as if it had been challenged to make all the traffic lights before they turned red.

Commander Fidel Castro welcomed me at his office. Jesús Montané Oropesa, a member of the Central Committee and one of Fidel's oldest comrades in the 26th of July Movement's struggle against the Batista dictatorship, was with him. A mild, almost sweet smell of cigars filled the room. I sat down in a leather armchair and, with a lump in my throat, heard the Commander explain that, due to the inauguration of the U.S. radio station, which had insulted Cubans by taking the name of José Martí, and also because of other work, it might not be possible to have the interview at that time. I would either have to extend my visit or return in a few weeks. The idea of the full, stifling agenda that awaited me in Brazil passed through my mind.

There was no possibility at all of my staying any longer on the island or of returning in a few months, because of serious work engagements. I insisted on taking advantage of the opportunity. He resisted, saying that he wanted to be better prepared for an interview on such a delicate and important topic as religion. Before the interview, he wanted to read Leonardo Boff's *Jesucristo libertador* (Jesus Christ the Liberator) and *Iglesia, carisma y poder* (The Church, Charisma and Power) and the Vatican II and Medellín documents, Spanish copies of which lay on top of his desk. He also wanted to study Gustavo Gutiérrez' works, and he needed a little more time to read the complete texts of the speeches given by John Paul II during his February 1985 tour of Latin America. I wondered how, with his tight work agenda, the Cuban leader could combine the countless tasks of government, his intellectual voracity for the most diverse topics and the pleasure of talking. I didn't recall ever meeting another person with such a sharp intelligence and inclination for personal talks. Joelmir had rightly noted and commented to me that Fidel enhanced everything, giving great importance to whatever topic was being discussed, from cooking to the Third World's foreign debt.

In view of my silent resistance, he requested that I read the questions I wanted to ask him. After hearing the first five, he immediately became interested. Those were the ones related to his personal history and the Christian education he had received. He had probably imagined an endless list of theological questions for which he would require a bibliographic preparation. He asked me to stay at least two more days in Cuba, so we could work better. His main difficulty was that he had to welcome a delegation of Latin American visitors who would arrive that Thursday, but he expressed his willingness to find some time for beginning the interview.

On Wednesday, May 22, 1985, I found out that the delegation had canceled its trip. That was good news for me. After dinner, I received a message that someone would call me that same evening for a meeting with the Commander. At 11:45 P.M. the Commander's Mercedes-Benz drew up at the door.

"Where are your parents?" Fidel asked.

I told him they had just gone to sleep but that I would wake them up. He wouldn't hear of it, and he invited me to go for a drive through the city. He'd just come from a dinner at the residence of the Papal Nuncio, given in honor of Monsignor Cordero Lanza de Montezemolo, Nuncio in Nicaragua and Honduras, who was visiting Cuba at the personal invitation of the Commander in Chief. We talked about the situation of the Church in Nicaragua, and I told him my opinion that the bishops' failure to explicitly and directly denounce the aggression promoted by the U.S. government was harming the life of faith of many Nicaraguan Christians, mainly the youth, who didn't feel supported by their parish priests. Anti-Communist prejudices were keeping the episcopate silent regarding the actions by the mercenary troops stationed in Honduras who go into Nicaraguan territory to murder farmers and even children. The victims included the Barredas; the husband had led a course on Christianity, and I had met him in Estelí during a pastoral meeting in 1981. Throughout history, men of the Church have committed a serious mistake by remaining silent in the face of the criminal elimination of human lives, in the name of the alleged defense of orthodox principles. My contact with the popular Christian communities in Sandino's homeland has taught me that all is not lost. Faith is reborn, with even greater strength, from these tests, with the awareness that the Church is not the exclusive preserve of the bishops and priests but belongs to all people of God in communion with their pastors and with the pastors at the service of the people.

The Commander listened to me. Then, before starting to talk about Cuba, he said, "I prefer not to meddle in the internal affairs of the Church."

Late that night, when he took me home, I insisted on waking my parents up. Quite surprised, in housecoat and pajamas, they greeted Fidel in the living room. When he found out that we were returning to Brazil via Mexico, he started reminiscing about when he had lived in the capital of that country and commenting with my mother about the preparation, seasoning and taste of Mexican food.

II
The Talks

One

T HURSDAY, May 23, 1985. I arrived at the Palace of the Revolution a little after 9:00 P.M. A heavy rain was falling in Havana, offsetting the drought of the last few days. Vilma Espín, president of the Federation of Cuban Women, was just finishing a meeting with Fidel when I got to his office.

We sat at the rectangular meeting table, Fidel across from me. He was wearing his olive-green uniform, with a red-and-black rhomboid emblem with a white star in the center, between two branches, on each shoulder. To his left, there was a box of cigars; to his right, a small white teacup with a gold rim. We began the interview. While speaking, he scribbled on a pad of paper; this seemed to help him systematize his ideas. It was the first time in history that a head of state—above all, the head of a revolutionary, Marxist-Leninist state, a Socialist country—had granted an exclusive interview on the topic of religion.

BETTO – Commander, I'm sure that this is the first time the head of state of a Socialist country has granted an exclusive interview focusing on the topic of religion. The only precedent is the document on religion issued by the National Leadership of the Sandinista National Liberation Front (FSLN) in 1980. That was the first time a revolutionary party in power issued a document on this topic. Since then, religion hasn't been dealt with in such an informative, in-depth and even historical fashion—and this at a time when religion is playing a major ideological role in Latin America, in view of the existence of many Christian Base Communities: of the Guatemalan Indians, Nicaraguan farmers, and workers in Brazil and many other countries. There is also the offensive that, beginning with the Santa Fe Document, imperialism has been waging in an attempt to directly attack Liberation Theology, the most theoretical expression of this Church which is deeply committed to the poor. I think that this interview and your contribution to this topic are very important.

Let's start with your background. You come from a Christian family.

CASTRO – Well, before I reply, now that you've provided an introduction, I'd like to explain that, knowing you were interested in an interview on this complex and delicate topic, I would have liked to have had more time to review some materials and give some thought to the matter. However, since the interview has coincided with a period of intense work for both of us and with your pressing need to return to your country, I agreed to discuss all these topics in a practically impromptu manner. It reminds me of a student who has to take an exam but hasn't had time to study the subject, or a speaker who has to deliver a speech but hasn't had the opportunity to familiarize himself a great deal with the topic and deepen his understanding of it, or a teacher who has to give a class without having had even a minute to review the subject matter. It is in these circumstances that I embark on this conversation.

I know that this is a topic you have mastered thoroughly. You have the edge on me. You've studied theology extensively, and you've also studied Marxism a great deal. I know some Marxism and really very little about theology. I know that your questions and statements will be serious and profound and that, even though I'm not a theologian but rather a politician—I also believe I'm a revolutionary politician who has always been very frank about everything—I will try to answer all your questions with absolute honesty.

You say that I come from a religious family. How can I respond to such a statement? I could say, first, that I come from a religious nation and, second, that I come from a religious family. At least my mother was a very religious woman, a deeply religious woman—more religious than my father was.

BETTO – Was your mother from the countryside?

CASTRO – Yes.

BETTO – Cuban?

CASTRO – Yes, from a farm family.

BETTO – And your father?

CASTRO – My father too came from a farm family. He was a very poor farmer from Galicia, Spain.

However, I wouldn't say that my mother was religious because she'd received any religious training.

BETTO – Did she have faith?

CASTRO – There's no doubt that she had a great deal of faith, and I'd like to add that she learned how to read and write when she was practically an adult.

BETTO – What was her name?

CASTRO – Lina.

BETTO – And your father's?

CASTRO – Angel.

My mother was practically illiterate. She learned how to read and write all by herself. I don't remember her ever having a teacher other than herself. She never mentioned one. With great effort, she tried to learn. I never heard of her ever having gone to school. She was self-taught. She couldn't attend school or church or receive religious training. I think her religious beliefs had their origin in some family tradition, for her parents—especially her mother, my grandmother—were also very religious.

BETTO – Was this religiousness limited to the home, or did she attend church frequently?

CASTRO – Well, it couldn't involve frequent church attendance, because there wasn't any church where I was born, far from any city.

BETTO – Where were your born?

CASTRO – In the north-central part of what used to be Oriente Province, near Nipe Bay.

BETTO – What was the name of the town?

CASTRO – Well, it wasn't a town. There was no church; it wasn't a town.

BETTO – Was it a farm?

CASTRO – Yes, a farm.

BETTO – And it was called—

CASTRO – Birán. It had a few buildings. There was the family house, and an annex containing a few small offices had been built on at one corner. Its architectural lines could be described as Spanish. You may wonder why a house built in Cuba should have Spanish architecture. It was because my father was a Spaniard, from Galicia. In the villages there, they had the custom of working a plot of land and keeping their animals under the house during the winter or in general. They raised pigs and kept some cows there. That's why I said my house was based on Galician architecture, because it was built on stilts.

BETTO – Why? As protection against floods?

CASTRO – No, there really wasn't any need for that, because there wasn't any flooding. Coincidentally, many years later, the blueprints that were drawn up in Cuba for the junior high schools in the countryside—very modern, solid buildings—called for piles, but not for the same reason. The idea was to eliminate the need for earth-moving operations to level the ground. Using a series of support columns in areas where the land sloped saved on such operations. Cement piles of different lengths were used to achieve a level base.

I've often wondered why my house had such tall stilts. Some of them were more than six feet high. The land under the house was uneven, so that, at the far end of the house, where the kitchen was located in an extension attached to the house, the stilts were shorter. At the other end, there was a slight inclination, and they were taller. But, as I've already explained, this wasn't so because of a desire to economize on earth moving. Even though, as a child, I never stopped to think about such things, I'm convinced it was because of the Galician custom. Why? Because I remember that, when I was very young—about three, four, five or maybe six years old—the cows used to sleep under the house. There were from 20 to 30 of them, and they were rounded up at dusk and driven to the house, where they slept below. They were milked there, and some were tied to the stilts.

I forgot to tell you that the house was made of wood. No mortar, cement or bricks. Plain wood. The stilts were made of hardwood, and they served as the foundation for the floor. It was a one-story house, and I imagine it was originally square. It was lengthened later on with the addition of a passage leading from one side of the house to several small rooms. The first room had cabinets where medicines were kept; it was called the medicine room. The next one was the bathroom. Then came a small pantry, followed by a hallway that led to the dining room and finally the kitchen. Between the dining room and the kitchen, there was a flight of stairs leading down to the ground. Another addition was made later on. A sort of office was built onto one corner. So, it was a square house on stilts with those additions. By the time I began to notice things around me, the kitchen had already been built. Above the square portion, there was another floor called the lookout, where my parents and their first three children slept until I was four or five years old.

BETTO – Did your mother have any religious statues?

CASTRO – Yes, I'm going to talk about that, but first I want to finish with the Spanish countryside architecture and other details.

My father built the house in keeping with the customs of his native region. He also had a farm background and didn't have any opportunity to study. So, like my mother, he learned how to read and write all by himself, through sheer determination.

My father was the son of a very poor farmer in Galicia. At the time of Cuba's last War of Independence, which began in 1895, he was sent here as a Spanish soldier, to fight. So, here my father was, very young and drafted into military service as a soldier in the Spanish Army. When the war was over, he was shipped back to Spain, but it seems he'd taken a liking to Cuba. Along with many other immigrants, he left for Cuba in the early years of this century. Penniless and with no relatives here, he got himself a job.

Important investments were made in that period. U.S. citizens had seized the best land in Cuba and had started to destroy forests, build sugar mills and grow sugarcane, all of which involved big investments in those days. My father worked in one of the sugar mills.

BETTO – When did the War of Independence take place?

CASTRO – The last War of Independence began in 1895 and ended in 1898. Spain had been virtually defeated when the United States staged its opportunistic intervention in that war. It sent soldiers; took over Puerto Rico, the Philippines and some other islands in the Pacific; and occupied Cuba. It couldn't seize Cuba permanently, because Cuba had been fighting for a long time. Even though their numbers were small, the Cuban people had been fighting heroically for many years. The United States didn't plan to seize Cuba openly, because the cause of Cuba's independence had extensive support in Latin America and the world as a whole. As I have repeatedly said, Cuba was the nineteenth century's Vietnam.

As I was saying, my father returned to Cuba and began working. Later, he apparently got a group of workers together. He managed them and contracted the men to work for a U.S. firm. He set up a sort of small enterprise that, as far as I can remember, cleared land to plant sugarcane or felled trees to supply sugar mills with firewood. It's possible that, as the organizer of that enterprise with a group of men under him, he began to make a profit. In other words, my father was clearly a very active, enterprising person, and he had an instinctive sense of organization.

I don't know very much about the early years, because, when I had a chance to inquire, I wasn't as curious as I am now about what my father did after reaching the age of reason. I couldn't do with him what you're doing with me, and, now, who could tell us about his experiences?

BETTO – When did your father die?

CASTRO – Much later, when I was 32. He died in 1956, before I came back from Mexico on the *Granma* expedition.

Now, allow me to finish up these details before answering your question.

BETTO – I thought you were 32 when the Revolution triumphed in January 1959.

CASTRO – Well, I was 32. I turned 33 in August 1959.

BETTO – But, if he died in 1956, then you were even younger —about 30 years old.

CASTRO – That's right. You're absolutely right. I forgot to include the two years of the war. The war lasted two years—25 months, to be exact. My father died on October 21, 1956, two months after my thirtieth birthday. In December 1956, when I came back from Mexico with my small expedition, I was 30. I was 26 when we attacked the Moncada Garrison, and I spent my twenty-seventh birthday in prison.

BETTO – And your mother; when did she die?

CASTRO – On August 6, 1963, four and a half years after the triumph of the Revolution.

I was about to finish your earlier point. Your questions have diverted me from the topic. We were talking about the country-side, where we lived, what the house was like, what my parents were like and the educational level they had achieved in spite of their very poor background. I told you all about the house and how it had incorporated Spanish traditions.

I can't really remember many indications of my father's being a religious person. I'd say there were very few of them. I couldn't even say whether or not he really had any religious faith, but I do remember that my mother was very religious, just like my grand-mother.

BETTO – Did he go to Mass on Sundays, for example?

CASTRO – I already told you there wasn't any church where we lived.

BETTO – How was Christmas celebrated in your house?

CASTRO – In the traditional way. Christmas Eve was a time for celebration. Then came New Year's Eve, which involved a party that would go on till past midnight. I think there was also a religious holiday on the day of *Santos Inocentes* (Holy Innocents' Day), which I think was celebrated on December 28. The custom was to play tricks on people, to pull their leg or tell them some tall tale, and say, "Fooled you, didn't I?" That was also part of the Christmas season.

BETTO – In Brazil, that day is April 1.

CASTRO – Well, here it was at the end of the year. Christmas was celebrated, as was Holy Week.

However, I still haven't answered your first question as to whether or not my family was religious.

There was no town—only a few buildings—where we lived. When I was a child, the cows were kept under the house. Later, they were moved somewhere else. In addition, there was always a small pen with pigs and poultry under the house, just like in Galicia. The place was inhabited by hens, ducks, guinea hens, turkeys, some geese and pigs—all kinds of domestic animals. Later, a barn was built around 30 or 40 meters away from the house. A small slaughterhouse was close by, and there was a small smithy, where tools, plows and other farm implements were repaired, in front of the barn. The bakery was around 30 or 40 meters away from the house in a different direction. The elementary school—a small public school—was around 60 meters from the house on the other side of the bakery, next to the main road. That mud and dirt road, which was called a highway, ran south from the municipal capital. The general store—the commercial center—was also owned by my family and had a leafy tree in front. The post office and telegraph office were opposite the store. Those were the main facilities there.

BETTO – Your family owned the store?

CASTRO – Yes, but not the post office or the little schoolhouse. They were public property. All the rest belonged to my family. By the time I was born, my father had already accumulated resources, a certain degree of wealth.

BETTO – When were you born?

CASTRO – On August 13, 1926. If you want to know the time, I think it was around 2:00 in the morning. Maybe that had something to do with my guerrilla spirit, with my revolutionary activities. Nature and the time of my birth must have had some influence. There are other factors that should be taken into account now, right—what kind of a day it was and whether or not Nature has anything to do with the lives of men. Anyway, I think I was born early in the morning—I think I was told that once. Therefore, I was born a guerrilla, because I was born at around 2:00 in the morning.

BETTO – Yes, part of a conspiracy.

CASTRO – A bit of a conspiracy.

BETTO – At least the number 26 seems to have had quite a bearing on your life.

CASTRO – Well, I was born in 1926; that's true. I was 26 when I began the armed struggle, and I was born on the thirteenth, which is half of 26. Batista staged his coup d'etat in '52, which is twice 26. Now that I think of it, there may be something mystical about the number 26.

BETTO – You were 26 when you began the struggle. The attack on the Moncada was on the 26th of July, and it gave rise to the 26th of July Movement.

CASTRO – And we landed in 1956, which is the round number of 30 plus 26.

Well, Betto, allow me to continue, because I still haven't answered your question.

I've been telling about what we had on the farm, but there's something else. The pit for cockfights was around 100 meters from the house, on the main road. During the sugar harvest, cockfights were held there every Sunday—cockfights, not bull-fights. In Spain, there would have been both, but what I saw there were cockfights every Sunday, on December 25, around New Year's time and every holiday. The cockfighting fans would gather there, and some of them brought their own fighting cocks. Others limited themselves to betting. Many poor people lost their small incomes there. When they lost, they went home broke; when they won, they immediately spent the money on rum and parties.

Not far from the pit, there were some poor dwellings, huts made of palm thatch with dirt floors. Most of them were inhabited by Haitian immigrants who worked on the farms and in the planting and cutting of sugarcane. They'd come to Cuba early in the twentieth century and led a miserable existence. Even way back then, there were Haitian immigrants in Cuba. It seems the work force in Cuba wasn't large enough, which is why Haitian immigrants came. The huts where the workers and their families lived were all over the place—along the main road and other roads, including the one that led to the railway that was used to transport the sugarcane, and even alongside the tracks.

The farm's main crop was sugarcane. Cattle was next, and, after that, truck farming. There were bananas, root vegetables, small plots planted with cereals, some vegetables, coconut trees and various fruit trees; there was a 10- to 12-hectare citrus grove near the house. The cane fields were farther away, closer to the railroad line that was used to take the sugarcane to the sugar mill.

By the time I started to take note of my surroundings, my family owned some land and leased some more. How much land did my father own? I'll tell you in hectares, even though we measure land in *caballerías* in Cuba. One *caballería* is equal to 13.4 hectares. My father owned around 800 hectares of land.

BETTO – Is the Cuban hectare similar to the Brazilian one?

CASTRO – A hectare is a square each of whose sides is 100 meters long—that is, 10,000 square meters.

BETTO – Ten thousand square meters, exactly.

CASTRO – That's a hectare.

Apart from that, my father leased some land. It wasn't as good as the land he owned, but it covered a much larger area, around 10,000 hectares.

BETTO – Commander, that's a lot of land in Brazil. Just imagine—

CASTRO – Well, he'd leased all that land. Most of it was hilly, with steep slopes, large areas densely wooded with pine trees and a plateau at an altitude of 700 to 800 meters. Up there, the soil is red, and there are large deposits of nickel and other metals. The Revolution has reforested that area. I liked that plateau very much, because it was cool. When I was around 11 years old, I used to go there on horseback. The horses had to struggle, climbing up the steep hillsides, but once they got there, they'd stop sweating and be dry in a matter of minutes. It was marvelously cool up there, because a breeze was always blowing through the tall, dense pine trees, whose tops met, forming a kind of roof. The water in the many brooks was ice-cold, pure and delicious. That whole area was leased. It didn't belong to the family.

Several years later, the family's income grew with a new asset: lumber. Some of the land that my father had leased included forested areas that were exploited for the lumber. Other sections consisted of hills where cattle were raised, and another part was used for raising sugarcane and other agricultural crops.

BETTO – So your father rose from being a poor farmer to a landowner.

CASTRO – I have a photo of the house in Galicia where my father was born. It was very small, about the size of this room— from 10 to 12 meters long and from 6 to 8 meters wide. It was made of stone, which was abundant in the area and was often used by the farmers for the construction of their rustic dwellings. That was the house where the family lived. A one-room house combining bedroom and kitchen. I imagine there were animals too. The family didn't own any land—not even a square meter.

In Cuba, he bought around 800 hectares of land and leased some more, from some veterans of the War of Independence. It would take a good deal of research, delving into history, to find out how these veterans of the War of Independence came to own 10,000 hectares of land. Of course, those two veterans had been high-ranking officers in the War of Independence. I never thought about doing any research on the matter, but I imagine it was easy for them to get it. There was plenty of land at the time, and, in one way or another—perhaps by paying a very low price for it—they managed to buy it. People from the United States bought extensive tracts of land at very low prices, but I can't imagine what money or other resources those veterans had that enabled them to buy the land. Afterwards, they got a percentage from the sale of the sugarcane that was grown there, plus a percentage from the sale of the lumber that was taken from their forests. They had independent means, lived in Havana and had other businesses on the side. I can't really say whether those people got title to that land legally or illegally.

That vast extent of land was of two types: the land that my father owned and the land that he leased.

How many people lived on that vast latifundium at that time? Hundreds of workers' families; many of them worked small plots that my father let them have so they could grow crops for their own consumption. There were also some farmers who grew sugarcane, who were known as *subcolonos*. Their situation wasn't as difficult as the workers'. How many families were there in all? Two hundred, maybe 300; when I was around 11 years old, around 1000 people lived in that vast area.

I thought it would be useful to explain all these things in order to give you an idea of the environment in which I was born and raised.

There wasn't a single church, not even a small chapel.

BETTO – Nor did a priest ever visit the place.

CASTRO – No, a priest used to show up once a year for baptisms. The area where I lived belonged to a municipality called Mayarí, and a priest used to come from the municipal seat, 36 kilometers away by the highroad.

BETTO – Were you baptized there?

CASTRO – No; I was baptized in Santiago de Cuba, several years after I was born.

BETTO – How old were you then?

CASTRO – I think I was around five or six. I was one of the last children in my family to be baptized.

Let me explain something: in that place, there was no church, no priests and no religious training whatsoever. Before going into the story of my baptism, I want to make it clear that there was no such thing as religious training there.

You asked me if those hundreds of families were believers. I'd say that, generally speaking, they were. As a rule, everybody there had been baptized. I remember that those who hadn't been baptized were called Jews. I couldn't understand what the term *Jew* meant—I'm referring to the time when I was four or five years old. I knew it was a very noisy, dark-colored bird, and every time somebody said, "He's a Jew," I thought they were talking about that bird. Those were my first impressions. Anyone who hadn't been baptized was a "Jew."

There was no religious training. The school was a small, nondenominational school. About 15 to 20 children went there. I was sent there because there wasn't any nursery school. I was the third-oldest child in my family, and my nursery school was that school. They sent me there when I was very young. They didn't have anything else to do with me, so they sent me there with my older sister and brother.

I can't even remember when I learned how to read and write. All I remember is that they used to put me in a small desk in the front row, where I could see the blackboard and listen to everything that was being said. So, it may be said that I learned in nursery school—which was the school. I think it was there that I learned reading, writing and arithmetic. How old was I then? Probably four, or maybe five.

Religion wasn't taught in that school. You were taught the national anthem and told about the flag, the coat of arms and things like that. It was a public school.

Those families had different kinds of beliefs. I remember what people in the countryside thought about religion. They believed in God and also in a number of saints. Some of those saints were in the Liturgy; they were official saints. Others weren't. Everybody had his own saint, after whom he was named. You were told that your saint's day was very important, and you were very happy when it rolled around. April 24 was my saint's day, because there's a saint called Fidel. There was another saint before me, I want you to know.

BETTO – I thought the name Fidel came from "he who has faith," which can also refer to fidelity.

CASTRO – In that case, I'm completely in agreement with my name, in terms of fidelity and faith. Some have religious faith, and others have another kind. I've always been a man of faith, confidence and optimism.

BETTO – If you didn't have faith, the Revolution might not have triumphed in this country.

CASTRO – Yet, when I tell you why I'm called Fidel, you'll laugh. You'll see that the origin of the name isn't so idyllic.

I had no name of my own. I was called Fidel because of somebody who was going to be my godfather. But, before we take up baptism once more, let me finish my description of the environment.

BETTO – And we have to get back to your mother, don't forget.

CASTRO – Certainly, but I want to describe the religious environment first.

At that time, those farmers had all kinds of beliefs. They believed in God, in the saints and in saints who weren't in the Liturgy.

BETTO – They believed in the Virgin.

CASTRO – Of course; that was a widespread belief. They believed in Our Lady of Charity, Cuba's patron saint. They were all fervent believers in her. They all believed in several saints who weren't in the Liturgy, including St. Lazarus the Leper. It was practically impossible to find anyone who didn't believe in St. Lazarus. Many people also believed in spirits and ghosts. I remember that, as a child, I heard stories about spirits, ghosts and apparitions. People believed in superstitions too. I remember some. For example, if a rooster crowed three times without getting an answer, that meant some tragedy might occur. If an owl flew over at night and you could hear the sound of his wings and his screech—I think they called it "the owl's song"—that too was a harbinger of tragedy. If a saltshaker fell to the floor and broke into pieces, the only way to forestall tragedy was to pick up some of the salt and throw it over your left shoulder. There were all kinds of very typical and very common superstitions. In that sense, the world I was born into was quite primitive, because there were all kinds of beliefs and superstitions: spirits, ghosts, animals that were harbingers of doom, everything. That's the environment I remember.

That environment was reflected in every family—including my own, to some extent. That's why I'd say they were very religious people. My mother was a Catholic Christian, and her beliefs and faith were closely associated with the Catholic Church.

BETTO – Did your mother teach her children to pray?

CASTRO – Well, not exactly. She did the praying. I couldn't say that she taught me, because I was sent to a school in Santiago de Cuba when I was about four and a half years old, but I heard her when she prayed.

BETTO – Did she say the rosary?

CASTRO – The rosary, Hail Mary and the Lord's Prayer.

BETTO – Did she have any statues of Our Lady of Charity?

CASTRO – There were many statues of saints: Our Lady of Charity, the patron saint of Cuba; St. Joseph; Christ; and other Madonnas. There were many statues of saints recognized by the Catholic Church. There was also one of St. Lazarus, who wasn't one of the official saints of the Catholic Church.

My mother was a fervent believer; she prayed every day. She always lighted candles to the Virgin and the saints. She requested things from them and prayed to them in all kinds of circumstances. She made vows on behalf of any family member who became ill or who was in a difficult situation. And she not only made the vows but kept them as well. One of those vows might be to visit the sanctuary and light a candle there or to help somebody out; this happened very frequently.

My aunts and my grandmother were also very firm believers. My grandmother and my grandfather—I'm referring to my maternal grandparents—lived about a kilometer away from our home at that time.

I remember when an aunt of mine died in childbirth. I remember her burial. If I could determine the exact date, I could tell you when I had my first image of death. I know there was great sadness, a lot of crying, and I even remember that, a small boy at the time, I was taken to the home of an aunt who had married a Spaniard and lived a kilometer away from my home.

BETTO – Did both the mother and the baby die, or was it only the mother?

CASTRO – The mother died, and the daughter—it was a girl— was raised with us. That is the first memory of death I have: that of my aunt.

My maternal grandparents were also very poor; they came from a very poor family. My grandfather hauled sugarcane in an oxcart. He, like my mother, was born in the western part of the country, in Pinar del Río Province. During the early years of the century, he and the rest of the family moved to what used to be called Oriente Province, 1,000 kilometers away from his home, in an oxcart, and settled there.

BETTO – Who moved?

CASTRO – My grandfather and his whole family: my mother and my uncles and aunts. Two of my mother's brothers also worked there as oxcart drivers.

As I was telling you, my grandmother was very religious. I'd say that my mother's and my grandmother's religious beliefs were the result of family tradition. Both of them were very fervent believers.

I remember that, after the triumph of the Revolution in 1959, I went to visit them once, here in Havana. They were together, and my grandmother had some health problems. The room was full of saints and prayer cards. Throughout the struggle, which entailed great risks, both my mother and grandmother made all kinds of vows on behalf of our lives and safety. The fact that we came out of the struggle alive must have greatly increased their faith. I was very respectful of their beliefs. They told me about the vows they had made and their deep faith. This was after the Revolution had triumphed in 1959. I always listened to them with great interest and respect. Even though I didn't share their concept of the world, I never argued with them about these things, because I could see the strength, courage and comfort they got from their religious feelings and beliefs. Of course, their feelings were neither rigid nor orthodox but something very much their own and very strongly felt. It was a part of the family tradition.

I think my father was more concerned about other matters —political issues, everyday struggles, the organization of tasks and activities. His comments referred mainly to other kinds of problems. Rarely, if ever, did I hear him make any religious comments. Maybe he was a skeptic in terms of religion. That was my father.

That was the environment I remember, my first memories about religious matters. In that sense, it may be said that I came from a Christian family, especially as regards my mother and my grandmother. I think that my grandparents in Spain were also very religious, though I never met them. I was aware of the religious feeling of my mother and her family.

BETTO – You were speaking about your baptism and your name.

CASTRO – Yes. The reason why they called me Fidel is interesting. Baptisms were very important ceremonies in the countryside, among all the farmers—even among those who had no religious background. Baptisms were a very popular institution. Since the risk of death was much greater and life expectancy in the countryside was low in those days, farm families believed that the godfather was the child's second father. He was supposed to help him. If the father died, his child would still have somebody who would help and support him. That was a deep-rooted feeling. They sought out their most trusted friends; sometimes the godfather was an uncle. I'd have to ask my older sister and Ramón, who was the second oldest, who their godfathers were, but I think they were some uncles.

We were the children of a second marriage. There were children from the first marriage, and I remember that we knew them. I was the third child of the second marriage, from which there were seven children in all: four daughters and three sons.

I had been chosen to become the godson of a friend of my father's. He was a very wealthy man who had some business dealings with my father. He sometimes lent him money for the house and other expenses. He lent my father money at a set rate of interest; he was something like the family banker. He was very rich, much richer than my father. People said he was a millionaire, and nobody ever said that about my father. To be a millionaire in those days was something really tremendous; it meant lots and lots of money. That was a time when people used to earn a dollar or a peso a day. A millionaire was somebody who had a million times as much as a person would earn in a day. At that time, my father's property couldn't be assessed at such a high price. Even though he was well fixed, my father wasn't a millionaire.

That man was chosen to be my godfather. He was a very wealthy, very busy man who lived in Santiago de Cuba and had business interests throughout the province. Apparently circumstances didn't favor simultaneous visits to Birán by that wealthy man, who was supposed to become my godfather, and the priest. While awaiting this coincidence, I remained unbaptized, and I remember that people called me a Jew. They used to say,

"He's a Jew." I was four or five and was already being criticized, for people were saying I was a Jew. I didn't know the meaning of the word *Jew*, but there was no doubt that it had a negative connotation, that it was something disgraceful. It was all because I hadn't been baptized, and I wasn't really to blame for that.

Even before being baptized, I was sent to Santiago de Cuba. My teacher had led my family to believe that I was a very industrious student. She made them believe that I was smart and had a talent for learning. That was the real reason why they sent me to Santiago de Cuba when I was around five; I was taken from a world in which I lived without any material problems and taken to a city where I lived poorly and was hungry.

BETTO – When you were five.

CASTRO – Yes, when I was five and had had no previous knowledge of hunger.

BETTO – Why were you poor?

CASTRO – I was poor because the teacher's family was poor. She was the only one earning any money. That was during the economic crisis of the thirties, around 1931 or 1932. The family consisted of two sisters and their father, and one of the sisters was the only one who had a job. Sometimes she wouldn't be paid or would be paid only after a long wait. During the great economic crisis of the early thirties, salaries often weren't paid, and the people were very poor.

I went to Santiago de Cuba to live in a very small frame house that leaked like a sieve when it rained. The house is still there; it's still standing. During the school year, the teacher kept working in Birán, and her sister had to live on that salary. My family sent 40 pesos for my board, an amount that had the same purchasing power as 300 or 400 pesos now. There were two of us, my older sister and me. In view of that poverty, their not receiving salaries and the fact that they wanted to save, not much money went for food. There were five people to be fed—later six, because my brother Ramón came too a few months later. We got a small container with a little rice, some beans, sweet potatoes, plantains and things like that. The container arrived at noon, and it was shared first by five and then by six people, for lunch and dinner. I used to think I had a huge appetite; the food always seemed delicious. Actually, it was just that I was always hungry. It was a rough period.

Later, the teacher's sister married the Haitian consul in Santiago de Cuba. Since I happened to be there at the time and my wealthy godfather hadn't materialized and the baptism hadn't been performed—I was around five years old and, as they said, a "Jew" because I hadn't been baptized and didn't even know what it meant—a solution had to be found for the problem. I guess that this use of the term *Jew* is also linked to some religious prejudices that we can discuss later on. Anyway, finally I was baptized, and the Haitian consul became my godfather, because he'd married the teacher's sister, Belén, who was a good and noble person. She was a piano teacher, but she didn't have any work or students.

BETTO – So it wasn't your father's wealthy friend after all.

CASTRO – No, it wasn't the rich man; it was the consul in Santiago de Cuba of the poorest country in Latin America.

The teacher was a *mestizo*, as was my godmother.

BETTO – Are they still living?

CASTRO – No, they died a long time ago. I don't feel any resentment toward them, even though the teacher was doing it to make a profit—my family paid 40 pesos for each of us every month. But that was a difficult period in my life.

One afternoon, they took me to the cathedral in Santiago de Cuba. I don't remember the exact date. I may have been six when I was finally baptized, because I'd already had some hard times before they took me to the cathedral in Santiago de Cuba. They sprinkled me with holy water and baptized me, and I became a normal citizen, the same as the rest, because, at long last, I'd been baptized. I had a godfather and a godmother, even though the former wasn't the millionaire they'd originally chosen, who was called Don Fidel Pino Santos. By the way, a nephew of his is a very valuable comrade of ours working for the Revolution: an outstanding economist, a hard worker, a very able comrade—an economist and a Communist. He's been a Communist ever since his youth, even though he was the nephew of that very wealthy man who was supposed to be my godfather but never was, even though he bequeathed me his name. He bequeathed me his name in that I'd been called Fidel because my godfather-to-be was called Fidel. So you can see how, by pure chance, you can receive a fitting name. That was the only fitting thing I received during that whole period.

BETTO – What was the consul's name?

CASTRO – Louis Hibbert.

BETTO – So you might have been named Luis Castro.

CASTRO – I could have been named Luis Castro if they'd chosen the consul to be my godfather at the beginning. Well, there've been some very prestigious Luises in history.

BETTO – Yes, quite a few.

CASTRO – A lot of Luises were kings and saints. Has there ever been a pope named Luis?

BETTO – I don't remember; I'm not that well versed in papal history. But I have a brother who's named Luis.

CASTRO – They could wait six years to baptize me, but they couldn't wait six years to give me a name. And that's the origin of my name. I owe it to a very wealthy man—not exactly the rich man in the Bible, though. It's sad to speak about people who've died a long time ago, but my potential godfather had the reputation of being a remarkably—excessively—thrifty man. I don't think he had anything in common with his biblical predecessor.

BETTO – I don't think so, either.

CASTRO – He didn't give me many gifts—none, in fact, that I can remember. He did lend my father some money at a set rate of interest, which was much lower than today's. I think the standard rate of interest that my father used to pay was 6 percent.

Later, that man became a politician; he even ran for Congress. Of course, you're going to ask his party affiliation. The ruling party; he always supported the ruling party. Later, a son of his was elected to Congress on the opposition party ticket, so everything evened out.

When the election campaign started, I remember that my father supported him. You can see the lessons in democracy I received at an early age. A lot of money circulated in my house at election time. To put it more accurately, my family spent a lot of money to help his friend in each election. In other words, my father spent a lot of money to help his candidate. That's what politics was like then.

Of course, as a landowner, my father controlled most of the votes, because many people didn't even know how to read and write. To be given ajob in the rural areas was considered a big favor then, as was being allowed to live on somebody else's land. Therefore, the farmer or worker for whom such a favor was done—and all the rest of his family—had to be grateful to his patron and vote for his candidate. In addition, there were ward heelers. Who were they? Experts in politics. This didn't mean they were advisers well versed in sociology, law or economics; rather, they were smart farmers in each area who obtained a specific government job or who were given money during the election campaigns to get votes for a councilman, a mayor, a provincial governor, a representative, a senator or even the President. There weren't any TV or radio campaigns then; I think they cost even more.

BETTO – That's the way it still is in Brazil.

CASTRO – I remember those election campaigns. I'm talking about when I was ten. I knew a lot about politics by the time I was ten, because I'd seen so many things!

I even remember that, when I was home on vacation during one election period—I'd been sent to the city to study when I was five—the safe that was kept in the room where I slept became a problem. You know that children like to sleep late, but I couldn't, because there was a lot of coming and going very early in the morning—around 5:30—during the election campaign. The safe was constantly being opened and closed, making an unavoidable metallic noise. The ward heelers would arrive, and they had to be given money. And let me tell you that all this was done in the most altruistic spirit, because my father did it out of friendship. I don't remember a single instance—apart from the loans—when Don Fidel solved any of my father's problems or gave him funds for political campaigns. My father undertook those expenses on his own. That's what politics was like, and that's what I learned as a child.

There were a number of people who controlled a certain number of votes, especially in the remoter areas, because the people who lived closer in were controlled directly by the most trusted employees on the farm. But ward heelers who controlled 80 to 100 votes would come from 30 to 40 kilometers away. Afterwards, those votes had to appear in the corresponding electoral college, or the ward heeler lost his prestige, award or job. That's what election campaigns were like in the country.

The man who was supposed to become my godfather became a representative. My real godfather, the poor one, the Haitian consul, had some difficulties then. In 1933, the Machado tyranny was overthrown by a revolution—I was seven in 1933—and, at the beginning, that revolution passed some laws of a nationalistic nature. At that time, many people were unemployed and were starving, while, for example, many stores in Havana that were owned by Spaniards would employ only Spaniards. There was a nationalist demand that a percentage of the jobs be given to Cubans. It may have been a fair demand in principle, but in practice, it gave rise to some cruel measures in certain circumstances, taking jobs away from people who, though they were foreigners, were very poor and had no other way to earn a living.

I can still remember with sorrow—with genuine sorrow—how, for example, in Santiago de Cuba and the rest of Oriente Province, they started to expel the Haitian immigrants who'd lived in Cuba for many years. Those Haitians had left their country years before, fleeing from starvation. They grew and cut sugarcane, making great sacrifices, tremendous sacrifices. Their wages were so low they were almost slaves. I think—in fact, I'm absolutely sure—that nineteenth-century slaves had a higher standard of living and better care than those Haitians.

BETTO – In terms of food and health.

CASTRO – Slaves were treated like animals, but they were given food and taken care of so they'd live and produce. They were preserved as part of the plantations' capital. But those tens of thousands of Haitian immigrants could eat only when they worked, and nobody cared whether they lived or died of starvation. They suffered from all kinds of deprivations.

The so-called 1933 revolution was, in fact, a movement of struggle and rebelliousness against injustice and abuse. It called for the nationalization of the electric company and other foreign enterprises and for the nationalization of employment. In the name of the nationalization of employment, tens of thousands of those Haitians were mercilessly deported to Haiti. According to our revolutionary ideas, that was an inhuman thing to do. What happened to them? How many of them survived?

My godfather was still the consul in Santiago de Cuba at that time, and a big ship with two smokestacks, called the *La Salle*, arrived in the city. I was taken to see it, because the arrival of a two-stack ship in Santiago de Cuba was a special event. The ship was full of Haitians who were taken back to Haiti on being expelled from Cuba.

Later on, my godfather lost his job and his consulate, and I think he had no income—nothing—and he too returned to Haiti. My godmother remained alone for many years, and it was only after a long time that he returned to Cuba. I was already an adult by then. He went to Birán, where he sought refuge and lived for a while. He had no way to earn a living.

BETTO – When did you enroll in a religious school?

CASTRO – When I went to the first grade.

BETTO – How old were you?

CASTRO – Well, I'd have to think. I must have been around six and a half or seven.

BETTO – Was it the Christian Brothers' school?

CASTRO – Yes. It's a long story.

During the period I told you about, I was sent to Santiago de Cuba while still very young. I had many unmet needs and went through a lot of hardship. Around a year later, things started to improve somewhat. At one point, my parents became aware of the difficulties I was facing. They protested and even made me return to Birán. But, after the protests, the teacher's explanation and the subsequent reconciliation, I was sent back to her house in Santiago de Cuba. The situation, of course, improved after the scandal. How much time did I spend there in all? At least two years.

In the beginning, I wasn't sent to school; my godmother gave me classes. Those classes consisted of having me study the addition, subtraction, multiplication and division tables that were printed on the cover of my notebook. I learned them by heart. I believe I learned them so well I've never forgotten them. Sometimes I calculate almost as quickly as a computer.

BETTO – Yes, I noticed that last night.

CASTRO – That's how it was. I had no textbook, only my notebook and some notes. And, of course, I learned arithmetic, reading, writing and taking notes. My spelling and handwriting must have improved a little. I think I spent around two years there, just wasting my time. The only useful aspect was the experience of tough, difficult conditions, hardships, and sacrifices. I think I was the victim of exploitation, in view of the income that family got from what my parents paid them.

I also remember the Three Wise Men. One of the beliefs that was inculcated in five-, six- and seven-year-olds was that of the Three Wise Men. Since you mentioned religious beliefs, one of the first things we were taught to believe in were the Three Wise Men. I must have been three or four the first time the Wise Men came. I can even remember the things they brought me: some apples, a toy car—things like that—and some candy.

BETTO – It's different in Brazil. In Brazil, presents are given at Christmas; here, it's on January 6.

CASTRO – January 6 was the Epiphany. We were told that the Three Wise Men, who'd traveled to pay homage to Christ when He was born, came every year to bring children presents.

I spent three Epiphanies with that family. Therefore, I must have been there at least two and a half years.

BETTO – So the capitalist Santa Claus never became popular in Cuba?

CASTRO – No, never. What we had were the Three Wise Men, who rode camels. Children wrote letters to the Three Wise Men: Caspar, Melchior and Balthazar. I can still remember my first letters. I wrote when I was five and asked them for everything—cars, trains, movie cameras, the works. I wrote long letters to the Three Wise Man on January 5. I looked for some grass, and I put it under my bed with some water. The disappointments came later.

BETTO – What's that about the grass?

CASTRO – Since the Three Wise Men rode camels, you had to provide them with some grass and water, which you put under your bed.

BETTO – All mixed up?

CASTRO – Either mixed up or the grass and water next to each other.

BETTO – How interesting! I didn't know that.

CASTRO – You had to provide food and water for the camels, especially if you wanted the Three Wise Men to bring you lots of presents, everything you'd asked them for in your letter.

BETTO – And what did the Three Wise Men eat?

CASTRO – Well, I don't know. Nobody remembered to leave food for the Three Wise Men. Maybe that's why they weren't very generous with me. The camels ate the grass and drank the water, but I got very few toys in exchange. I remember that my first present was a small cardboard trumpet; just the tip was made out of metal, something like aluminum. My first present was a small trumpet the size of a pencil.

For three consecutive years, three times, I was given a trumpet; I should have become a musician. After all. . . . The second year, the Three Wise Men brought me a trumpet that was half aluminum and half cardboard. The third time, it was a trumpet with three small keys, made completely of aluminum.

I was attending school by then. When I finished my third year there, I was sent away to school, and then the changes began.

BETTO – Which school?

CASTRO – The La Salle School. After being in Santiago de Cuba for a year and a half or two years—I can't remember exactly; I'd have to find out—I was sent to the La Salle School, which was six or seven blocks away. I went to school in the morning and went home for lunch. We had lunch then; there wasn't any more hunger. Then I went back to school. The Haitian consul, my godfather, was still with us when I enrolled in the school. It was a big step forward, because I at least went to a school.

There, they systematically taught the catechism, religion and some elements of biblical history. I was in the first grade. I must have been around six and a half or seven, because they'd kept me back. I'd learned to read and write very early, yet they'd made me waste almost two years. I could have been in the third grade.

Once I started attending school, the education was systematic, but the most important thing was the material and environmental improvement; for the first time, I had teachers, classes, friends to play with and many other activities that I'd lacked when I was a single student studying arithmetic from the cover of a notebook. That new situation lasted up until I launched my first act of rebellion, when I was still very young.

BETTO – What caused it?

CASTRO – I was tired of the whole situation. At the teacher's house, I'd be spanked every so often, and if I didn't behave perfectly, they threatened to send me to boarding school. Then, one day, I realized that I'd be better off in boarding school than in that house.

BETTO – Who threatened you? Your brother and sister?

CASTRO – My godmother, my godfather, the teacher when she was on her vacation—everybody.

BETTO – Your godmother and the other adults.

CASTRO – Yes.

BETTO – How did you rebel?

CASTRO – Those people had had a French education. They spoke perfect French. I guess that's how they got to know the consul. I don't remember exactly how it was they'd gotten a French education. I don't know if they'd been to France or had attended a school in Haiti. They knew how to speak French and had perfect manners. Of course, I was taught those manners when I was very young. Among other things, you weren't supposed to ask for anything. The very poor children used to have a penny to buy a *rayado* or *granizado*, which is what they called sno-cones, but I couldn't ask them for anything; that was forbidden, according to the rules of French education. If I asked another boy to give me some, the children, with the selfishness inherent to that age and the desperate poverty in which they lived—they knew the rules I had to follow—used to say, "You're begging! I'm going to tell on you!"

That family had its code, and I'm not criticizing it. You had to do this, and that, and the other thing. You were subjected to a lot of discipline. You had to speak in an educated way. You couldn't raise your voice. Naturally, you couldn't use improper language. When they threatened to send me to boarding school, I was already tired and had become aware of what had happened before. I even realized that I'd been starving and that I hadn't been treated fairly. I haven't told you everything in full detail, because I don't want to make this an autobiography; I just want to touch on subjects you're interested in. So, one day when I got to school, I deliberately started to break all the rules and regulations. In what amounted to a conscious act of rebellion aimed at having them send me to boarding school, I raised my voice and said all the words I'd been forbidden to use. That's the story of my first— though not my last—rebellion, which took place when I was in the first grade. I must have been seven at most; my age could be verified.

BETTO – So you were finally sent to boarding school?

CASTRO – Yes, and I began to be happy. For me, boarding school meant freedom.

BETTO – How long were you at the La Salle boarding school?

CASTRO – Nearly four years. I was there for the second half of the first grade, second grade and third grade. Because of my good grades, I was promoted to the fifth grade straight from the third grade, so I made up for one of the years I'd lost.

BETTO – What was the religious training like? Was religion presented as something good and joyful, or was there a lot of talk about hell, punishment and God? What was it like? Was a lot of emphasis placed on going to Mass, making sacrifices and doing penance, or were things more positive? How do you remember it?

CASTRO – I remember different periods, because I was in three different schools at various times in my life. It was really very hard for me to have any opinion on the matter during that first period. I'll have to think back to how it was.

First of all, I remember that I was away from my family. I'd been sent to Santiago de Cuba, and this, in itself, caused some problems. I was away from my family, my home, the place I loved, where I used to play, run around and enjoy freedom. Then, suddenly, I was sent to a city where I had a difficult time, faced with material problems. I was far from my family, with people who weren't my relatives placed in charge of me. I had some material living problems. The thing I was most interested in was solving those problems. Yes, I was tired of that life, that house, that family, those rules. My problems were of a different kind. I didn't have any religious problems; rather, I had material living problems and a personal situation that needed solving and that I wanted to solve. Acting by instinct—or, rather, on intuition, which was how I really functioned—I disobeyed that authority.

Then things changed. There was a distinct material improvement when I went to boarding school. After class, I could play in the school yard with all the other boys. I wasn't alone any more, and once or twice a week we were taken to the countryside and the ocean. We went to a small peninsula on the Bay of Santiago de Cuba, where there's an oil refinery and some other industrial projects now. The Christian Brothers rented a spot there near the beach. They had a resort and sports facilities. They'd take us on Thursdays, because we didn't have class on Thursday or Sunday. They divided the week into two parts: three days of classes, a break and then two more days of classes. I was very happy at the boarding school, going to the beach every Thursday and Sunday and being free, fishing, swimming, hiking, taking part in sports— all those things. I was more interested in and concerned about those things.

The religious training, catechism, Mass and other activities were normal parts of everyday life, just like classes and study periods. Then, as now, with too many meetings, what I liked most were the recesses. Religious training in those days was a natural thing; I couldn't make any value judgments at that time.

BETTO – Talk of sin didn't make you afraid? Wasn't it stressed?

CASTRO – I didn't become aware of those problems until later on—not during the first phase.

At that time, I studied religion just as I studied the history of Cuba. We accepted all those things about the beginning of the world, what we were told existed in the world, as natural facts. They didn't make us reason this out, and I was more concerned about sports, the beach, nature and studying the different school subjects—that kind of thing. I didn't really have any special religious inclination or vocation. That's a fact.

We usually had a vacation every three months, when we went home, to the countryside. The countryside was freedom.

For example, Christmas Eve was a wonderful thing, because it meant 15 days of vacation—and not just 15 days of vacation, but 15 days of a festive atmosphere and treats: cookies, candy and nougats. We had a lot of them at my house. Many traditional Spanish products were always bought for the Christmas season. When that time came, you were always excited, from the time you took the train and then continued on horseback until you finally arrived. In those days, you had to take a train and then a horse to get home—both things. The roads were nothing but huge mudholes. During the first few years in my house, there weren't any cars or even electricity. We got electricity a little later. We used to use candles for light in the countryside.

So, for us, since we'd experienced hunger and confinement in the city, having that open space, guaranteed food and the festive atmosphere that was created around Christmas, Christmas Eve, New Year's Day and the Epiphany—all those things—was very attractive. We quickly learned that there weren't any Three Wise Men, however. That was one of the first things that made us skeptical. We began to discover that there weren't any Three Wise Men, that our parents were the ones who brought the toys. The adults themselves robbed us of our innocence too soon. It's not that I'm against the custom—I'm not making a value judgment about that—but we quickly learned that some trickery had been involved.

Christmas vacations were happy times. Holy Week was another wonderful time, because we had another week of vacation at home. And, of course, summer vacation, when we went swimming in the rivers, running through the woods, hunting with slingshots and riding horses. We lived in direct contact with nature and were quite free during those times. That's what my childhood was like.

I'd been born in the countryside and had lived there before the problems arose that I've already told you about. When you enter the third or fifth grade, you begin to learn a lot more and to observe things.

Holy Week in the countryside—I remember from when I was very young—were days of solemnity; there was great solemnity. What was said? That Christ died on Good Friday. You couldn't talk or joke or be happy, because Christ was dead and the Jews killed Him every year. This is another case in which accusations or popular beliefs have caused tragedies and historic prejudices. I tell you, I didn't know what that term meant, and I thought, at first, that those birds called *judíos* (Jews) had killed Christ.

BETTO – And you had to eat very little.

CASTRO – You had to eat fish—no meat. Then came Holy Saturday, which was a day of festivity, even though, as I understand it, the Resurrection hadn't taken place yet. But the people used to say, "Holy Saturday, day of celebration; Good Friday, day of silence and mourning." There, in the countryside, the stores were busy on Holy Saturday, and there were parties and cockfights that continued into Easter Sunday.

I'd say that, during that period, I was more absorbed in the things I've told you about; I wasn't in a position to evaluate the religious training then. But I did realize, after a while, that everything was taught like arithmetic: 5 times 5 is 25. That's how religion was taught.

BETTO – Did the Brothers seem more like teachers than

religious workers, or did they also appear to be good religious workers?

CASTRO – Well, the Christian Brothers weren't really priests; they hadn't been trained for the priesthood. It was a much less demanding, less strict Order than the Jesuits'. I realized that later on, when I went to the Jesuits' school.

BETTO – How old were you?

CASTRO – Well, when I went to the Jesuits' school—

BETTO – Was it junior high?

CASTRO – I was in the fifth grade when I first went to the Jesuits' school.

Conflicts arose in the Christian Brothers' school. I had my second rebellion there. The education in that school wasn't bad, nor was the organization of the students' activities. There were around 30 boarding students, and we used to be taken out on Thursdays and Sundays to rest, as I told you. The food wasn't bad. Life in general wasn't bad.

BETTO – You're talking about the Jesuits' school?

CASTRO – No, not yet.

BETTO – The La Salle School?

CASTRO – Yes. Those people hadn't had the training that the Jesuits had. Moreover, they used really censurable methods at times. Some teachers or authorities at the school hit the students every so often. My conflict there was over that, because of an incident with another student. It was a small quarrel typical of students of that age. I had the opportunity to see how violence is used against students in what would now be called bad teaching methods. That was the first time the Brother monitor in charge of the students hit me with a fair amount of violence. He slapped both sides of my face. It was a degrading and abusive thing. I was in the third grade, and I never forgot it. Later, when I was in the fifth grade, I was hit on the head twice. The last time I wouldn't put up with it, and it ended up in a violent personal confrontation between the monitor and me. After all that, I decided not to go back to that school.

I also saw some forms of favoritism at that institution that were shown toward some students at times. I also saw how money played a role. I was perfectly aware that some of the Brothers displayed a great deal of interest in us and my family and gave us special treatment because we had a lot of land and were said to be rich. In other words, I saw that material interest and deference related to money. I saw this very clearly.

They weren't as disciplined as the Jesuits. I'd say they were less strict and less ethically solid than the Jesuits. I say this as a criticism, while also recognizing the positive things: the students' contact with the countryside, the scheduling of activities, a good education, a number of things. But hitting students is infamous and unacceptable. There was discipline; I'm not against the imposition of discipline. They had to discipline us. But you're older in the fifth grade; you have a sense of personal dignity; and violent methods, physical punishment, seem inconceivable to me.

I also saw their interest in money, and I noticed some privileges and favoritism at that school.

BETTO – Let's go on to the Jesuits. What was the school called?

CASTRO – It was the Colegio de Dolores [School of Our Lady of Sorrows] of Santiago de Cuba, a prestigious upper-class school.

BETTO – When did you start boarding there?

CASTRO – First I went through a trial period; I wasn't sent there to board.

BETTO – Where did you live?

CASTRO – In the home of a businessman who was a friend of my father's. There, again, I had to confront another new experience: changing schools. It was a much more rigorous school, and I found a lot of misunderstanding on the part of the adults who were caring for me. It was one of those families that takes in somebody who isn't its child as a matter of friendship. It wasn't really a matter of kindness. There were economic interests at play in those situations, and, at any rate, a different relationship. I wasn't their son; they couldn't treat me like a son.

It's better to board at school, I'm convinced, than to be sent to the home of a friend, a family friend. Staying with family friends isn't advisable unless the people are kind—and such people do exist. The society in which I lived was a society with many difficulties; the people had to make many sacrifices. That society engendered tremendous selfishness—I say and think this on reflecting about it. As a general rule, that society made people selfish, turned them into people with an ax to grind, who tried to gain something out of every situation. That society wasn't characterized by encouraging feelings of kindness and generosity in the people.

BETTO – And that society was considered Christian?

CASTRO – There are many people in the world today who call themselves Christians but do horrible things. Pinochet, Reagan and Botha, for example, consider themselves Christians.

The people I was living with practiced Christianity. That is, they went to Mass. Could anything particularly bad be said about that family? No. Nor could I say that my godmother was a bad person, because she went hungry along with the rest of us. She didn't have control in that house at the time. Her sister was in control. Her sister was the one who received the salary, the income, and managed it. She was really a good, noble person. But this situation involved not a son—with whom another relationship generally exists—but rather a stranger who was there in that home.

When I was in the fifth grade, then, I went to live in the home of a businessman's family. I couldn't say they were bad people, but they weren't my family; they couldn't have the same interest, and they applied some strict—even arbitrary—rules. For example, they didn't take into account the fact that I'd had problems in my other school, as I've already explained, and that I'd transferred to a more rigorous school. They didn't consider the psychological factors involved in the adaptation to a new, more demanding school and new teachers. They wanted me to get the highest grades; they demanded it. If I didn't get the highest grades, I didn't get that week's ten cents for going to the movies, five cents for buying ice cream after the movies and five cents on Thursday for buying some comic books. I remember that clearly. There were some comic books that came from Argentina, a weekly called *El Gorrión* (The House Sparrow). I read some novels there too. *De tal palo, tal astilla* (Like Father, Like Son) was one of them. Five cents. The normal weekly allowance was 25 cents. If you didn't get the highest grades, you didn't get the 25 cents. That measure was arbitrary and completely unfair, because they didn't take my new circumstances into account. It wasn't the right psychological approach to an 11-year-old.

Why did they want me to get good grades? It was mainly a matter of pride and vanity, but other factors were involved too. It was a rather upper-class school. The people who had children in that school, boarding or otherwise, viewed it with vanity, as a kind of social achievement. As a child, I suffered from many such things, for there was no one to guide me.

I began as a day student at the school, after Christmas vacation—and also after arguing a lot at home. I had to argue at home and demand that I be sent away to study. That's when I launched my battle to study. I had to struggle, because the people at my old school had told my parents that I'd behaved badly, and those arbitrary reports had influenced my family. I said I wouldn't accept not being allowed to study. I knew what the problem was and what was behind the conflict. It stemmed from an abusive, violent act, the physical punishment of a student. I think I had very clear ideas about the matter—the result of instinct; because of some notions of justice and dignity that I was acquiring; or perhaps because, when I was still quite young, I'd begun to see some incorrect, unfair things by which I was victimized. I began to acquire values. I was very aware of them, and I had to demand very firmly that I be sent away to study— perhaps not so much out of a love of study but rather because I felt an injustice had been committed against me. And I was sent away to study; my mother supported me. I convinced her, first, and then she convinced my father, and they sent me to Santiago de Cuba again, but as a day student. When I got there, I began to have the problems I told you about.

Summer came, and they left me there because my older sister was there, studying. A black teacher from Santiago de Cuba came to tutor my sister. She was very well trained. Her name was Professor Danger. She became interested in me. Since I had nothing else to do during my vacation, I went to class with my sister, who was preparing for high school. I answered all the questions in all the subjects the teacher taught, and this made her genuinely interested in me. I wasn't old enough to enter high school, so she began to draw up a study plan for both before and during the first year of high school at the same time. Then, when I got old enough, I could take the exams. She was the first person I ever met who encouraged me; who set a goal, an objective, for me; and who gave me impetus. She got me interested in studying when I was that young. I think you can stimulate children at that age with a specific objective. How old was I? Ten or maybe 11.

Then a new phase began. We studied with the teacher that summer, but when school began, I had to go to the hospital to have my appendix out. I hadn't had anything more than mild discomfort, but in those days, everybody had his appendix out. The wound got infected, and I spent three months in the hospital. The teacher's plan was forgotten, and I had to begin the sixth grade almost at the end of the first quarter.

After that, I decided to board at the school. I was tired of that situation, and at the end of the first quarter, I suggested—or rather, firmly demanded—that I go as a boarder. I was already an expert in those disputes. I decided to create a situation in which they had no alternative but to send me to school as a boarder. Thus, between the first and sixth grades, I had to wage three battles to solve three problems.

By the time I started to board in the sixth grade, I was getting excellent grades, and in the seventh grade, I was among the top students in my class. I also gained a lot in other ways, because the world of sports and trips to the countryside and the mountains was within reach. I liked sports a lot—especially basketball, soccer and baseball.

BETTO – There was soccer?

CASTRO – Yes, and I liked it a lot.

BETTO – Better than volleyball?

CASTRO – Well, I really liked soccer, but I liked basketball too. I also played baseball and volleyball. I played everything. I always liked sports a lot. For me, they served as a diversion, and I put my energy into them.

I was in a school with more demanding, better trained people with a much greater religious vocation. They were more devoted, able and disciplined than those in the other school; they were incomparably better. I think it was good for me to go there. I met a different kind of people—teachers and other men who were interested in molding the students' character. They were Spaniards. In general, I think that, with regard to the things we've been talking about, the traditions of the Jesuits and their military spirit—their military organization—go with the Spanish personality. They were very rigorous, demanding people, who were interested in their students and in their character and behavior.

In other words, I acquired ethics and norms that weren't just religious. I got a human influence from the teachers' authority and the values they attached to things. They encouraged sports and trips to the mountains, and I liked sports, excursions, hikes and mountain climbing—it was all very attractive to me. Sometimes I even made the whole group wait two hours while I climbed a mountain. They didn't criticize me when I did something like that, when I was late because I was making a great effort. They saw it as proof of an enterprising, tenacious spirit. Even if the activities were risky and difficult, they didn't discourage them.

BETTO – They never dreamed they were training a guerrilla.

CASTRO – Nor did I dream I was preparing to be a guerrilla, but every time I saw a mountain, it was a challenge to me. The idea of climbing that mountain, of reaching the top, would seize me. How did they encourage me? I think they never put any obstacles in my way. Occasionally, the bus with the rest of the students would wait for two hours, and I still wouldn't be back. At other times, when there were heavy downpours, I would swim across swollen rivers—not without risk. They always waited and never criticized me for this. In other words, if they noted characteristics in their students that they liked—a spirit of adventure, sacrifice or effort—they encouraged them. They didn't turn students into weaklings. Nor did the others, but the Jesuits were much more concerned about their students' character.

I disagree with the political ideas I learned then, though; they were the prevailing ones. And I also disagree with the way religion was taught.

From the things I've told you, you can draw some conclusions about how my character was shaped by the problems and difficulties I had to overcome and by my trials, conflicts and rebellions, when I didn't have a mentor or a guide to help me. I never really had a mentor. The person who came closest to being one was that black teacher from Santiago de Cuba, who gave private classes preparing students for high school and tutoring students in high school as well. She was the one who set a goal and inspired me, but everything fell apart when I got sick at the beginning of the school year and spent three months in the hospital. I missed that long period of classes in the sixth grade. Then I decided to go to school as a boarder. I made that decision.

As you can see, the misfortunes in my life didn't create favorable conditions for a strong religious influence; instead, they must have strongly influenced my political and revolutionary vocation.

BETTO – I understand.

What do you remember about the Jesuits' religious mission? Was it good, bad, tied to real life or more oriented to heaven and the saving of souls? What was it like?

CASTRO – I can judge better now. I also went to a Jesuit high school. Looking back on what influenced me, I think that, in some ways, it wasn't positive; everything was very dogmatic—"This is so because it has to be so." You had to believe it, even if you didn't understand it. If you didn't, it was a fault, a sin, something worthy of punishment. I'd say that reasoning played no role. Reasoning and feelings weren't developed.

It seems to me that religious faith, like political belief, should be based on reasoning, on the development of thought and feelings. The two things are inseparable.

BETTO – I don't want to get into a centuries-old squabble between the Jesuits and the Dominicans, but the Dominicans are noted for placing greater value on the intelligence of faith, while the Jesuits place more emphasis on willpower.

CASTRO – I accept that some people may have a special leaning, a mystical spirit, a great religious vocation, a greater predisposition to religious faith than other people with different characteristics. I could have been open to reason, and I think I was open to developing feelings, but it wasn't possible to inculcate a solid religious faith in me, because things were explained in an entirely dogmatic way. "You have to believe this, because you have to believe it." Not to believe it was a serious fault, a terrible sin deserving of the worst punishment.

If you have to accept things because you're told they are a certain way, you can't argue or reason them out. Moreover, if the main argument used is reward or punishment—punishment more than reward—then it's impossible to develop the reasoning and feelings that could be the basis of a sincere religious belief. That's what I think, in retrospect.

BETTO – What was the punishment, and what was the reward?

CASTRO – Well, the reward was very abstract. For a child, abstract rewards based on contemplation, on a state of happiness you had to imagine for all eternity, were more difficult to perceive than punishment. Punishment was easier to explain. A child is better prepared to understand punishment, everlasting hell and pain, suffering and eternal fire. Much more emphasis was placed on punishment. I really think this is a bad way to develop any kind of deep conviction in a human being. Later on, when I had to form a belief and faith in the political arena, I firmly upheld specific values; I've never been able to imagine how a belief might be based on something that isn't understood or that's inspired by fear of something or by a reward.

I believe that people's religious beliefs should be based on understandable reasons and the intrinsic value of their actions.

BETTO – Unrelated to reward or punishment?

CASTRO – That's right. I think that what's done out of fear of punishment or in search of reward isn't entirely kind or noble. It isn't really worthy of praise, admiration or esteem. In my revolutionary life and revolutionary concepts, when I've had to involve people in very difficult situations and very hard tests and they endured them with total self-sacrifice and altruism, the most admirable thing was that they weren't motivated by the idea of reward or punishment. The Church has also gone through trials; it did so for many centuries. It suffered martyrdom and confronted it. I feel that this can only be explained by deep conviction.

BETTO – Which is the opposite of fear.

CASTRO – I think conviction is what makes martyrs. I don't think anybody becomes a martyr simply because he expects a reward or fears punishment. I don't think anybody behaves heroically for such a reason.

BETTO – I've always said that the opposite of fear is not courage but faith.

CASTRO – I think all of the Church's martyrs were impelled by feelings of loyalty, because they believed strongly in something. The idea of the hereafter, where their actions would merit reward, might have been of some help, but I don't think it was the main reason. People who do something out of fear generally fear the fire, the martyrdom and the torture even more. They don't dare to defy them. People who are concerned about obtaining material possessions, pleasure or rewards try to save their lives, not sacrifice them. I think that throughout the

Church's history its martyrs must have been motivated by something more inspiring than fear or punishment. It's much easier for me to understand that.

I've called for self-sacrifice and, at times, for martyrdom, heroism and death. I think it's a great merit for a man to give his life for a revolutionary idea and to fight, knowing he may die. Even though he knows there's nothing after death, he upholds the idea, the moral value, so firmly that he defends it with everything he has—his life—without expecting reward or punishment.

Basically, I'd say that those were the weakest points in the religious teaching we were given. I don't think they produced many saints from among us. There weren't many boarding students in that school—only about 30—and there were around 200 students in all. When I went on to the main Jesuit school, there were 1,000 students, 200 of whom were boarders. Not many priests must have come out of there. It would surprise me to know if even ten priests came out of that 1,000. I'd be surprised.

BETTO – Was there any social and racial discrimination?

CASTRO – Unquestionably. In the first place, the institution itself was private. The Jesuits weren't motivated by profit, however. The Christian Brothers weren't motivated by it very much either, but they did attach some importance to the social prestige of money. Tuition wasn't expensive. I remember, for example, that board at the Jesuit school in Santiago de Cuba costs 30 pesos. A peso was equal to a dollar at the time. I'm speaking of 1937, when I was 10½ or 11 years old.

BETTO – Thirty pesos a month.

CASTRO – Equal to $30 a month.

That included room and board—the meals weren't bad—and outings. Some health care was provided too, and the students paid to join a cooperative medical society. What are they called?

BETTO – Mutual benefit societies.

CASTRO – A mutual benefit society. I belonged to it. For anything more serious, we were sent to the hospital. We had water. Of course, if we wanted our clothes washed, we paid separately; textbooks were extra too. But, for classes, food, sports and everything else we did there, 30 pesos wasn't expensive. Thirty pesos isn't much when you think of the personnel needed to cook, provide transportation and do the maintenance work for the school.

That was possible because those priests didn't earn anything—that is, they weren't paid a salary. They were just fed; they lived very austerely. There were some lay teachers—who, naturally, received a small salary—and a rigorous administration. The Jesuits were untouched by the profit motive, and there was very little of it at the La Salle School. Austere, strict, self-sacrificing and hardworking, the Jesuits contributed human effort, cutting costs. If they had been men who earned salaries and all that, the tuition wouldn't have been just 30 pesos. It would have been double or triple that, even though the purchasing power of money was much greater then. If all those priests had earned salaries, the school couldn't have been so inexpensive. They had no profit motive.

But, even so, 30 pesos was within the reach of only a few families in that society. Day students paid 8 or 10 pesos, more or less. This means that for 20 pesos more I got everything else; I lived at school, was fed, and was provided with water and electricity. This was clearly due to the self-denial and austerity of those men. But, still, few could afford it.

BETTO – Were any of your schoolmates blacks?

CASTRO – Let me explain. To begin with, the school itself was very exclusive, confined to the few families who could pay for it—from the countryside, where I was from, or from small towns in the province's interior. As I've said, there were around 200 day students from Santiago de Cuba and 30 boarders. Not many families could afford to send their children to the school, because they also had to pay their travel and clothing expenses. It cost a family at least 40 pesos a month. If the child got some money for buying ice cream, candy or something like that, it could cost as much as $50, and there were few families that could pay that.

That is, the institution, as a private school, was the privilege of a small minority, and the students boarding there were the sons of businessmen and landowners—moneyed people. A worker's son—even a professional's—couldn't have gone there as a boarder, though he could have gone as a day student if he were the son of a professional who lived in Santiago de Cuba.

But a teacher couldn't send a child to one of those schools, because a teacher earned around $75. He couldn't send a child there. Many doctors and lawyers couldn't send their children. They'd have had to have been eminent—very eminent—lawyers or doctors to have been able to send a child to those schools. Usually, only a family that had an estate, a factory, a coffee processing plant, a shoe factory, a distillery or some other important business could send a child there. Of course, if a family lived in Santiago de Cuba, there wasn't any need to send the child as a boarder; he could be a day student. He wasn't boarding; he went home every day. A bus picked him up every morning and took him home in the evening. A family with a more modest income could pay the fees charged for a day student; even some not very prominent professionals could afford it if it were $8 to $10. But you had to be an eminent doctor or lawyer or the head of an affluent family to afford the fees charged for a boarding student.

I can remember the social origins of almost all my schoolmates there, both day students and boarders. Those schools were very exclusive; they were upper-class schools, but even our class had two categories: the children of businessmen, manufacturers and professionals who lived in Santiago de Cuba proper and those who lived in the rich Vista Alegre section—the middle bourgeoisie and the very rich bourgeoisie. The very rich bourgeoisie had an aristocratic spirit. They considered themselves different from the rest of us—superior. So, in that exclusive school, there were two groups —the division wasn't entirely based on money, though money lay at the root of it; rather, it was based on social status, the houses where they lived and tradition.

My family may have had as many resources as some of the ones in that social group had, but, fortunately, I wasn't in that category. Why not? Because my family lived in the countryside. There, we lived among the people, the workers, all of whom were very poor. As I told you, we even had animals under the house— the cows, pigs, chickens and all.

I wasn't the grandson or great-grandson of a landowner. Sometimes the great-grandson of a landowner didn't have money anymore, but he kept the culture of the aristocratic or rich oligarchic class. Since my mother and father had been very poor farmers who managed to acquire some money and accumulate some wealth, my family didn't have the rich people's landowners' culture as yet. They were people who worked every day in harsh conditions. They had no social life and hardly any relations with people like themselves. I think that if I'd been the grandson or great-grandson of a landowner, I might possibly have had the misfortune of acquiring that class culture, mentality and consciousness. I might not have had the privilege of escaping bourgeois ideology.

There was a whole group of students at that school who had that bourgeois, aristrocratic mentality. They looked down on the other rich children who were less ostentatious about it. I noticed it. I didn't attach much importance to it, but I noticed it. And I noticed that those in the second group competed with the very rich ones and held themselves apart. Even among the rich students, there were divisions that led to rivalry. I was perfectly aware of that.

You had to be from a relatively rich class to be at that school at all, and you breathed in an awareness of class distinction, the bourgeois institution and privilege. It wasn't a school for workers or proletarians or poor farmers—not even for professionals, except for the very exclusive ones.

There were some black students at the La Salle School, though. In that regard, it was more democratic. There weren't any black students at the Colegio de Dolores; all were supposedly white. This puzzled me several times, both there and at the Havana school that I attended later on. I wondered why there weren't any black students. I remember that the only answer I was given was "Well, it's really because there are very few of them, and a black child here among so many white ones would feel bad." So, in order to keep them from feeling bad, it wasn't a good idea to have one or two black children together with 20, 30 or 100 white ones. That was the argument I was given. I was told that it was really for that reason. I asked several times and always got the same answer. I didn't know that racial discrimination existed. How could anybody who was still in the sixth grade—especially if he wasn't from a workers' family or a family that could explain the problem to him—have known about it? I asked why there weren't any black children out of sheer curiosity. I was given an explanation, and I accepted it, more or less. Essentially, I was told, "The poor little children who are black are going to feel bad here, because they aren't the same color as most of the students."

I don't remember seeing even one black student while I was there. They might not even have accepted a mulatto. Of course, they didn't do a blood test on everybody who entered the school, as Adolf Hitler's SS would have demanded, but if you didn't look white, you didn't get in. I don't know how many cases there were or if any families challenged this. I had no way of knowing how many students were rejected because they weren't pure white.

But that's another matter, that enters the sociopolitical realm. In short, the schools were exclusive. I can talk about their good and bad aspects without bitterness. To the contrary, I feel grateful to those teachers and institutions, because they didn't frustrate some positive things I had in me, but rather developed them. Personal factors, personal circumstances, also influenced me a lot. I think that man is the product of struggle and difficulties, that problems gradually mold him in the same way a lathe shapes a piece of material—in this case, the matter and spirit of a human being.

BETTO – Tell me a little about the religious retreats—

CASTRO – Well, the religious retreats belonged to a later stage.

At that school, on my own, I decided to go on to the Jesuits' school in Havana. I hadn't had any conflicts there; I was completely successful academically and in sports. I had no problems in the sixth or seventh grades or in the first and second year of high school, as I was there until the end of the year. I consciously decided to seek new horizons. I may have been influenced by the prestige of the other school in Havana, by its catalogues and buildings and the books written about it. I felt motivated to leave the school I was in and go to the other one. I made the decision and suggested it at home, and I was allowed to transfer to the other school.

BETTO – In Havana?

CASTRO – Yes.

BETTO – What was the name of the school?

CASTRO – The Colegio de Belén. It belonged to the Havana Jesuits and was the best Jesuit school in the country—perhaps the best school in Cuba in general, because of its material base and facilities. It was a huge place, a center with great prestige, where the cream of the aristocracy and the Cuban bourgeoisie went.

BETTO – Does the school still exist?

CASTRO – After the triumph of the Revolution, it became a technological institute, and now it's a college of military technology, the Military Technological Institute, at the university level. It's a huge center and has been enlarged. For a while, it was a technological institute, but because of the need to develop the Armed Forces, we decided to locate the Military Technological Institute, known as the ITM, there.

When I was a student, there were around 200 boarders and around 1,000 students in all, including boarders and day students. It was a little more expensive, around $50 a month. It had more lay people, much more space and greater expenses. The food may even have been better, and there were excellent sports fields. I think that $50 was cheap for that institution. I say "dollars" because, with the current inflation in Latin America, nobody knows what a peso means. Once again, the spirit of self-sacrifice and Jesuit austerity made relatively low fees possible.

BETTO – Fifty dollars a month.

CASTRO – Yes.

The Jesuits' spirit of self-sacrifice and austerity, the kind of life they led, their work and their efforts made a school of that caliber possible at that price. A school like that in the United States today would cost $500 a month. There were several basketball courts, baseball fields, track and field facilities, volleyball courts and even a swimming pool. It was a wonderful school.

I was a little older then, a junior in high school. I'd never been to the capital of the Republic. I went to Birán for my summer vacation and was given some money for buying clothes and other things. I also had to buy textbooks and pay my tuition and other expenses. I packed my suitcase and went off to Havana for the first time.

BETTO – How old were you?

CASTRO – I'd just turned 16. I was born in August, so that September I was 16.

BETTO – Classes begin here in September?

CASTRO – Yes, and my birthday's August 13.

I joined the basketball team and some other teams in the 16-year-old age group. I began to take an active part in sports and became quite good in basketball, soccer, baseball, and track and field—nearly everything—right from the start. When I arrived, I found a wide range of activities. My favorites were sports and the Explorers. I maintained my old love of the mountains, camping and things like that, which I continued to do on my own. There was an Explorers' group there. It seems that during our first excursions the teachers decided I was good, and they promoted me, until one day they made me the head of the school's Explorers—the Explorers' General, as it was called.

BETTO – What does "Explorers" mean?

CASTRO – The Explorers were a group—not exactly like the Boy Scouts, but something like them. We had our own uniforms and went camping in the wilderness, using tents. We used to go for one or two days. We had to do guard duty and things like that, and I added some other activities, such as mountain climbing.

While at this school, I climbed the highest mountain in the west. We had a three-day holiday, and I organized a trip to Pinar del Río Province with three of my friends. The expedition lasted five days instead of three, because the mountain was in the north, and I didn't know where it was exactly. We went out to look for it and to explore it. We took a train that went south, but the mountain was in the north. We began the trip at night and hiked for three days before reaching the mountain—Pan de Guajaibón, which was quite a difficult one to climb. We reached the top but got back to school two days after classes had started. Everyone was worried, because they didn't know if we were lost or if something had happened to us.

During that period, I was very active, mainly in sports, the Explorers and mountain climbing. I didn't know—nor could I have imagined, then—that I was preparing myself for the revolutionary struggle. And I studied. That was always a question of honor. It wasn't that I was a model student. I wasn't, because my interest in sports and activities of that kind meant that I spent a lot of time either taking part in them or thinking about them. But I attended classes punctually and was disciplined. I paid attention —sometimes more, sometimes less. I always had a lot of imagination, and sometimes I managed to escape mentally from class and go around the world, being completely unaware of what the teacher was saying for the next 45 minutes. Now, I think the teachers were partly responsible.

Something happened there. Since I was an athlete and a somewhat outstanding one, they weren't very strict with me during the competition times, but they were later on. When the glories of the championships, medals and contests had faded away—competitions and rivalry were part of the history, prestige and name of schools of that kind—then they were demanding. Of course, I'm referring to the academic side, because they were generally very strict with regard to the students' behavior.

Several priests were very highly trained; scientists; people who were very knowledgeable in physics, chemistry, mathematics and literature, though they were still very backward politically. I'm referring to a period beginning in 1942, from 1942 to 1945. I was graduated from high school in 1945, when World War II ended. Also during that period, a few years earlier, the Spanish Civil War had ended, and all those priests and the ones who hadn't yet been ordained but who were already teaching were Nationalists—or, more frankly, pro-Franco—politically speaking. Except for a very few Cubans, they were all Spaniards. Just after the Spanish Civil War, there was a lot of talk about the horrors of the war, about Nationalists—even priests—who had been shot by firing squads. Very little was said about the Communists and other Republicans who had been shot. It seems that the Spanish Civil War was very bloody, and there were excesses on both sides.

BETTO – Was that the first time you heard about communism?

CASTRO – Well, I'd been hearing for some time that communism was a terrible thing. Communism was always described in those terms. I could tell you a lot of things about that, and we'll talk about it some other time, when we're discussing politics.

All those Jesuits were rightists. Some were obviously kind people who expressed solidarity with others; they were exemplary in many ways. But, ideologically, they were right-wing, pro-Franco reactionaries. There wasn't even one left-wing Jesuit in Cuba at that time. I know that there are many left-wing Jesuits now, and I think you could point to some examples in the past. But at the school where I studied, just after the Spanish Civil War, there wasn't a single left-wing Jesuit. It was the worst period of all in that regard.

I took note of it but didn't question it very much. As I said, I was involved in sports. I was also trying to do well in my studies. Even though I wasn't a model student, I felt morally obligated to pass all my exams. For me, it was a question of honor. In general, I got good grades, even though my attention wandered in class and I had the bad habit of depending on last-minute cramming. We criticize this now, and rightly so.

I had some duties at school, because students used to be assigned specific tasks. If you were in charge of a classroom or study hall, you had to turn out the lights and close the doors and windows. I was in charge of the main study hall where we stayed for a while after dinner before going to bed. During exam time, I had to be the last to leave. I used to stay there for two, three or four hours, going over my notes. Even though it wasn't exactly right, it was allowed—perhaps because it didn't hurt anybody. During exam time, I studied all the time—before and after lunch and during recess. I studied the textbooks to learn everything I was supposed to know but didn't about mathematics, physics, chemistry and biology. I'm self-taught in all those subjects; somehow, I managed to understand them. I developed a capacity to unravel the mysteries of physics, geometry, mathematics, botany and chemistry with textbooks alone. I usually got excellent grades, which were often higher than those obtained by the best students. Teachers from state institutes came to give us the examinations, and the school was very interested in the results.

BETTO – What were those institutes?

CASTRO – The state high schools. Don't forget that that was during World War II, when people's fronts had been created, and some countries enacted laws to regulate their educational systems. Our 1940 Constitution included some advancements regarding education and lay schools, and, according to Cuban law, the private schools—which clearly served the more privileged sectors of the population—had to comply with the law and follow the state high schools' program. There was only one program, and when the teachers in the state high schools—who had their pride, selfesteem and prestige as educators to maintain —came to test those privileged students in the Jesuit and other private schools, they gave hard exams, some more so than others. Perhaps some of them were more understanding than others. That was the time, I repeat, of the people's fronts and the anti-Fascist alliance. The Communist Party, which had already participated in drawing up the 1940 Constitution, exerted some influence on the government later on and contributed to the ratification of some laws.

So the teachers came and gave their exams, which were usually tough. It seems that my specialty was those exams given by the state teachers. Often, when the best students became confused and didn't answer correctly, I managed to get the highest grades in subjects that were considered difficult. I remember when I got the only high grade on a Cuban geography exam; it was 90. Our school complained to the state high school teachers, pointing to the low marks, and they replied, "The textbook the students used isn't very good." Then our teachers said, "Well, there's one student who used that same textbook and got a 90." The thing is, I used a little imagination and made an effort to explain the answer. For me, the exams were a question of honor.

In short, I was very involved in sports, the Explorers, all kinds of outdoor activities and cramming during that period, but I got good grades.

I also made a lot of friends among my fellow students. Without trying—and without even realizing it—I became popular as a sports enthusiast; an athlete; an Explorer; a mountain climber; and also as an individual who, in the end, got good grades. Some political virtues may also have been apparent, without my being aware of them.

BETTO – You were going to talk about the religious retreats.

CASTRO – I went on religious retreats during that period. It goes without saying that the religious training remained the same as what I've already described when telling you about the Colegio de Dolores. The same system prevailed, even though we were studying logic and philosophy.

We went on religious retreats for three days every year. Sometimes they were held at school, but sometimes we went somewhere else. All the students in the same grade were isolated for three days for religious lectures, meditation, spiritual communion and silence. Silence was the cruelest part. All of a sudden you had to become a mute and not say a word. Even so, though, that stillness had some pleasant aspects. I remember that so much philosophizing gave me a tremendous appetite. As a result, lunch and dinner were two wonderful hours; that gave me a lot of pleasure and satisfaction. The spiritual exercises began early.

Naturally, I had to go to Mass every day in those schools.

BETTO – Every day?

CASTRO – Yes. This was another policy that I think was negative: forcing students to go to Mass every day.

BETTO – At Dolores as well as Belén?

CASTRO – Yes. I don't remember what it was like at La Salle, but I know—I remember this clearly—we had to go to Mass every day at Dolores and Belén.

BETTO – In the morning?

CASTRO – Yes, before breakfast. Every day, we had the same ritual. I think it was mechanical. Having to go to Mass every day was overdoing it, and I don't think it helps a child.

Along with Mass, there were prayers. Now, as I see it, repeating the same prayers over and over 100 times, saying the Hail Mary and the Lord's Prayer mechanically, had no positive effect; that's the best I can say. How many times I must have said them in the course of all those years! Did I ever stop to think what the prayer meant? For example, later on I noticed a form of praying in other religions in which the person seemed to be talking spontaneously with somebody; he used his own words and ideas to make a plea or a request, to express his will or a feeling. They never taught us that; rather, they just told us to repeat the written words, to repeat them absolutely mechanically one, ten, fifty or a hundred times. To me, that's not really praying; it may be good exercise for the vocal cords, the voice or whatever—of patience, if you will—but it's not praying.

BETTO – It's a mechanical thing.

CASTRO – Often, I had to recite the litany in Latin and Greek, and I didn't know what the words meant: "*Kyrie eleison, Christe eleison.*" One person would say the litany, and another would respond: "*Ora pro nobis,*" etc. I almost remember the litany. We didn't know what it meant or what we were saying; we just kept on repeating it mechanically. Over the years, we grew accustomed to it. I tell you quite frankly that that was a great defect in the religious training I received.

BETTO – I think so too.

CASTRO – When we were 16, 17 or 18, our spiritual exercises included meditation. During those three days of the religious retreat, we meditated on philosophical and theological topics, but usually the theme was punishment—which was most likely, according to all indications, in the circumstances—and reward. The reward didn't inspire our imagination, but the punishment was described in such a way as to do just that.

I remember long sermons for meditation on hell—its heat and the suffering, anguish and desperation it caused. I don't know how such a cruel hell as the one that was described to us could have been invented, because such severity is inconceivable, no matter how great a person's sins may have been. Moreover, the punishment for venial sins was way out of proportion. Even to doubt something that wasn't understood regarding a certain dogma was a sin. You had to believe it, because if you didn't and had a fatal accident or died for any other reason while in that state of sin, you could be condemned to hell. There was really no proportion between the individual's sins and eternal punishment.

The idea was to arouse the imagination. I still remember an example that was often given in those spiritual exercises. There was always some written material, some theses or commentaries, but we were told, "so you may have an idea of eternity, my children, imagine a steel ball the size of the world [and I tried to imagine a steel ball the size of the world, with a circumference of 40,000 kilometers] whose surface is grazed by the proboscis of a fly once every 1,000 years. Well, the fly will wear away the steel ball—that is, that steel ball the size of the world will disappear as a result of the fly's slight touch once every 1,000 years—before hell ends, and, even after that, it will go on forever." That was the nature of meditation. I'd describe it as a form of mental terrorism; sometimes those explanations turned into mental terrorism.

It's near the end of the twentieth century, and, not so long—only 40 years (I'm amazed at what a relatively short time)—ago, one of the best schools in our country provided this kind of an education. I don't think it was a good way to foster religious feeling.

BETTO – Was the Bible mentioned a lot?

CASTRO – It was mentioned, but not very much. The meaning of a parable or a passage from the Gospels might be explained. We just kept on studying biblical history throughout that period. The editions of the book were larger every year. That is, we started with a slender volume, and each year more subject matter was added. Biblical history was always in the curriculum and was very interesting. I always liked biblical history, because its content was fascinating; it was wonderful for children and adolescents to know everything that had happened from the creation of the world to the Flood.

There's something I've never forgotten about biblical history, though. I'm not sure if it's actually mentioned in the Bible or not, but, if it is, I think it will require some analysis. It's this: after the Flood, one of Noah's sons—was it one of Noah's sons?—mocked his father. Noah made wine from grapes and drank so much that he became drunk. One of his sons made fun of him, and, as a result, his descendants were condemned to be black. I can't recall if the son mentioned in biblical history was Canaan. Who were Noah's sons?

BETTO – Shem, Ham and Japheth. In the Bible, in Genesis, Canaan appears as the son of Ham—and, therefore, as one of Noah's offspring. Noah cursed Canaan and condemned him to be the last of the slaves. Since the slaves in Latin America were blacks, some old translations use the term *black* as a synonym for *slave*. Moreover, Canaan's descendants became the people of Egypt, Ethiopia and Arabia, who are dark-skinned. But, in the Bible, his descendants weren't included in the curse, unless you make a slanted interpretation, in order to seek religious justification for apartheid.

CASTRO – Well, I was taught that one of Noah's sons was punished by having black descendants. Somebody should check to see if this is being taught today and if it's really proper for a religion to teach that being black is a punishment of God. I remember that problem in biblical history.

All those stories fascinated me, though: the building of the Ark, the Flood, all the animals, the landing of the Ark, what life was like, Moses' travails, the crossing of the Red Sea, the promised land, and all the wars and battles described in the Bible. I think I first heard about war in biblical history. That is, I became interested in the art of warfare. I was fascinated by it, from Joshua's destroying the walls of Jericho to the sound of trumpets, to Samson's herculean strength, which allowed him to tear a temple down with his bare hands. Those deeds were really fascinating. The entire period covered by the Old Testament was marvelous to me—Jonah and the whale that swallowed him, the punishment dealt by Babylon, and the prophet Daniel. Of course, we could have studied other stories—those of other peoples and their interpretations—but I believe that few are as fascinating as the ones in the Old Testament and biblical history.

BETTO – Was there also a book called *Imitation of Christ*?

CASTRO – I think I've heard of it.

After biblical history came the New Testament, with its many parables. These were repeated and generally explained to us with the terms used in the Bible, which were interesting. The crucifixion and death of Christ, with all the explanations that were given, always had an impact on the children and young people.

BETTO – When did you begin to feel sympathy with the cause of the poor?

CASTRO – I'll have to go into my childhood experiences. First of all, where I was born and raised, we lived among poor people; all of the children went barefoot. Now, I realize they must have had a lot of hardships. Now, I think of the diseases that struck them and their suffering. I wasn't aware of all this then, but we had a very close relationship. They were my friends and comrades in everything. We went to the river, the woods and the fields together to hunt and to play. During my vacations, they were my friends and buddies. I didn't belong to another social class. We were always together and had all kinds of relationships. I had a very free life there.

There was no bourgeois or feudal society in Birán. There weren't 20 or 30 landowners whose families would get together, always forming the same group. My father was an isolated landowner. Sometimes a friend would visit him, but we hardly ever visited anybody. My parents usually stayed home; they didn't go to visit other families. They worked all the time. So, the only people we saw were the ones who lived there. I used to go to the Haitians' quarters, to their huts, and sometimes I was scolded for it, but only because I ate the dry corn they cooked. I got into trouble because I ate with them—for health, not social, reasons. Nobody at home ever said, "Don't go near so-and-so." Never. They weren't class-conscious; they didn't have a rich people's or landowners' mentality.

I wasn't aware of the privilege of having many things. My family had everything and was always treated with respect, but I was raised and grew up with these people without any prejudices or bourgeois culture or ideology. This must have had an influence.

My ethical values were created at school, by the teachers, and even at home, by the members of my family.

I was told very early in life that I shouldn't lie. I was undoubtedly taught ethical values at school and by my parents and the other members of my family. There were clearly ethical values. They weren't Marxist, and they didn't stem from an ethical philosophy. They were based on a religious ethic. I was taught what is right and wrong, things that should and should not be done. In our society, the first notion children got of an ethical principle may have been based on religion. In the prevailing religious environment, people absorbed a number of ethical values as a matter of tradition, even though there were some irrational beliefs, such as thinking that the flight and screeching of an owl or the crowing of a rooster could foretell disaster.

Later on, the life I've described to you also began to create a feeling of what was wrong, the violation of an ethical standard, an injustice, abuse or fraud. I received not only a set of ethical values but also some experience in what the violation of ethical standards was and what unethical people were like. I began to have an idea of what was fair and unfair. I also began to have a concept of personal dignity. It would be very difficult to give a complete explanation of what a sense of personal dignity is based on. There may be men who are more sensitive than others to this. People's character also has an influence. Why is one person more rebellious than another? I think that the conditions in which a person is educated can make him more rebellious or less rebellious. Character and temperament also play a role. Some people are more docile, more receptive to discipline and more obedient than others. But the fact remains that you gradually develop a sense of justice, of what is fair and what is unfair.

In this regard, I think I've always had a sense of justice—from very early on, because of what I saw and experienced. I also feel that physical exercise and participation in sports can teach us a lot: rigor, endurance, determination and self-discipline.

Undoubtedly, my teachers, my Jesuit teachers—especially the Spanish Jesuits, who inculcated a strong sense of personal dignity, regardless of their political ideas—influenced me. Most Spaniards are endowed with a sense of personal honor, and it's very strong in the Jesuits. They valued character, rectitude, honesty, courage and the ability to make sacrifices. Teachers definitely have an influence. The Jesuits clearly influenced me with their strict organization, their discipline and their values. They contributed to my development and influenced my sense of justice—which may have been quite rudimentary but was at least a starting point.

Following this path, I came to view abuse, injustice and even the humiliation of a fellow man as inconceivable. These values were developed gradually in my conscience and stayed with me. Several things contributed to my developing a certain set of ethical values, and life itself kept me from acquiring a class culture, a sense of belonging to a different, superior class. I think this was the basis from which I later developed political awareness.

If you mix ethical values with a spirit of rebellion and rejection of injustice, you begin to appreciate and place a high value on a number of things that other people don't value at all. A sense of personal dignity, honor and duty form the main foundation that enables people to acquire political awareness. This was especially so in my case, since I didn't acquire it by having poor, proletarian or farm origins—that is, through social circumstance. I gained my political awareness through reasoning, thinking, by developing feelings and deep conviction.

I think that what I was telling you about faith—the ability to reason, think, analyze, meditate and develop feelings—is what makes it possible to acquire revolutionary ideas. In my case, there was a special circumstance: nobody taught me political ideas. I didn't have the privilege of having a mentor. Most of the people who have played a role in our history had mentors, outstanding teachers or professors. Unfortunately, I've had to be my own mentor all my life. How grateful I would have been if somebody had taught me about politics, if somebody had taught me revolutionary ideas!

Nobody could instill religious faith in me through the mechanical, dogmatic, irrational methods that were employed. If somebody were to ask me when I held religious beliefs, I'd have to say, "Never, really." I never really held a religious belief or had religious faith. At school, nobody ever managed to instill those values in me. Later on, I had other values: a political belief, a political faith, which I forged on my own, as a result of my experience, analysis and feelings.

Political ideas are worthless if they aren't inspired by noble, selfless feelings. Likewise, noble feelings are worthless if they aren't based on correct, fair ideas. I'm sure that the same pillars that sustain the sacrifices a revolutionary makes today sustained the sacrifices made in the past by a martyr who died for his religious faith. I think that religious martyrs were generous, selfless men; they were made of the same stuff of which revolutionary heroes are made. Without those qualities, there can be no religious or political heroes.

I've had to continue on my way—a long way—to develop my revolutionary ideas, and they have the immense value of conclusions reached on my own.

BETTO – Were there any Christians in the group that attacked the Moncada Garrison in 1953?

CASTRO – Definitely yes, but we never asked anybody about his religious beliefs. Yes, there were Christians. I already had a Marxist ideology, however, when we attacked the Moncada.

BETTO – Your ideology was already Marxist?

CASTRO – Yes. I had a Marxist-Leninist ideology, quite a well-developed revolutionary ideology.

BETTO – Did you have it when you were going to the university?

CASTRO – Yes. I acquired it as a university student.

BETTO – In the political struggle at the university?

CASTRO – Through my contact with revolutionary literature.

There's a curious thing, however: as a result of studying capitalist political economy, I started drawing Socialist conclusions and imagining a society whose economy would operate more rationally, even before I discovered Marxist literature. I started off as a utopian Communist. I didn't come in contact with revolutionary ideas, revolutionary theories, *The Communist Manifesto*, or the first works by Marx, Engels and Lenin until I was a junior in the university. To be quite frank, the simplicity, clarity and direct manner in which our world and society are explained in *The Communist Manifesto* had a particularly great impact on me.

Naturally, before becoming a utopian or a Marxist Communist, I was a follower of José Martí's; I mustn't omit that. I've been a follower of Martí's ideas ever since I was in high school. Martí's ideas impressed all of us a lot; we admired him. Also, I always wholeheartedly admired our people's heroic struggles for independence in the past century.

I've spoken to you about the Bible, but I could also tell you about our country's history, which is extremely interesting, filled with examples of courage, dignity and heroism. Just as the Church has its martyrs and heroes, so too the history of any country has its martyrs and heroes; it's almost part of a religion. Something very like veneration filled my heart when I listened to the history of General Antonio Maceo, the Bronze Titan, who waged so many battles and performed so many feats; or when I was told about Ignacio Agramonte; or Máximo Gómez, that great Dominican internationalist and brilliant military commander who fought on the Cubans' side from the beginning; or the innocent medical students who were shot in 1871 for having allegedly desecrated a Spaniard's grave. We heard about Martí and Carlos Manuel de Céspedes, the Father of his Country, so, together with the biblical history we were talking about, there was another history that we considered sacred: our country's history, the history of our nation's heroes. I got that not so much from the other members of my family as at school, from books. Gradually, I came in contact with other models of people and behavior.

Before becoming a Marxist, I was a great admirer of our country's history and of Martí. I was a disciple of Martí's. Both Marx and Martí begin with an "M," and I think they resemble each other greatly. I'm absolutely convinced that, if Martí had lived in the same environment as Marx, he would have had the same ideas and acted in more or less the same way. Martí had great respect for Marx. He once said of him, "Since he sided with the weak, he deserves honor." When Marx died, Martí wrote some very beautiful things about him.

I think that Martí's thinking contains such great and beautiful things that you can become a Marxist by having his ideology as a starting point. Of course, Martí didn't explain why society was divided into classes, though he was a man who was always on the side of the poor and who bitterly criticized the worst vices of a society of exploiters.

When I first got hold of *The Communist Manifesto*, I found an explanation, and, in the midst of that forest of events, where it was very difficult to understand phenomena and where everything seemed due to the wickedness of men—their defects, perversity and immorality—I started to identify other factors that weren't dependent on man, his morals and his individual attitude. I began to understand human society, the historic process and the divisions that I saw every day. After all, you don't need a map, a microscope or a telescope to see class divisions, with the poor going hungry while others have more than they need. Who could know this better than I, who'd experienced both realities and who had even been, in part, a victim of the two? How could I fail to understand the experiences I'd gone through, the situation of the landowner and of the landless, barefoot farmer?

Maybe I should have added something when I spoke to you about my father and Birán. Even though he was a big landowner, my father was a very kind—an extremely kind—man. His political ideas, of course, were those of a landowner, because he'd already developed those views, and he must have been aware of the conflict between his interests and those of the wage earners. Even so, he was a man who never said no to anybody who asked him for something, to anybody who came to him for help. That's very interesting.

My father's land was surrounded by latifundia owned by U.S. citizens. He owned large tracts of land, but they were surrounded by three big sugar mills, each of which had tens of thousands of hectares of land. One of them alone had over 120,000 hectares, and another, around, 200,000. It was a chain of sugar mills. The U.S. owners had very strict standards for managing their property. They were ruthless. The owners didn't live there; they lived in New York. They had an administrator who was given a budget for expenses, and he couldn't spend even a penny more.

During the dead season, after the sugar harvest, many people used to come to our place. They spoke to my father, saying, "I've got such-and-such a problem; we're hungry; we need something, some help, some credit at the store," and so on. Those who didn't usually work there would go to him and say, "We need work; give us work." My father's sugarcane fields were the cleanest in all of Cuba. While others had their fields weeded only once, my father organized three or four weedings, so as to give those people work. I can't recall his ever failing to find a solution whenever somebody asked him for something. Sometimes he grumbled and complained, but his generosity always got the upper hand. That was a characteristic of my father's.

During my vacations, I had to work. When I was an adolescent, my father used to take me to the office or have me work at the store. I had to spend part of my vacation doing that work, which wasn't at all voluntary—I had no alternative. I'll never forget the many poor people who came there—barefoot, ragged and hungry—looking for a chit so they could buy at the store. However, that was an oasis compared to the way the workers were treated on the U.S.-owned latifundia during the dead season.

By the time I started having revolutionary ideas and discovered Marxist literature, I'd already had a very close look at the contrast between wealth and poverty, between a family with large tracts of land and those who had absolutely nothing. Who had to explain a society divided into classes and the exploitation of man by man to me, since I'd seen it all with my own eyes and even suffered from it, in a way?

If you have certain traits of rebelliousness, certain ethical values, and you come across an idea that gives you greater insight—such as the ones that helped me to understand the world and the society in which I lived, what I could see all around me—how can you fail to feel the impact of a veritable political revelation? I was deeply attracted to that literature; it completely won me over. Just as Ulysses was ensnared by the Sirens' songs, I was captivated by the irrefutable truths of Marxist literature. Immediately, I began to grasp, understand and see things. Later on, many compatriots who had no previous idea of these topics but who were honest men eager to end the injustices that existed in our country also had that same experience. As soon as they were provided with some elements of Marxist theory, they felt the same impact.

BETTO – Didn't this Marxist awareness breed prejudices in you with regard to the Christian revolutionaries who joined the 26th of July Movement—such as Frank País, for example? How was it?

CASTRO – Let me tell you. Neither I nor any of the other comrades ever had any conflict—not that I can recall—with anyone over religious matters. As I told you, I already had a Marxist-Leninist ideology. I was graduated from the university in 1950, and I'd acquired a fully revolutionary outlook—not just in terms of ideas, but also in terms of purposes and how to implement them, how to apply it all to our country's conditions—in a very short period. I think that was very important.

When I enrolled in the university, I first became involved with an opposition party that was very critical of political corruption, embezzlement and fraud.

BETTO – The Orthodox Party?

CASTRO – Yes. Its official name was the Cuban People's Party, and it had broad mass support. Many well-meaning, honest people belonged to that party. The main emphasis was placed on criticizing corruption, embezzlement, abuse and injustice, constantly denouncing Batista's abuses during his previous term. This was linked at the university to a tradition of struggle, including the martyrs of the School of Medicine in 1871 and the struggles against Machado and Batista. Also during that period, the university took a stand against the Grau San Martín Administration, because of its fraud and embezzlement and the frustrations it caused the country.

Like many other young people at the university, I'd already established relations with that party almost at the beginning, before I had any contact with the literature I was telling you about. When I was graduated, my ties with the party were very strong, but my ideas had developed much further.

After graduation, I wanted to take some graduate courses. I was aware that I needed more training before devoting myself fully to politics. I especially wanted to study political economy. I'd made a great effort at the university to pass the courses that would enable me to obtain degrees in law, diplomatic law and social sciences, in order to get a scholarship. I was already living on my own; my family gave me some help during the first few years, but, when I was finishing college—I'd even gotten married—I couldn't think of continuing to receive help from my family. Even so, I wanted to study, and the only way to do it was by getting a scholarship abroad. To get that scholarship, I had to get those three degrees. The scholarship was already within my reach. I had to take only two more courses out of the 50 I had had to pass in two years. No other student in my class had done this, so there was no competition. But then impatience and my contact with reality forced me to act. I didn't have the three years I needed to continue my studies—as you did as a friar of the Dominican Order during the years you devoted to the study of theology—the ones I needed to study economics and improve and deepen my theoretical knowledge.

Rather well equipped with the main ideas and with a revolutionary outlook, I then decided to put them into practice. Before the coup d'etat of March 10, 1952, I already had a revolutionary outlook and even an idea of how to implement it. When I entered the university, I didn't have any revolutionary culture yet. Less than eight years passed between the development of that outlook and the triumph of the Revolution in Cuba.

I've said that I had no mentor. The effort to think through, develop and apply those ideas in such a short time was very great. What I had learned of Marxism-Leninism was decisive in this. I believe that my contribution to the Cuban Revolution consists of having synthesized Martí's ideas and those of Marxism-Leninism and of having applied them consistently in our struggle.

I saw that the Cuban Communists were isolated—by the atmosphere with which imperialism, McCarthyism and reaction enveloped them. No matter what they did, they remained isolated. They'd managed to become strong within the labor movement; a large number of Party members had worked with the Cuban working class, devoting themselves to the workers, and had done a great deal for them and won great prestige among them, but I didn't see any political possibilities for them under those circumstances.

So, I worked out a revolutionary strategy for carrying out a deep social revolution—but gradually, by stages. I basically decided to carry it out with the broad, rebellious, discontented masses, who didn't have a mature political awareness of the need for revolution but who constituted the immense majority of the people. I said, "The rebellious masses, the untainted, ordinary people, are the force that can make the revolution, the decisive factor in the revolution. They must be led to revolution, but they must be led by stages." Such an awareness couldn't be created overnight, with mere words. It was clear to me that the masses were the basic factor—the still-confused masses in many cases, prejudiced against socialism and communism; the masses who hadn't been able to receive any real political education, influenced as they were from all quarters by the mass media and other resources: radio, television, movies, books, magazines, newspapers and reactionary anti-Socialist preaching everywhere.

Socialism and communism were depicted as the enemies of mankind. This was one of the arbitrary, unfair uses made of the mass media in our country, one of the methods used by the reactionary society in Cuba, like everywhere else. Very early in life you'd hear that socialism denied the homeland, deprived farmers of their land and people of their personal property, divided families, and soon. In Marx's time, socialism was accused of communizing women—a charge that was given a devastating rebuttal by the great Socialist thinker. The most horrible, most absurd things were invented to poison the people against revolutionary ideas. Many people who were part of the masses might be anti-Communist: beggars, hungry people and the unemployed might be anti-Communist. They didn't know what communism or socialism was all about. However, I could see that the masses were suffering from poverty, injustice, humiliation and inequality. The people's suffering wasn't just material; it was moral, as well. You don't suffer just because you're getting 1,500 calories and you need 3,000. There's another sort of suffering too—social inequality, which makes you feel constantly debased and humiliated as a human being, because nobody thinks anything of you and you're treated like dirt, as if you didn't exist: somebody else is everything, but you're nothing.

Then I realized that the masses were decisive, that the masses were extremely irritated and discontented. They didn't understand the social essence of the problem; they were confused. They attributed unemployment; poverty; and the lack of schools, hospitals, job opportunities and housing—everything, almost everything—to administrative corruption, embezzlement and the perversity of the politicians.

The Cuban People's Party that I mentioned earlier had harnessed much of that discontent, but it didn't blame the capitalist system and imperialism for it very much. I'd say that this was because we'd been taught a third religion: the religion of respect for and gratitude to the United States. That was something else.

BETTO – Because of its nearby, constant presence?

CASTRO – "The United States gave us our independence. It is our friend; it helped us and is still helping us." This appeared quite frequently in official texts.

BETTO – Many American tourists used to come here too.

CASTRO – Of course they used to come, but I'm trying to explain a historic reality. We were told, "Independence began on May 20, 1902," the day when the United States handed us a neocolonial republic with a constitutional amendment that gave it the right to intervene in Cuba. By the way, May 20 was the day they chose for initiating the broadcasts of Radio Goebbels, Radio Reagan, Radio Hitler—I'm not going to call that subversive radio station Radio Martí. When the United States imposed the Platt Amendment on Cuba, it had already been occupying our territory for four years. It occupied the country for four years and then imposed its infamous right to intervene in our country. It intervened more than once and seized our best land, our mines, our trade, our finances and our economy.

BETTO – When was that?

CASTRO – It started in 1898 and culminated on May 20, 1902, with the caricature of a republic, the political expression of the U.S. colony established in Cuba. That was when it began the massive appropriation of Cuba's natural resources and wealth. I told you about my father, who worked for a famous U.S. company, the United Fruit Company, which was established in the northern part of Oriente Province. My father was a United Fruit worker. That's where he started working in Cuba.

Textbooks praised the American way of life. Those books were complemented with all sorts of literature. Now, even the children know that all that was a great big lie.

How do you go about destroying all those lies, all those myths? How do you destroy them? I remember that the people didn't know anything, but they suffered. The people were confused, but they were also desperate and able to fight and to move in a given direction. The people had to be led to the road of revolution by stages, step by step, until they achieved full political awareness and confidence in their future.

I worked out all those ideas by reading and studying Cuban history, the Cuban personality and distinguishing characteristics, and Marxism.

BETTO – Were you in the left wing of the Orthodox Party?

CASTRO – Some people knew what I thought, and some were already trying to block me. They called me a Communist, because I explained everything to everybody rather candidly. But I wasn't preaching socialism as the immediate objective at that time. I spoke out against injustice, poverty, unemployment, high rent, the eviction of farmers, low wages, political corruption and ruthless exploitation everywhere. It was denunciation, preaching and a program—for which our people were much better prepared and where I had to start working in order to lead them in a really revolutionary direction.

I noticed that, even though it was strong and had influence among the workers, the Communist Party was isolated. I saw it as a potential ally. Of course, I couldn't have convinced a Communist Party member of the fact that my theories were right. I didn't even try to do that. What I did was to pursue those ideas after I already had a Marxist-Leninist outlook. I had a very good relationship with them. Almost all of the books I read were bought on credit at the Communist Party bookstore on Carlos III Street. I also had a very good relationship with Communist leaders at the university; we were allies in almost every struggle. But I would think, "There is a possibility to work with the large, potentially revolutionary masses." I was putting those ideas into practice even before Batista's coup on March 10, 1952.

BETTO – Did the members of the group that attacked the Moncada Garrison belong to the left wing of the Orthodox Party?

CASTRO – They came from among the young people in that party whom I knew. I also knew what they thought. When the coup was staged, I started to organize them.

BETTO – Under what name?

CASTRO – I was organizing combat cells.

BETTO – Was that what they were called, "cells?"

CASTRO – I was setting up a military organization. I didn't have an independent revolutionary plan as yet, because that was in the first few months after the 1952 military coup. I'd had a long-term strategic plan since 1951, but it called for a preliminary political period.

Just after the coup, I was proposing a revolutionary movement. I even had some political strength. The Orthodox Party was going to win the election. I knew that its leadership in almost all the provinces—all except Havana Province—was already in the hands of the landowners and bourgeoisie, as was always the case. The People's Party was virtually in the hands of the reactionary elements and electoral machines—except for Havana Province, where a group of honest, prestigious politicians, intellectuals and university professors prevailed. There was no machine, though some rich people were coming up and trying to take control of the party in the province, using the traditional methods of machines and money.

The party was quite strong in Havana. It had 80,000 members who'd joined spontaneously. That was a considerable number. It grew—especially after the death of its founder, a militant man with great influence among the masses who killed himself as the result of a controversy with a government Minister. He'd charged the Minister with having purchased property in Guatemala with embezzled funds, but he couldn't prove it. He fell into a trap, starting a controversy over that issue, for—even though corruption was rampant in the country—he couldn't provide any concrete evidence. He grew desperate and committed suicide. The party was virtually without leadership, but it had enormous strength.

I was already saying that that party was going to win the June 1952 presidential election. I also knew what was going to happen with that government: it would end up in frustration. However, I was already thinking of a preliminary political stage, for preparing the movement, and a second stage of seizing power in a revolutionary way. I think that one of the key things that Marxism taught me—and that I also new intuitively—was that power had to be seized in order to make the revolution and that nothing could be accomplished through the traditional political methods that had been used up until then.

I was thinking of using certain positions as a platform from which to launch a revolutionary program—initially, in the form of legislative bills—that later came to be the Moncada Program. It wasn't a Socialist program yet, but it could win the support of large masses of the population, and it was the first step toward socialism in Cuba. I'd worked out the ideas of the Moncada Program long before Batista's coup. I was already organizing a powerful base with poor suburban Havana residents and other low-income sectors in the city and province. I also worked actively with Orthodox Party members.

Since I already was a lawyer, I had close contact with those sectors in an active, dynamic, energetic struggle, supported by the efforts of a small group of comrades. I didn't hold any leadership posts, but I had broad mass support in that party and a revolutionary outlook. When the coup took place, everything changed. It became impossible to carry out that initial program, in which I'd even included the soldiers, as I considered them to be victims of exploitation—they were put to work on the private farms of magnates, the President and the colonels. I could see all that, and I denounced it and even had some subtle influence among their ranks. At least, they were interested in the denunciations. I planned to include the soldiers in that movement—soldiers, workers, farmers, students, teachers, professionals and the middle class—all in a broad program.

When the coup took place, everything changed. As a first step, I thought we'd have to go back to the previous constitutional stage. The military dictatorship would have to be defeated. I thought we'd have to recover the country's previous status and that everybody would join forces to wipe out Batista's infamous, reactionary coup. I started to organize ordinary militant members of the Orthodox youth group on my own, and I also contacted some of the leaders of that party. I did that on my own. Some of the leaders said they favored armed struggle. I was sure that we would have to overthrow Batista by force of arms in order to return to the previous stage, to the constitutional regime, and I was convinced that that was the objective of all the parties. I'd already worked out the first revolutionary strategy with a large mass movement that would initially be implemented through constitutional channels. I thought that everybody would unite to overthrow Batista's regime—all the parties that had formed part of the government and all the opposition parties: everybody.

I began to organize the first combatants, the first fighters—the first cells—within a few weeks. First, I tried to set up a small, mimeographed newspaper and some underground radio stations. Those were the first things. We had some run-ins with the police that served as useful experience later on. When it came time to apply that experience, we were extremely careful in choosing cadres and in protecting the security of the organization. That's when we became true conspirators and started organizing the first nuclei for what we thought would be a united struggle by all the parties and all the other forces. That's how I began in that party, where I met a lot of earnest young people. I looked for them in the lowest-income sectors in Artemisa and Havana, among the workers, with several comrades who supported me right from the beginning: Abel Santamaría, Jesús Montané, Ñico López and some others—a very small group.

I became a professional cadre. At the beginning, that movement had one professional cadre: me. Up until just before the attack on the Moncada Garrison, we had just one professional cadre—one. Abel joined me a few days before the attack, so there were two of us cadres during the last month.

We organized that movement in just 14 months, and it came to have 1,200 men. I talked to every one of them and organized every cell, every group—1,200 men! Do you know how many kilometers I drove before the attack on the Moncada Garrison? Forty thousand. All that effort was devoted to the organization, training and equipping of the Movement. How many times I met with the future fighters, shared my ideas with them and gave them instructions!

By the way, that car hadn't been paid for. Since I was a professional cadre and there were always bills outstanding, Abel and Montané supported me and paid for the car.

In this way, we created a disciplined organization with honest, determined young people who had patriotic, progressive ideas. Of course, we were organizing to fight the dictatorship.

We didn't intend to lead that struggle; we simply wanted to cooperate with all our forces. There were plenty of well-known political chiefs and personalities already. Then the stage came when we concluded that everything was a fraud, a falsehood and an impossibility and decided to work out our own plans. That changed everything.

We ended the first part of the interview. I realized that I no longer retained the supposed neutrality of my days as a journalist, for I was very moved by what I had just heard. It was nearly 3:00 A.M. when we said good-bye.

Two

T HE second part of the interview began at 4:45 P.M. on Friday, May 24, 1985.

BETTO – We were talking about the Moncada. Specifically, I'd like you to talk about some of the revolutionaries at that time, such as Frank País, and about another who wasn't at the Moncada but was in Havana—José Antonio Echeverría, who was known to be a Christian. What impression did his being a Christian make, and what kind of relationship did he have with the people who already had a Marxist viewpoint?

CASTRO – Let me tell you. At the time of the attack on the Moncada, only a very small group of those with the greatest responsibility and authority had a Marxist training. I'd worked with a nucleus of the most responsible people in this regard.

Now, the qualities we needed from those comrades were, first of all, patriotism, revolutionary spirit, seriousness, integrity, willingness to struggle, and acceptance of the goals and risks of the struggle, because it was an armed struggle against Batista. Those were the elements, the fundamental traits. Nobody was asked whether or not he was religious; that question was never mentioned. I don't remember a single case of that. Whether or not a person believed in God was his own business, and— though there are no data or statistics on this, because, as I told you, nobody took a survey on these matters—undoubtedly, many of the participants in the attack on the Moncada were believers.

You've mentioned some cases. At the time of the attack, Frank País had no relations with us. He was very young and didn't join the Movement until several months after the attack, and he soon began to be outstanding. I think that he'd received some religious training through his family.

BETTO – Wasn't his father a minister?

CASTRO – Yes, but we never discussed religion.

BETTO – There wasn't any antireligious proselytizing?

CASTRO – There couldn't have been; it wouldn't have made sense. We were looking for people who were willing to struggle. That question never arose.

I also understand that Echeverría had received some religious training. I don't know, because I never talked with him about it, either. We talked about the struggle against Batista. One day, though, on the anniversary of his death—this was published somewhere; it was March 13—I criticized somebody very strongly because he left out an invocation to God that Echeverría had made in his political testament.

BETTO – What had he made?

CASTRO – A declaration that he'd written shortly before the action that led to his death.

Several years later, there was a ceremony on the anniversary, and I was going to speak. Well, I noticed that, in the reading of his testament, the invocation of a religious type which he'd made—an invocation to God—was omitted, and I was very irritated. When I spoke, I criticized this—it must have been in the newspapers—and asked how it was possible that the invocation had been skipped. I said that it was an act of fraud with regard to the document and asked why we had to be worried about the invocation. It didn't detract from Echeverría's merits, and it shouldn't have been omitted. I criticized it both from the point of view of historical truth, which must be respected, and as an indication of prejudice —of thinking that the invocation couldn't be repeated because it would detract from or take away his merits, that the thing could be misunderstood. This led me to make a strong public statement. It must have been in the newspapers; there's proof of all this. I don't know if you ever heard of it.

BETTO – Yes, I'd been told about it.

Now, after you were jailed. What did the Bishop of Santiago de Cuba do on behalf of the Moncada attackers?

CASTRO – In order to understand this, you have to bear in mind that when the Moncada Garrison couldn't be taken—for reasons that were accidental but turned out to be decisive—our forces withdrew. Our people were in different positions, and when the order was given to withdraw, some of them went back to the house we'd set out from, in Siboney.

I was still thinking about organizing another action, for I was concerned about the people in Bayamo—who, if they'd carried out their mission, were going to end up isolated. I was thinking about regrouping a number of comrades for an action against a smaller garrison, with an eye to backing up the people in Bayamo. Even though we'd had no news of them, I supposed they'd been able to complete their task and had taken the Bayamo garrison.

BETTO – A historical question: I visited that small farm in Siboney. I imagine that some of your comrades didn't go to the farm because they'd already been taken prisoner.

CASTRO – No.

BETTO – No? I wondered if you weren't afraid that they would talk and that all—

CASTRO – No, not then. I didn't even consider that problem, because I didn't think the enemy had had time to react to such a surprise action that might well have been traumatizing, since it was an attack on its main fortress in Santiago.

We headed for the house we'd set out from, thinking that many people were on their way there. And, in fact, a group did go there. I tried to organize the group. We took some ammunition and exchanged some weapons for others that seemed to be more effective for the new plan for those who were determined to go on to the mountains.

More exactly, I'd intended to go to Caney, which was a few kilometers north of Santiago de Cuba, to make a surprise attack on that smaller garrison with a group of about 20 or 30 men. Then I saw that the cars—we weren't in touch with one another right then—were heading for the farm we'd left. So we went to the farm too, because it was where the others had gone. That is, initially, I couldn't count on a minimum number of people for an action against the Caney garrison, which was what I planned to do at that time to support the Bayamo group.

BETTO – How many attacked the Moncada?

CASTRO – Around 120 in all.

BETTO – How many of them died?

CASTRO – I'll explain that later.

Some took up positions in some buildings, such as the court, which dominated the garrison at one angle. Others went to occupy buildings that were behind it, and my group went to the entrance to force our way in from the front. I was in the second car. The shooting broke out there, when we ran into a patrol. The group that entered—or that should have entered—there had about 90 men. The caravan that was coming down the avenue had to turn to head for the garrison, and, since some of our people weren't very familiar with the streets, some of the cars—several cars— kept going instead of turning, so only 60 or 70 men arrived at the main spot.

That was the group that was with me. The ones who were in other areas—in the court and in the hospital—knew the plans. We expected to take the command post and were then going to force the soldiers to retreat toward the rear. Those of us who entered at the guard post and those who, from their positions, dominated the area behind the garrison, where the soldiers slept, were going to take prisoners.

When the clash with the patrol took place, the fighting began outside the garrison rather than as planned. The soldiers mobilized. There were more than 1,000 men, the surprise factor was lost, and it became impossible to carry out the plan. Even so, the first car had managed to seize and control the entrance to the garrison. When we withdrew, there was a moment when I got out of the last car and gave my place to a comrade who'd been left there. Then a comrade from Artemisa got me out when it occurred to him to go back in and pick me up.

That's why, when I left by the same street on which we'd entered and was thinking of going to the Caney garrison, I couldn't count on the people, because some of them—around half of those 60 or 70 men, maybe fewer—had gone on ahead and were returning to the house we'd set out from in Siboney. There, after the failure of the action—remember, they were civilians, and, even though they were organized, it was the first time they'd ever gone into action—some of them were discouraged and began to take off their uniforms, but there was still a group that was determined to keep on fighting. The ones in that group went with me toward the mountains, the Sierra Maestra, which were near Santiago de Cuba. We weren't familiar with the area. We took off, armed, for the mountains—the group that wanted to continue with me.

The weapons that would be good for a head-on practically hand-to-hand clash—some .22-caliber automatic rifles and some 12-gauge semiautomatic shotguns with heavy shells, which were undoubtedly effective for the action we'd had in mind (anyway, we didn't have any others)—weren't very appropriate for fighting in the open. We set off for the mountains with a bunch of small-caliber rifles and shotguns.

We didn't know the terrain, and, by nightfall, we still hadn't made it to the heights. By that time, the enemy had deployed troops throughout the area, and all the key points in the range in that zone had been taken. In spite of that, with the experience we now have, we could have outflanked their positions, but our lack of experience and unfamiliarity with the area forced us, when we couldn't find ways to skirt the main heights that had been taken, to return to the lower ranges. Then we drew up a plan for reaching the Sierra Maestra from the other side of the Bay of Santiago de Cuba—that is, west of the city.

If we couldn't defend the city, if the general strike we were going to call didn't come off and the country wasn't paralyzed, and if the enemy was able to counterattack with sufficient force so we couldn't hold the city, our original plan called for falling back to the Sierra Maestra with 2,000 or 3,000 armed men. That was the idea. Of course, it was based on the premise that we would have the support of the city of Sanitago de Cuba once we had taken the garrison.

With the knowledge we gained later, we could have laughed at all those positions and all those soldiers, but, because of our inexperience and ignorance at that time, we thought it was impossible to cross to the other side of the Sierra Maestra to get away from that mass of deployed forces, and we came up with the plan of crossing the Bay of Santiago de Cuba; going west;

and getting into the steeper, more strategic part of the Sierra Maestra.

It was a small group; it even included some men who'd been wounded—though not seriously. But then an accident took place: a comrade fired his gun and was seriously wounded, and we had to try to find some way to save him, leaving him with some of the others who'd been wounded. As a result, the small group began to get smaller. Other comrades were obviously very exhausted. I didn't feel that they were in shape to withstand the hardships of a struggle in the mountains. I decided that the comrades who were so exhausted they could hardly move around should return to Santiago de Cuba.

How was it possible that they could return at that time? In the hours and days following the attack, the Army began to capture a lot of people: some who'd gotten lost on the way to the Moncada and others who'd been in other positions on the other side of the fortress and apparently didn't learn in time that the key operation had gone wrong. Some of them fell back in time, but others, who delayed, were surrounded. Still others were captured in different ways: dressed as civilians, when they tried to go to a hotel, to seek refuge or to get out of the city of Santiago de Cuba. Still others were captured in the countryside. Different comrades were captured in different places.

BETTO – Your group was in uniform?

CASTRO – Yes. The number who fell in the fighting was very low. The enemy had a relatively high number of casualties. If I'm not mistaken, there were 11 dead and 22 wounded.

BETTO – How many of your men were killed?

CASTRO – I only heard of two or three comrades who were killed in the initial fighting, and some were wounded. Yet, by Monday, Batista was announcing 70 rebels killed—that is, 70 casualties among the revolutionaries. It's possible that, by Monday, they still hadn't killed all of the 70—a total of 160 had participated in the Santiago de Cuba and Bayamo actions—but they were talking about 70 dead rebels. By Sunday afternoon, they'd managed to take several dozen comrades prisoner, and they were murdered. For almost an entire week—the first four or five days—all of the prisoners were subjected to horrible torture and murdered.

All this triggered great opposition by the people of Santiago de Cuba and a national uproar. The city began to find out that every prisoner who was taken was being murdered. The citizens organized, mobilized and went to see the archbishop, Monsignor Pérez Serantes—the Archbishop of Santiago de Cuba, who was of Spanish origin—and he intervened for humanitarian reasons to save the lives of the survivors. Remember that there were 40 comrades in Bayamo. They too had had problems in carrying out their mission, and a number of them were taken prisoner in various places.

The general rule applied by Batista's Army was to spread a bunch of lies in order to make the soldiers hate us. It spread an infamous accusation that we had cut the throats of soldiers who were patients in the Santiago de Cuba hospital. What really happened was that, as I told you, the fighting began outside—not inside, as was planned—because of an accidental meeting with a patrol. The patrols usually didn't pass by there; the one that met us had been assigned simply because it was a Sunday during the carnival season.

BETTO – A patrol from the garrison?

CASTRO – Yes. It was carnival time, and that patrol had been placed there. Even though the first car had taken the guard post, there was a clash between the second car—where I was—and the patrol. When our car stopped, since all those were military installations, the men in the cars behind mine got out and advanced toward positions to their left. A group even went into the hospital, believing it was the garrison. As soon as I realized this, I went into the hospital and brought them out, trying to reorganize the group again. The attack had stopped, and our impetus and the surprise factor had been completely lost. We tried to resume the attack on the fortress, but it wasn't possible. The troops were up and had taken defensive positions. That was what made success impossible; it could only have been done by surprise. Once the troops were alerted and had taken up positions, it was impossible. We had neither the kind of weapons nor the number of men required to seize the fortress.

Somebody fired a gun very close to me—it nearly deafened me—aimed at a man in a military uniform in the hospital. As a result, a paramedic was killed or wounded, but the enemy used the fact that some of our men went into the hospital—though only on the ground floor, in the lobby—to launch a huge slander campaign, saying that we'd cut the throats of soldiers who were hospitalized. That was nothing but a big lie, but many soldiers believed it. Batista did this to stir the soldiers up and arouse their hatred. He also played on the Army's traditional brutality, saying that its dignity had been insulted by the attack launched by some civilians who'd dared to stand up against them, to serve his purpose.

The Army systematically murdered the prisoners it took. Some were taken, subjected to questioning, and then tortured atrociously and killed.

Under those circumstances, with public opinion aroused, as I said, the Archbishop of Santiago de Cuba, as an ecclesiastical authority, got involved and made efforts, together with other prominent figures in the city—he was the most distinguished of them—to save the survivors' lives. And, in fact, some survivors were saved as a result of the efforts made by the archbishop and that group of prominent figures, together with the fact that the people of Santiago de Cuba were very indignant. In view of the new situation, it was decided that those of the comrades who were with me whose physical condition was the most serious should present themselves to the authorities, through the archbishop. It was a group of six or seven comrades.

I stayed with two other leaders. That was the small group that intended to cross the bay, reach the Sierra Maestra and reorganize the struggle. The rest were exhausted, and we had to find a way to save their lives.

We discussed the matter with a civilian, who arranged a meeting between the group and the archbishop. We went close to a house and talked with the people who lived there. Then we left the group of six or seven comrades, whom the archbishop was to pick up at dawn. The two other comrades and I withdrew to about two kilometers from the house, intending to cross the road that night and reach the Bay of Santiago de Cuba.

It's certain that the Army knew of this. It may have tapped the phone. It seems that it listened in on a telephone conversation between that family and the archbishop, and, very early, before dawn, it patrolled the whole area near the highway.

We were two kilometers away, and we made a mistake that we hadn't made in all the days we'd spent there. We were tired.

We had to sleep on the hillside, in very bad conditions. We had no blankets, nothing. That night we found a thatched-roof hut. It was quite small, about four meters long and three meters wide, the type we call *vara en tierra*. It's more like a shed for storing things. Seeking shelter from the fog, the mist and the cold, we decided to stay there until dawn. What happened was that, precisely at dawn—before we woke up—a patrol came into the hut, and we woke up with their rifles against our chests. The most disagreeable sensation there can be is to be awakened by the enemy like that. It was the result of a mistake we should never have made.

BETTO – Nobody was on guard?

CASTRO – No. The three of us were asleep. We were a little too confident; a week had already passed, and they hadn't been able to find us. No matter how much they searched, we'd evaded capture. We underestimated the enemy. We made a mistake and fell into their hands.

They must have tapped the telephone. I don't want to think that the people we made contact with gave us away. I don't believe they did, but they must have done something indiscreet, like talking on the phone. This put the Army on the alert, and patrols were sent there. As a result, they captured us.

That was how they took us prisoner. Some of them were undoubtedly bloodthirsty and would have murdered us on the spot.

Then, by chance, something incredible happened. There was a black lieutenant called Sarría who seemed to have some authority and who wasn't a killer. The soldiers wanted to kill us; they were enraged and were looking for a pretext. Their rifles were ready to fire, and they tied us up. First they asked us our names, but we didn't tell them our real names; we gave some other ones. I'm positive that the soldiers didn't recognize me at first; they didn't recognize me.

BETTO – Were you already well known in Cuba?

CASTRO – Relatively well known, but for some reason or other, those soldiers didn't recognize me—but they wanted to kill us anyway. If we'd given them our names, we would have been shot then and there. We got into an argument with them, because they called us murderers. They said that we'd gone there to kill soldiers and that they were the followers of the Liberation Army, so we got into an argument. I lost my patience and argued with them. I told them that they were the followers of the Spanish Army and that we were the true followers of the Liberation Army. That made them even more furious.

We were convinced they were really going to kill us. Of course, I didn't feel there was even the remotest chance of surviving. I started to argue with them, and then the lieutenant said, "Don't shoot; don't shoot." He put pressure on the soldiers, and then, more quietly, he repeated, "Don't shoot. You can't kill ideas; you can't kill ideas." Notice what this man said. He repeated this around three times: "You can't kill ideas."

One of the two comrades—Oscar Alcalde, who is president of the People's Savings Bank now; he was an accountant, in charge of the Movement's funds—happened to be a Mason, and, on his own initiative, he told the lieutenant this, which increased our chances or gave the lieutenant greater assurance, because many of the soldiers were Masons too. Anyway, they made us stand up and start moving, all tied up. When we'd walked a few steps and I'd seen the lieutenant's attitude, I called him over and said, "I've seen your behavior, and I don't want to deceive you. I'm Fidel Castro." He said, "Don't tell anybody; don't tell anybody at all." He himself advised me not to tell anybody.

We walked a little further, and there were some shots, 700 or 800 meters away. The soldiers spread out; they were very nervous, and they hit the ground.

BETTO – How many soldiers were there?

CASTRO – Around 12.

BETTO – How old was the lieutenant?

CASTRO – He must have been 40, maybe 42.

When I saw that they'd spread out, I thought it was a pretext for shooting us, and I remained standing. Everybody spread out, and I remained standing. The lieutenant came to me again, and I told him, "I won't hit the ground. If they want to kill us, they'll have to shoot at us standing up." Then the lieutenant said, "You're very brave, boys; you're very brave." Imagine that! I think that must have been one chance in a thousand, but that didn't mean we were saved; no. That didn't mean our survival was guaranteed. The lieutenant saved our lives yet again.

BETTO – Again?

CASTRO – Yes, he saved us once more. Before the archbishop arrived, the other group—that was near the highway—was found and taken prisoner. That was the reason for the shooting I just mentioned. Then we were kept together there. The lieutenant looked for a truck. He put all the other prisoners in the back and made me ride between him and the driver, in the cab, up front.

Farther on, we came across a major. His name was Pérez Chaumont, and he was one of the most bloodthirsty army men, one of the ones who'd killed the most people. He ran into our truck, made it stop and ordered the lieutenant to take us to the garrison. The lieutenant argued with him and didn't obey; instead, he took us to the city jail in Santiago de Cuba. If we'd been taken to the garrison, they would have put us through a meat grinder.

By then, the people in Santiago de Cuba knew that we'd been taken prisoner and that we were there. All the city knew it, and they put on a lot of pressure to save our lives. Naturally, the commanding officer of the regiment went there to question us. That was very important, because the soldiers, the military men themselves, were very impressed by that action. Sometimes they even showed a kind of respect, a kind of admiration, together with their satisfaction because the invincible Army had repelled the attack and captured the prisoners. Another psychological element was added to this: they already had a guilty conscience, because, by then, they'd murdered between 70 and 80 prisoners, and the people knew about it.

BETTO – Were those prisoners your comrades?

CASTRO – Yes, the ones who'd been captured before. They'd murdered between 70 and 80 of the ones they'd captured at different times. A few managed to escape, and a few had remained prisoners, including the group that was with me and some others whom they captured in different places. It was just by chance that they weren't killed, also thanks to the public protest and, of course, because of the action taken by the archbishop and other prominent figures, who'd become involved and had been echoing that protest. They'd managed to save more; some had surrendered directly to the Army or through the archbishop. But, for our small group, when we were taken prisoner, the decisive factor was that army lieutenant.

BETTO – What happened to that lieutenant after the triumph of the Revolution?

CASTRO – Well, after that, years before the triumph of the Revolution, he was blamed for our not having been killed. He was blamed for the fact that they hadn't murdered us.

They made some other attempts to kill me later on, but they failed. Then came prison, release from prison, exile, the *Granma* expedition and the struggle in the mountains. Our guerrilla army was organized, and again, at the beginning, there were new setbacks. They thought they'd crushed the guerrilla army then too, but it rose again out of its ashes, became a real force and fought with prospects for winning.

During that period, the lieutenant was discharged from the Army. After the triumph of the Revolution, we took him back in the Army and promoted him to the rank of captain. He served as the head of security for the first President appointed by the Revolution. He was in the Presidential Palace, heading the President's security guard. Unfortunately—this is why I think he must have been about 40—eight or nine years after the triumph of the Revolution, he got cancer, and he died on September 29, 1972. We couldn't save his life. He died as an army officer, much respected by everybody. His name was Pedro Sarría.

It seems that this man had been at the university. Before that, he had been self-taught and studied on his own. I'm sure he must have met me or seen me at some time at the university. Obviously, he had an inclination for justice; he was an honorable man. But the surprising thing, what reflected his way of thinking, was that, at the most critical moments, he kept repeating to me quietly—I could hear him when he was telling the soldiers not to shoot—that ideas can't be killed. Where did he get that phrase? Maybe some of the journalists who interviewed him later know; I never asked him. I thought he'd live a long time. In the early years of the Revolution, we always thought there was a long time in which to do many things, investigate things and clear things up. But where did he get that phrase? "Don't shoot. You can't kill ideas." That's the phrase which that honorable officer repeated several times.

Besides that, there was that other gesture, when I told him who I was and he said, "Don't tell anybody; don't tell anybody at all." And then that other phrase, when they all hit the ground, when the shooting took place, and he said, "You're very brave, boys; you're very brave." He repeated that twice. Unquestionably, that man—one in a thousand—sympathized in some way with or had a moral affinity for our cause. He was really responsible for our survival at that moment.

BETTO – Then you went to prison and spent 22 months there, on the Isle of Pines.

CASTRO – Yes, starting around August 1.

BETTO – You were released as the result of a national amnesty campaign. Do you remember if the Church took part in it?

CASTRO – The amnesty was granted in response to a very broad movement of public opinion. All of the opposition political parties, civic groups, social organizations, prominent figures, intellectuals, journalists and many others were involved in the campaign. The Church must have backed it, but the Church wasn't at the center of that campaign. Undoubtedly, the Church gained prestige thanks to Pérez Serantes' actions and conduct in Santiago de Cuba right after the attack on the Moncada—the efforts he made and the lives he saved. That was acknowledged throughout the country.

In addition to that strong public pressure, the amnesty was determined, in the long run, by several factors. The murders that had been committed aroused great indignation among the people. At the beginning, only the people in Santiago de Cuba knew about them. I denounced those murders at the trial, even though there was tight censorship of the press. I was arbitrarily separated from the others at the trial. In the first few days, I was taken to two or three hearings. I was defending myself and proving all their crimes. We took the position of assuming full responsibility for our act of rebelliousness and of defending it morally, legally and constitutionally. That was our position; nobody evaded that honorable responsibility. We all said that we accepted responsibility for and were proud of what we had done. That was the stand we took. Afterwards, all of the documents were circulated clandestinely. All the people learned of the monstrosity of those crimes, which were some of the most horrible crimes committed in Cuba's history. Meanwhile, the government thought that its power was already consolidated.

All the other political forces that had supposedly taken a stand for armed struggle did nothing and gradually became deactivated. Many of them joined in the electoral farce while we were still in prison. Then Batista thought his position was consolidated and wanted to legalize his power. He wanted to turn his de facto, transitional government into a constitutional, elected one. He programmed an election in which he was the candidate, certain that he could legalize his government. On the one hand, many forces abstained, for the opposition was very discredited; on the other, a group of parties supported him and he could draw on the government's resources. He wanted to give his regime a legal veneer.

That factor was very influential, because it was traditional in Cuba's history that it was inconceivable to have an election without an amnesty. So the amnesty was partly the result of public pressure and partly due to other factors: awareness of the crimes that had been committed; the campaign that we waged from prison to denounce those crimes and guide the people; and Batista's wish and need to give his government a legal veneer, which made him call an election. All those factors were decisive, as was his underestimating that small group that survived—a group of around 20 comrades. Believing the armed action had been crushed and that we had no resources, no strength, he passed the amnesty law.

BETTO – When you were there, was it called the Isle of Pines?

CASTRO – Yes.

BETTO – Was that where you first got in touch with Father Sardiñas, who took part in the Sierra Maestra campaign later on?

CASTRO – It's possible. While I was there in prison, some nuns visited me once or twice.

I spent only a very short time with the rest of my comrades.

BETTO – You were in solitary confinement?

CASTRO – Approximately three months after I got there, or it may have been earlier, Batista visited the prison on the island that's now known as the Isle of Youth in order—ridiculously enough—to inaugurate a power plant with a capacity for turning out a few dozen kilowatts of energy. Many units with a capacity for turning out tens of thousands of kilowatts were later built here, and no inauguration ceremonies were held, because there simply wasn't enough time, yet Batista went there to inaugurate that tiny plant. Of course, the prison authorities made preparations to welcome and honor Batista, and we reacted against that. We even decided not to eat on the day Batista arrived and not to go out into the yard; then they locked us in. The power plant was very near the pavilion where we were, and one comrade, Juan Almeida, looked out a window and saw Batista when he went into the plant. We waited until he came out, and then we sang the "26th of July Anthem."

At first, Batista thought it was all part of the welcoming ceremony or that it was perhaps a chorus singing his praises. At first, he was happy, and he told the others who were with him to be quiet. Then he grew silent and began to get irritated when the words of our anthem spoke of the "insatiable tyrants who have plunged Cuba into evil." Almeida saw everything from the window. Then the police came, but we kept on singing, even though a terrible thug, a killer called Little Pistol, was there. We were locked in, and, besides that, I was isolated from the others until the end of our prison term. I'd been kept in solitary confinement in Santiago de Cuba until I was tried, so I must have spent 19 of the 22 months I was in prison in solitary. Near the end, my isolation was ended because they sent Raúl to the place where I was, several months before the amnesty.

Therefore, I can't answer your question. I think you'll have to ask Montané, who's from the Isle of Youth, if Father Sardiñas had already made contact with the Moncada prisoners at that time.

BETTO – Do you recall how Father Sardiñas joined the group in the Sierra Maestra? What do you remember about him?

CASTRO – I don't remember any details; his joining us wasn't anything unusual, because we were getting more and more support from the population. That was at a time when the guerrilla force was being consolidated in the Sierra Maestra. All sorts of people arrived—sometimes a doctor, sometimes a technician. We appreciated doctors the most, because of the services they rendered to the troops and to the population. One day, halfway through the war, Father Sardiñas, a revolutionary priest who sympathized with our cause, joined our guerrilla force. He spent quite a lot of time with us.

BETTO – It's interesting that he joined the guerrilla force at a time in the life of the Church when no priests were in favor of socialism, yet he had the support of his bishop; his action wasn't just a personal, isolated act.

CASTRO – He joined not as a soldier but as a priest. He was there with the troops, living with us, sharing our daily lives. He had everything he needed to carry out his duties; he could even celebrate Mass. Somebody was assigned to help him, because our troops moved about a great deal. When we controlled more territory, he used to stay in one place, 10 or 15 days in the same place. He was warmly received by all the troops. Besides, as I told you before, baptism was a social institution here. Farmers gave it a lot of importance. A lot of families wanted me to be their children's godfather, and Father Sardiñas baptized scores of children there. That was one of the things he used to do: baptize. Families went to see him. They took their children and asked me to be their godfather, which in Cuba is like being a second father. I have a lot of godchildren in the Sierra Maestra. Many of them may already be army officers or college graduates. In short, the farmers established very close ties with us; it was more than friendship, more like a family relationship.

BETTO – Did he preach to the farmers? Did he explain the struggle to them from the standpoint of faith?

CASTRO – At that time, of course, he was in favor of the Revolution politically and supported the Revolution. He showed this with his own willingness to join our cause. He went through a lot of hardships with us at the time. Of course, he didn't preach in the same way it's done today or the way that a priest who's been with the guerrilla movement preaches, because, by the time Father Sardiñas joined us, the farmers who'd stayed in the area already had close ties with our forces. Some of the farmers had left the Sierra Maestra because they were afraid of the bombing raids and the other repressive measures taken by the Army, which burned houses and killed farmers. The ones who remained were very close to us.

As far as I remember, he didn't do that kind of work there. He often stayed among the farmers. I imagine he preached to them on matters of faith; it was mainly religious, not political work. And then, since no priests ever went to the area, as I've already told you, baptism was very important to the farmers; it was a social ceremony of great significance.

I'd say that his presence and the fact that he was working there as a priest, baptizing a lot of children, helped to strengthen the people's ties with the Revolution, the ties between the families and the guerrillas. It linked the population and the guerrilla command more closely. His preaching or political work in favor of the Revolution was of an indirect nature. He was very popular; everybody loved him. Everybody tried to do things for him.

BETTO – Later on, did he become a major?

CASTRO – Yes. He was given that rank for the time he was in the war and for his meritorious conduct. There were no army chaplains, properly speaking; he was made a major in recognition of his hierarchy and his merits.

BETTO – Did you wear a small cross on your guerrilla uniform?

CASTRO – Well, the people of Santiago de Cuba sent me many presents. Many people—both children and adults—sent me all kinds of presents, and a little girl from Santiago de Cuba sent me that chain with a cross and a very affectionate message, so I wore it. Yes, I wore it. If you were to ask me if it was a matter of faith, I'd have to say "No." It wouldn't be honest to say it was a matter of faith. I did it more as a gesture to that little girl. However, we had a priest with us, and I was the godfather of many of the farmers' children. There was absolutely no prejudice in that regard.

BETTO – Was she a friend of yours?

CASTRO – Yes, a sympathizer, a little girl from Santiago de Cuba.

BETTO – I thought your mother had sent it to you.

CASTRO – No. We weren't in touch. It was very difficult, because she was under constant surveillance. It wasn't easy. But my mother made countless vows.

BETTO – Now let's go a little more deeply into the Revolution's relations with the Church after the Revolution triumphed. How did the Church react? How did Christians react to the Revolution? What were their relations like at the beginning, and when did the crisis begin and why?

CASTRO – At the beginning, the Revolution's relations with all the social sectors were very good. It may be said that Batista's toppling was welcomed with joy by every social group without exception, including the elements that had been committed to Batista's regime, the people who had grown wealthy through dishonest means, who had stolen, and some sectors of the upper bourgeoisie that had been closely associated with Batista's regime. At least 95 percent of the population—several polls were taken at the time—were glad to hear the news, were overjoyed at the triumph, because everybody hated Batista's regime. It had committed many crimes and other abuses. The people regarded the triumph of the Revolution as a ray of hope, and, above all, they were glad to be rid of that regime of terror, which had lasted for seven years and had shed so much blood during the last few years.

The difficulties began with the first revolutionary laws.

BETTO – For example?

CASTRO – Well, one of the first laws—it didn't affect that many people—confiscated everything that had been obtained illegally. Everything that had been stolen during the tyranny was confiscated: farms, businesses, industries—everything they hadn't been able to take out of here, from Batista's, March 10, 1952, coup on, was confiscated. The law was limited to that period because several parties that had been in the government before then had supported or cooperated in one way or another with the struggle against Batista. If we had extended the law, many more people would have been affected, so we granted a kind of amnesty for the embezzlement committed prior to Batista's tyranny, so as not to create divisions, so as not to weaken the Revolution and so as to promote the unity of all the political forces that had opposed the regime. Therefore, only those things that had been embezzled from March 10 on were confiscated. If we'd gone farther back, to the beginning of the Republic, we'd have had to confiscate illgotten goods from the grandchildren of those who'd stolen them, and there'd been a tremendous number of thieves. So, we limited it to Batista's period, from March 10, 1952, on.

Our second step, which also received the people's full support, was to try all those who had been responsible for the tortures and other crimes that had been committed; thousands of people had been tortured and murdered. I should point out, however, that the repression which existed at that time wasn't as refined as it has come to be in other Latin American countries, such as Chile, Argentina and Uruguay. It wasn't as sophisticated then as it is today; the cases in Cuba took place in the fifties, while the ones I'm referring to in the other countries occurred nearly 20 years later, when U.S. troops had experienced the Vietnam War and the CIA had acquired a lot of technological know-how concerning repression and torture and had passed it on to the Latin American repressive forces, police and armies. In

Vietnam, U.S. imperialism perfected its techniques of crimes and terror. So, later on, in the seventies, those countries had to deal with repressive bodies that used much more refined, much more technical methods.

Really, even though the repression that Batista unleashed meant a lot of bloodshed for our people, the repression that has existed in some of these countries since then has undoubtedly been much worse. The United States and the CIA are responsible for this, because they were the ones that instructed those people in the art of killing, torturing and murdering people and making them disappear. The diabolical practice of making people disappear was practically unknown during the time of Batista. Only on rare occasions did the bodies of the murder victims fail to appear.

BETTO – In my home town, in Brazil, Dan Mitrione tortured beggars in order to teach the military men those techniques.

CASTRO – You told me that the last time you were here. It's deplorable, but it happened. Anyway, Batista killed a lot of people —students, farmers and workers. He committed all kinds of crimes. For example, one time, one of Batista's troops killed 62 farmers—all of the men in a hamlet in the Sierra Maestra. I don't know where they got that idea—maybe from the Nazis' example of Lidice, Czechoslovakia, because this was after a battle in which an army column had fallen into an ambush. It was a farm village that didn't have anything to do with it, a hamlet—there weren't any real villages there; the farmers usually lived off by themselves, but sometimes there were small hamlets—and they killed all the men. In some families, they killed the father and five or six sons; it was an atrocity.

Even before the triumph of the Revolution, in the Sierra Maestra, when what we had was an embryonic state, we drew up penal laws for punishing war crimes. This wasn't like Nuremberg; at Nuremberg, they didn't have any laws on the books under which to try the war criminals. The Allied powers agreed to try them—I'm not saying it was wrong to punish them; I think the people who were punished deserved their punishment; but, juridically, the way in which it was done wasn't very defensible, because there's a juridical principle that the laws must exist prior to the crime. I repeat: right from the beginning, in the Sierra Maestra, we, who had juridical criteria, decreed laws for punishing war criminals. When the Revolution triumphed, the country's courts accepted those laws as valid—validated by the victorious Revolution—and many war criminals who couldn't escape were tried by the courts and, by virtue of them, were given severe sentences: capital punishment in some cases and prison sentences in others.

That's when the first campaigns against the Cuban Revolution began abroad—especially in the United States, which quickly understood that it was dealing with a different kind of government (not a very docile one) and began a furious campaign against the Revolution. Even so, this didn't create any problems with sectors inside Cuba—not even with the wealthy class or with the Church. To the contrary, all sectors (the polls taken during that period show this) were in agreement with those two laws: the confiscation of property obtained illegally from March 10 on and the exemplary punishment of those who had engaged in torture and committed other war crimes.

After this, some laws of an economic nature were promulgated—such as the reduction of the electricity rates, which were slashed practically in half. The people, who hated the abusive prices charged for electricity, had been demanding this for a long time. Other measures and laws that Batista had passed for the benefit of the transnationals, such as the telephone company, were also struck down. That began to create conflicts with the foreign companies in our country. Then came the rent reduction law, which was very important socially and economically. All rents were slashed by almost 50 percent. That law made millions of people very happy. Later, it was even made into a law which said that, because of the rent they'd been paying, those people could acquire title to their homes. That was the first Urban Reform Law.

Together with these laws, we took another series of measures. We put a halt to the firing of workers, and we reinstated workers who'd been laid off during the tyranny. These were basic measures to rectify the situation in a fair way. We began to build sports installations and recreational facilities at the beaches; we opened all the beaches and other public places to everybody. That is, right at the start, we called a halt to and eliminated all discriminatory measures in clubs and at beaches. Many of the country's best beaches were private. Blacks were excluded from many hotels, bars and recreational facilities. All of this was eliminated with the triumph of the Revolution.

In some places, this wasn't easy. There were some parks in Cuba—for example, in Santa Clara—where whites habitually went to one section and blacks to another. Some comrades took immediate measures against that. We recommended that they be prudent and pointed out that these measures couldn't be imposed by force but had to be implemented largely by persuasion. That is, they couldn't force the people to mix in the parks. The prejudices existed; they'd been created by bourgeois society and the influence of the United States, which had introduced these prejudices here. They couldn't be changed overnight.

Certain irritating discriminatory practices began to disappear. This began to erode the whites' privileges, since whites-only clubs and beaches weren't tolerated any longer. This wasn't done in a drastic way, however; if you apply drastic measures in these situations, you can aggravate the problem instead of solving it. The legal measures have to be accompanied by discussion, persuasion and political work, since they touch on prejudices that are rooted quite firmly.

I myself was surprised to see just how much racial prejudice existed in our country. Right away, the first insidious campaigns began: that the Revolution proposed that whites should marry blacks, that we were going to insist on mixed marriages. That kind of insidious campaign. I had to go on television more than once to explain these problems, saying that this was a lie, that it was insidious, that we respected the freedom of each person in all decisions of this kind—but that we wouldn't permit injustice and discrimination on the job, at school, in industry or in recreational facilities. I had to argue and explain, because all sorts of insidious slander campaigns began. Undoubtedly, the privileged sectors began to feel affected by the Revolution.

The Agrarian Reform came later. That was the first law that really established the break between the Revolution and the country's richest, most privileged sectors and the break with the United States and the transnational corporations. Right from the beginning of the Republic, the best land had been owned by U.S. companies that had seized it or bought it for next to nothing. Our law didn't seem very radical, because it established a maximum limit of 400 hectares. We even made an exception for very well organized areas of intensive farming, permitting individual owners to retain up to 1,200 hectares. I don't know if there were landlords at the time of the Chinese Revolution who owned 400 or 1,200 hectares of land. But, in our country, this was a very radical law. There were U.S. companies that owned up to 200,000 hectares of land here.

This law affected the land owned by my own family. The family property was limited to 400 hectares. We lost half of the land we owned and all of the property we'd leased, which I spoke to you about earlier.

This law affected a few hundred companies and perhaps 1,000 owners—not many, because the landholdings were large. The privileged sectors began to realize that there really had been a revolution, and U.S. citizens too began to realize that there was a different kind of government.

What we did at first was implement the Moncada Program. That's the program that I told you I'd had in my head since 1951 and that I put forth in 1953 at the time of the attack on the Moncada. It contained an agrarian reform and a series of social measures that we applied in the first phase of the Revolution. Many people may have been confident that none of those programs would be applied, because programs had been spoken of many times in Cuba yet hadn't been implemented when the governments took power. Many of the wealthy couldn't even conceive of a revolution in our country 90 miles from the United States; they didn't believe that the United States would permit a revolution in our country. They thought that perhaps it was the excitement of young revolutionaries—there'd been a lot in the history of Cuba who never put anything into practice.

But then all those sectors that were accustomed to running the government began to realize that this was a different kind of government, which they couldn't run and which wouldn't allow the United States to run it either—a government that began to act honestly, with justice. The people began to see that there was a government that defended them, that really identified with their interests.

Even though everybody supported and applauded, there was generalized moral support rather than revolutionary militancy among the people at the beginning. When the first revolutionary laws were passed, the Revolution began to lose some of its support. That is, while 95 or 96 percent of the population supported it at first, that figure began to drop to 92 or 90 percent. But the support grew deeper. That 90 percent became more revolutionary and more and more committed to the Revolution.

The series of measures that I've mentioned—the end to racial discrimination, the reinstatement of workers who'd been fired under Batista, rent reductions, protection for workers and the agrarian reform—began to have the desired effect.

Also, the workers—who had been repressed—began to make demands after the Revolution triumphed. Moreover, many industrialists, some seeking to curry favor, began to give in to demands of all kinds. More than those of us in the government, it was the businessmen who began to give in to the workers' demands, and the unions, on their own, began to win many victories for labor in that first period.

I even had to meet with all the sugar workers, because they were demanding a fourth shift in the sugar mills, where there'd only been three shifts. Since we had many unemployed in the country, this demand gathered great strength. I had to meet with the delegates from all over the country in a theater where, up until then, they'd been deliriously supporting the fourth shift— even the people in our organization were wildly supporting it. I had to meet all night and speak at great length with the workers, explaining why I didn't think this was the way to solve the problem of unemployment. This wasn't easy, because the companies were still privately owned and it might appear to be a contradiction between the companies' and the workers' interests. I explained that the resources saved, the profits earned, had to be invested in development; we weren't going to allow them to be taken away—they had to be invested in the country's development. Even though I already had Socialist ideas, I didn't think it was the moment to begin to apply a Socialist program.

It's easier to explain things to a worker from a Socialist position—to ask for understanding and for sacrifices—than to explain things in a situation in which the workers see their interests as conflicting with those of the company, with those of the private owners, and see every peso less that they earn as a peso more for the owners' profits. In those circumstances, I explained the problems to the workers clearly and objectively; I've always tried to avoid demagogy, not to resort to demagogy. It wasn't easy.

From the economic point of view, some measures—such as the rent cuts—were what we would call inflationary today, in the sense that they freed a lot of money, but this was an old demand. The people had been terribly victimized by rent gouging. That demand had strong backing.

BETTO – What were the tensions with the Church like at that moment?

CASTRO – The tensions with the Church emerged when the Revolution clashed with those privileged sectors. That is the historic truth.

In the first place, the Archbishop of Havana, who later became a cardinal—I think he became a cardinal before the Revolution—had excellent official relations with the Batista dictatorship.

BETTO – What was his name?

CASTRO – Manuel Arteaga. He had excellent relations with Batista. That was one of the things he was criticized for.

I remember that in the early days of the Revolution I met with all the authorities. In those early days, a lot of people started requesting meetings, and, out of courtesy, I tried to see everybody who wanted to meet with me. That's when I had a lot of meetings with representatives of the classes that considered themselves responsible for progress: the president of the industrialists' association, the president of the merchants' association, the presidents of other associations and the high-ranking ecclesiastical hierarchy. All of those institutions started requesting meetings with me, and I saw everybody who wanted to see me.

I remember the early days in Havana. After three or four weeks, when we'd managed to establish some order, I tried to organize my work and found myself with an enormous agenda of interviews. This went on for about 15 or 20 days, two or three weeks, until I discovered that my life was the most sterile thing in the world and that, if I went on that way, I'd be doing nothing but meeting with prominent figures—the ones who met with the government—even though I didn't hold any executive position. The government was operating; I had my post as Commander in Chief of the Rebel Army and was very careful not to meddle in government affairs.

BETTO – Urrutia was President?

CASTRO – Yes, there was a provisional President, a judge who'd had a correct attitude in Santiago de Cuba and who'd won prestige because he'd acquitted some revolutionaries—those were his merits. We promoted him to that post without his having had any participation in the revolutionary process—among other things, because we wanted to make it absolutely clear that we weren't after public positions. So, as soon as the Revolution triumphed, we handed the government over to him. The problem is, he was somewhere up in a cloud; he was totally unrealistic. He started to create difficulties right from the beginning. He even adopted attitudes against the workers. He created some very difficult situations. I had to meet with the workers and explain that they had to be understanding, patient; I also had to meet with the Council of Ministers and say, "Political problems are being created."

There were no problems with the first laws passed by the Revolution, but the judge was what we might call a right-wing President. At one point, this led to a serious conflict. He started making anti-Communist statements, dancing to the tune of the U.S. campaigns and the most reactionary sectors and splitting the revolutionary forces—this was some time later—and this created a conflict. I said, "What do we do now?" The people were with us, nearly all of the people. The Revolution had around 90 percent of the people's support—maybe more. They supported the Revolution, the Rebel Army and the revolutionary leadership, but they didn't support Urrutia. If Urrutia imagined for one second that that support was for him, something that belonged to him personally, it was the wildest idea anyone could have conceived of, but it seems that, at one point, he actually believed that and started to act accordingly; that created a conflict. I said, "How can we solve this? This can't be solved by force. It's impossible. What kind of a situation are we going to end up in if a conflict arises between the revolutionary force and the President, and we have to remove him from office? It's going to look as if we're having a coup d'etat in this country." I thought about this a lot.

Previously, I'd been appointed Prime Minister—that was before the revolutionary laws were decreed. The Ministers themselves had asked me to accept. The one who was Prime Minister asked me on behalf of the rest, and he brought this request to Urrutia and the Council of Ministers. I set just one condition. I said, "I'll accept the position of Prime Minister, but you must entrust me with the responsibility for determining the policy to be followed—the revolutionary laws that are going to be passed." That was my condition, and it was accepted. As Prime Minister, I was responsible for the revolutionary decrees that would be issued.

After that, a number of revolutionary laws were passed. Later, however, an institutional contradiction arose between the Prime Minister and the President of the Republic. I gave the issue a lot of thought. I didn't let myself be swayed by any kind of provocation, and I decided to resign—to resign seriously— and that's what I did. I said, "I'd rather resign than have something like a coup d'etat." So I resigned, and it came out in the papers. I called in the television people and explained why I'd resigned. President Urrutia was at the Presidential Palace, and I was on television.

BETTO – When was that? How long after the victory?

CASTRO – It must have been at least five months after the victory, maybe more. I'd have to look it up.

BETTO – Still in 1959?

CASTRO – Yes, still in 1959. A few months later.

He was at the Palace, and I was on television. I explained why I'd resigned, and he called in the journalists to make a statement. I was informed of this while I was speaking, and I said, "No, send the television crew there. Let's discuss this publicly, on television, in front of all the people." He didn't want to discuss it on television in front of all the people, and, a few hours later, pressured solely by public opinion, he resigned. A prestigious comrade who *had* participated in the Revolution was appointed President by the Council of Ministers. Then some time passed in which I didn't have any participation in the government, because I didn't want to accept the position of Prime Minister again. I didn't want it to appear as if my resignation had been a tactic for solving the problem. I said, "Rather than see us compelled to resort to force, I resign." Of course, I wasn't renouncing the Revolution. I made that clear: I wasn't renouncing the Revolution. But, at least, I resigned because, under the circumstances, I couldn't go on carrying out my duties. I was determined not to use force to solve that contradiction.

The people solved it. The people are capable of solving many problems. Afterwards, I put up some resistance to going back to that post, until it became almost absurd, in view of the pressures that the comrades and all the people exerted on me. So I accepted the post of Prime Minister again and have had the main responsibility in the government ever since.

BETTO – You were going to refer to the contacts with the cardinal.

CASTRO – Well, I was telling you that, in the first few days, I'd discovered—it must have been in February—that my life was going to be the most sterile thing on earth, that I'd have to devote myself to affairs of protocol and meeting with prominent figures. More than once, two chubby characters came up requesting interviews. I asked, "Who are they?" "They're the cardinal's nephews." The cardinal's nephews wanted to see me. So, I said, "Well, I'll have to devote myself to meeting with the cardinal's nephews." They were interested in things because they had business ventures; in addition, being mentioned in the papers was a social coup. The next day, the newspapers would report, "So-and-so met with Castro." I never liked that, but, fortunately, I soon managed to quit that style of work. I said, "Now, I'm going to meet with the people I'm interested in seeing, go to the places I want to visit and not be enslaved by meetings with all these characters who produce nothing and solve nothing and just want to see me." So I changed the approach. But I still recall those two chubby boys who kept requesting interviews every so often, and it would seem as if I'd have to devote myself just to that. The cardinal was also on very good official terms with the Revolutionary government.

This didn't create any problems. The problems stemmed from the passing of the revolutionary laws: the Urban Reform Law and the Agrarian Reform Law.

BETTO – The problem of the schools: when was the law on taking over the schools passed?

CASTRO – It wasn't done at the beginning. Our first measures didn't include the nationalization of private schools, nor was that considered part of an immediate program. What we had foreseen was launching the Literacy Campaign and sending teachers all over the country.

Parallel to these revolutionary measures, we started building roads, hospitals, polyclinics and other health centers in the mountains, and schools there and in the rest of the countryside. Ten thousand new jobs for teachers were created. That was another measure that was implemented in the early months of the Revolution: 10,000 jobs were created, and teachers were sent throughout the country.

The revolutionary laws produced conflicts, without a doubt, because the bourgeois and landed sectors, the rich sectors, changed their attitude toward the Revolution and decided to oppose it. Together with them, the institutions that served all those interests started launching campaigns against the Revolution. That's how the initial conflicts with the Church began, because those sectors wanted to use the Church as a tool against the Revolution.

How was it that they could attempt that? Because of a factor that was characteristic of Cuba but not of Brazil, Colombia, Mexico, Peru or many other Latin American countries: the Church in Cuba wasn't popular; it wasn't a Church of the people, the workers, the farmers, the low-income sectors of the population. Here, in our country, something that was already in vogue and which later became common practice in most of the Latin American countries had never been applied: that of priests working side by side with the villagers and workers, priests working in the fields. In our country, where 70 percent of the people lived in the countryside, there weren't any rural churches. This is an important piece of information: there wasn't a single church in the countryside, not a single priest in the countryside! And that was where 70 percent of the people lived. The same thing was true of the place where I was born—I told you about this yesterday; there was no evangelical—or apostolic; I don't know what you call it—work, no religious education for the population.

BETTO – Evangelization.

CASTRO – Evangelization.

As I was saying, allegedly, it was a Catholic society, and it was customary to baptize children and do all those things I told you about yesterday, but there was no real religious education or religious practice.

Religion in Cuba was disseminated, propagated, mainly through private schools—that is, schools run by religious Orders—the schools I mentioned yesterday, which were attended by the children of the wealthiest families in the country, the members of the old aristocracy, or those who considered themselves aristrocrats, the children of the upper middle class and part of the middle class in general. As I told you yesterday, a doctor could perhaps afford to send his child to a school as a day student and pay the equivalent of $10 a month for tuition. That was the main vehicle for religious dissemination in our country, and, consequently, those children were the only ones who received a religious education and engaged in religious practices, though not very methodically or rigorously. Perhaps one of the characteristics of those classes was their laxness, the absence of discipline in terms of religious practice. For example, some of them didn't even go to Mass—devout Catholics don't miss Mass on Sunday—and many others went to Mass on Sunday only as a social practice or because it was the *in* thing, and then, after that, just went about enjoying their own well-to-do life and wealth. They weren't noted for their faithful observance of religious principles.

Those were the sectors that constituted the nucleus of the Catholic Church in our country. They were the ones with the closest ties to the parishes—which were generally located in the rich neighborhoods. Of course, some churches had existed in the ordinary urban areas for quite some time, and wherever there was a new residential development for the upper bourgeoisie—for the wealthy—excellent churches were sure to be built. Religious service was guaranteed for them. In the slums, in the poor neighborhoods, no religious services were guaranteed. As a rule, the rich classes had family ties with bishops, with the Church hierarchy.

Besides, a large part of the clergy was of foreign origin. As I said yesterday when I was telling you about the Jesuits, most of them were Spaniards who held reactionary, right-wing, Spanish-Nationalist—even pro-Franco—ideas. Our first conflicts with the Church arose when they tried to use the Church as a tool, as a party against the Revolution.

Of course, the Catholic Church wasn't the only one that had private schools. Some Protestant churches had them too—not many, just a few—and they had made quite a name for themselves. For example, there was a school in El Cristo, in Oriente Province—where my youngest sister studied, by the way—a Protestant school that was quite prestigious. It wasn't very expensive; in fact, it was rather economical. I don't know if it received any assistance from the Church or not.

In Cárdenas, there was a school called Progresiva, which was also Protestant. It had a lot of prestige, and many of its alumni are now with the Revolution. For example, Comrade Pepín Naranjo attended that school. The most renowned principal of that school is still living and has always supported the Revolution: Emilio Rodríguez Busto. There were no problems; it was a lower-income sector.

There were some Protestant schools in Havana too; some of them had English names. One of them, if I remember correctly, was called Candler College; it was quite a swanky school, and its name was English. I remember it well because we played against its teams in basketball and baseball meets when I went to Belén. There were nondenominational private schools too. Almost all of the schools were Catholic, like the one I attended. At the end, it had 1,000 students. It was the biggest school in the country. Now we have several schools with 4,500 boarding students each. That school had around 1,000 students, around 150 or 200 of whom were boarders. It was the Colegio de Belén, the biggest and one of the most prestigious schools in the country.

Those schools were the sources that nourished the Church. I'm not considering other beliefs—what might be called popular beliefs. All the fervor of Our Lady of Charity was popular fervor; the fervor for St. Lazarus—people lit candles to him—was also popular, as was the masses' tradition of baptism.

BETTO – You don't deny that there's a diffused religiousness in the Cuban people's culture? This can be seen in Martí's works, for example, even though people often try to give the impression that the people here were always nonclerical, that they never had a religious tradition. From the little I know about the country, I have the impression that *santería* was influential, that the Afro religions were influential, and that there's a diffused religiousness in the culture. Would you ratify this?

CASTRO – It's what I was trying to explain: the cult of Our Lady of Charity, St. Lazarus and various other saints. I've already explained that spiritualism was also widespread; there were all sorts of beliefs. We also had an African legacy, a legacy of animist religions that later mixed with the Catholic and other religions. You're speaking about a diffused religiousness. Well, I believe that every people in the history of the human race has had some diffused religiousness.

When Columbus arrived here with his church—the Catholic Church—he came bearing the sword and the cross. With the sword, he sanctified the right to conquer; with the cross, he blessed that right. The Indians who lived here had their own religious beliefs, all of them.

When Cortes arrived in Mexico, he found that culture and religion were widespread, even more than in Spain. I might even say that the Aztecs were more religious than the Spaniards. They were so religious that we're still impressed by the degree to which those priests devoted themselves to religion, with human sacrifices. And the governments were theocratic. Books and other works have been written in which those methods are widely analyzed. So, the Christians arrived with their morality and said the Indians were cruel. If an Aztec had gone to Spain, he might have thought it very cruel to have a priest wearing a cassock in the summer heat, or he might have thought that other things were very cruel. He would have formed judgments, and the Spaniards would have seemed barbarians to the Indian because they didn't offer sacrifices to the gods but burned heretics alive at the stake, instead.

You have to analyze how much savagery there is in each, how much cruelty in each. The Aztecs didn't sacrifice human lives as an act of cruelty against another person; rather, they considered it the greatest privilege for the victim. This is like some Asian religions, in which it is considered a privilege for a widow to be burned together with the body of her dead husband. They considered that being sacrificed to stone gods was the greatest happiness, the greatest joy and the greatest gift. It's difficult to find a more religious people than the Aztecs or the Mayas. They filled Mexico with pyramids and religious buildings, and when you ask about some great pyramid or some other great work they built, you find that everything had a religious purpose. That is, the Aztecs were more religious than the Spaniards.

In Peru, the Incas too were more religious than the conquistadores, than Pizarro and all those people. Pizarro gave more thought to gold than to the Bible, and all the conquistadores were mainly concerned with gold. They criticized the others for worshiping stones, while they themselves worshiped gold. They criticized those who made human sacrifices to stone idols, while they made thousands of human sacrifices to the god of wealth and gold, for they killed millions of Indians by making them work in the mines, and they killed Spaniards too. Atahualpa himself was taken prisoner and deceived—after they collected the ransom (a room filled with gold objects), they murdered him.

So, you can't even say that those who came to conquer this hemisphere were more religious. I don't think that those conquistadores were very religious at all.

When you analyze the history of India, of China or of Africa —of all the peoples—the first things you find is religiousness. Moreoever, you find it combined with great purity—even if we don't understand it; even if their ways may seem savage and their things may seem ridiculous to us; even if, on many occasions, it's said, "They're savages; they believe in the moon or an animal or a thing." Throughout the history of the human race, the first thing you see everywhere is diffused religiousness. It's not a principle that can be applied to a particular people. Rather, all peoples, in one way or another, have had religiousness, and, undoubtedly, there was religiousness in Cuba. What we didn't have was a tradition of organized, systematic, methodical religion; religious practice; or active participation in Church affairs. We did have a great mixture of religions and a spirit that was generally influenced by religious ideas and beliefs.

I think that very few societies have escaped this situation. In Mexico, for instance, there is more religiousness than we had here, and the same is true of other Latin American countries. In Spain, itself, there was a greater sense of that diffused religiousness you were talking about, but it was expressed in a thousand different ways other than the systematic practice of religion.

BETTO – Right.

Now, I'd like to go back to the initial tensions—for instance, the problem of teaching in the schools. I think that this must have been one of the most difficult problems in the relationship between the Revolution and the Church.

CASTRO – When the conflicts arose—they were really class conflicts, because, as I was explaining, the wealthy class had a monopoly on the Church; it tried to use it and to lead bishops, priests and ordinary Catholics to take counterrevolutionary positions—this also produced an opposite reaction in other Catholic sectors, middle-class Catholic sectors and lower-income sectors that didn't accept this counterrevolutionary attitude. An active group of Catholics, largely composed of women—who were always very sensitive to the work of the Revolution—established an organization called With the Cross and With the Homeland, that firmly supported the Revolution. Many of them were founding members of the Federation of Cuban Women.

The Protestant churches took a different attitude, however. I could see—I've always observed this—that, as a rule, the Protestant churches spread more among the low-income sectors of the population, and they also had more active religious practice. What I mean is, I observed more discipline in the Protestant churches—in their ideas, their styles, their methods and their way of praying.

BETTO – More coherence.

CASTRO – Yes; they were more consistent in their religious practice. There weren't many of those people, but, in general, the ones belonging to such a school or such a Protestant church— there are a lot of them—were much more consistent in their religious feelings and ideas than the Catholics were; they were more disciplined. No problems arose with those Protestant sectors; to the contrary, our relations with them were always good and easy in general.

There were no problems, either, with animist beliefs or with any other kind of belief. Nor were there any problems with Catholic beliefs; the problems that arose concerned Catholic institutions, but that's something else.

Within the Protestant churches, there are some groups with which—due to their special characteristics—the Revolution did have some difficulties, as was the case of the Jehovah's Witnesses —but I've read that Jehovah's Witnesses usually cause problems everywhere.

BETTO – Everywhere—even with the Brazilian military men.

CASTRO – They enter into conflict with a country's symbols, schools, public health and defense—with many things—and, in this regard, we were highly sensitive. Threatened by the United States, we needed to apply a strong defense policy—and we found ourselves faced with a doctrine that opposed conscription. We didn't have any trouble over beliefs; rather, all our problems were over ideas—and you don't know whether they're religious or political. In Cuba's special conditions, antagonism arose between the Revolution and those ideas, and we had a couple of problems with the Protestant churches.

Disputes also arose with the Catholic institutions. Undoubtedly, there were confrontations—not violent ones, because there were no violent confrontations of any kind, but there were political confrontations. At the beginning, the nationalization of private schools hadn't been foreseen or analyzed. By revolutionary definition, we logically wanted to develop state schools so they'd be as good as or better than the best private schools. I think we've succeeded in this, for we now have thousands of schools. Cuba now has over a million students in its nursery schools, full-day school programs with lunches and scholarship schools.

As I was telling you, just one of our big vocational schools, with 4,500 students, has more boarding students than there used to be in the entire country. Among the schools that used to have the largest enrollments, the Colegio de Belén had about 200 boarding students, and the Colegio de Dolores, in Santiago de Cuba, had 30. I'm just mentioning two of the schools I knew about. I don't think that, in the past, there were 2,000 boarding students—what we call scholarship students—but now we have 600,000 of them, who receive not only a free education, room and board but also clothes, books, medical care and transportation; they receive everything. We must have around 300 times as many scholarship students as the number of boarding students that the bourgeoisie and landowners had. So, today, the son or daughter of a farmer, of a family living in the mountains—the Sierra Maestra mountains, for example—or of a worker who lives in the countryside for any reason can receive a better education than the sons and daughters of the country's privileged minority used to receive.

Now, Cuba has around 1,000 nursery schools; there weren't any before the Revolution. Now, we have special schools, with an enrollment of 42,000, for students who are deaf, dumb or blind or who have some other handicap. Now, we have many preschool centers. We have tens of thousands of scholarship students at the university level. That is, after 26 years of the Revolution, we've been able to apply the principle of making better schools available to the lowest-income families than the privileged families used to have. And it's all provided by society, by the Socialist state.

If it hadn't been for those disputes, we wouldn't have had any need to nationalize those schools. Instead of paying for a private school, many people would probably have preferred a state school—after all, most Latin American professionals studied at public universities—or perhaps there would have been healthful competition between those schools and ours. We hadn't decided to nationalize the private schools. The conflicts that occurred at that time, before we'd built the new schools, created the need to nationalize the private schools, because the sons and daughters of the wealthy families who opposed the Revolution attended them—most of those schools were Catholic—and turned them into centers of counterrevolutionary activity. All this brought about the need to nationalize the schools, but there was no discrimination. It wasn't a question of nationalizing the Catholic schools; Protestant and private lay schools were nationalized too. It wasn't just the Catholic and Protestant schools; all the schools were nationalized.

I'd have to review and analyze all that. Remember, I'm talking off the cuff. I'm telling you what I remember about what gave rise to that process. Otherwise, if you were to ask me if those schools would still exist now, 26 years later, I'd say that perhaps they would. That is, I'm not saying, stating or suggesting that private schools must necessarily be nationalized if the families that send their children to those schools have no antagonism toward the Revolution. But, if the schools become hotbeds of counterrevolutionary activities—especially when those activities become violent and are linked to sabotage, bombs and other CIA activities, with the CIA moving around everywhere, plus U.S. attacks and economic blockades that force the country to defend itself—there's no choice. If you have cordial relations within society, you may be able to decide, from the economic viewpoint, that if you have 300 million pesos for education, you can assign 200 million to the sectors that can't pay for private schools and can save 100 million—that you can then assign to public health, to the building of homes or to economic development, because it won't be necessary to assign it to the sectors that can afford to pay private schools' fees. Even today, there are families in Cuba that could afford to pay private schools' fees— not because they're industrialists or landowners, but because they have monthly incomes of 1,000 pesos, because they're doctors, engineers or workers. There are many families here that have monthly incomes of over 1,000 pesos because several members of the family are working, and, if there's only one child, they could pay 50 or even 100 pesos for schooling.

The Socialist state could even have schools that charged fees, if this were deemed advisable, as long as there were enough free schools for the rest of the children and the free ones weren't worse than the others. If there were private religious schools in a country that was beginning a revolutionary process, it might be considered that they were contributing to the country's education and helping to defray educational costs. Third World countries, developing countries that don't have a lot of money but do have many needs, might decide to use this $100 million for other purposes.

So, far from being dogmatic about the need to nationalize the private schools, I can even view them as a contribution by certain sectors to the country's economy and as an aid, so the money that would otherwise have had to be used for those schools could be allocated for meeting other important needs. I don't consider this question to be a matter of revolutionary dogma. I'm talking about our particular experience, which was different. We've established what we might call an ideal: to give all the children in the country the same chance to get a high-quality education.

BETTO – Commander, when I was a child, I used to hear some priests say that we had to struggle against communism and socialism, because the arrival of socialism would mean that the churches would be closed, priests would be murdered, nuns would be raped and bishops would be hanged. Now I'm asking you: were the churches closed down in Cuba? Were the priests executed? Were the bishops tortured, as happened in Brazil during the military regime? What was it like in Cuba?

CASTRO – I think that serious conflicts between the revolution, the political movements and the Church have occurred in the classical historic revolutions. Sometimes, this involved the Catholic Church; in the old empire of the czars, it happened with the Orthodox Church.

BETTO – And in Mexico, at the time of the Mexican Revolution.

CASTRO – Yes, I was about to mention that, but I was going farther back into the past. Even the Reformation gave rise to a series of violent clashes with the emergence of Luther's and Calvin's movement and the appearance of various churches. The reforms led to violence and bloodshed. I was still a child when I first heard stories about St. Bartholomew's Night, in France. That's part of history. Thousands of people were murdered in those religious conflicts. In other words, there was violence not only in the political and social conflicts but also within the ranks of the religious movements. I don't know if anybody has ever figured out how many people were sacrificed for those reasons.

BETTO – By the Inquisition.

CASTRO – Yes; and since the Inquisition, by one side or another. As I understand it, everyone resorted to violence of one kind or another. Sometimes it was the state; at others, the Church. In other words, violence was present—not just in the political conflicts. It was also present—this is what I want to emphasize—in the religious movements themselves. It's obvious that with the appearance of Christianity millions of people were sacrificed in the name of the old pagan church of Rome. Nobody knows how many Christians were sacrificed by the Roman Empire in the course of 300 years, beginning with Christ, down to the last one before Christianity became the Empire's official religion.

Even in the Church's own clashes, there was a lot of violence. There was violence against the Church, and the Church also applied violence to a considerable extent. This is why it's not strange for violence to surface in clashes between the revolutionary political movement and the Church.

Let's take the classical revolutions. The French Revolution, which was a major historical event, was marked by violent clashes between the Revolution and the Church—only part of the Church, however, because we should never forget that the French Revolution stemmed from an Assembly in which three estates were represented: the nobility, the clergy and the Third Estate (the merchants, professionals, craftsmen, etc.; what we would call the middle class). The priests and lower clergy—and some bishops too—formed the majority of the Third Estate. Then, when that Assembly, called by the king, was convened, even some members of the nobility expressed their support for the middle class. The majority was composed of the lower clergy, priests and a number of bishops, but we shouldn't overlook Lafayette and several others who also supported the Revolution. That was the first classical revolution of our time, and it was a violent one. Bishops and priests were sacrificed in the struggle by one side or the other—by both sides, not just one. We shouldn't forget that the priests played a decisive role in the emergence of the French Revolution.

These conflicts were repeated in one way or another in the second great social revolution of our time, the Bolshevik Revolution. I'm not very familiar with this aspect, but I imagine that, as in every revolution, there must have been clashes between the Church and the Revolution, and some priests may have been executed. I'm not positive about this, since you don't pay much attention to the details in these great historical processes. I have more information about what occurred in this regard in the French Revolution—many books have been written about it—but there was conflict there too.

The Mexican Revolution, which took place in our hemisphere, was also a social revolution—not a Socialist revolution, but a social one—and all sorts of things happened. A part of the Church was with the Revolution, and another part was against it, which gave rise to serious conflicts and violence. It was a bloody conflict.

When I recall the Spanish Civil War, I realize that it too was marked by bloodshed. Both sides applied violence, and priests—and perhaps bishops too—were executed by one side, and it's likely that priests were executed by the other side as well.

Now, let's take our Revolution. It's a profound social revolution, yet no bishops or priests have been executed, and no priests have been manhandled or tortured. The most important thing, I'd say, is that no priests or lay people have been manhandled or tortured. When we were in the Sierra Maestra, we enacted laws against torturers and murderers—I've told you about those laws—and promoted deep respect for human life, for the individual, and rejection of high-handedness, injustice and violent treatment of people, of prisoners, among all our fighters.

We won the war not only by fighting but also because we knew how to treat prisoners. No enemy soldiers whom we captured were executed, and none of them were tortured—not even to try to force them to give us important informaion. Of course, we had our laws. When we discovered a spy, we could try him, sentence him and even execute him, but we never tortured anybody in order to get information. As a rule, those people were so demoralized that we'd have been ashamed to do such a thing.

Our people were inspired by their hatred of torture and crime; how could we possibly have set an example of torture and crime for our soldiers? It would have had a demoralizing effect. Those who don't understand that morale is a fundamental factor in a revolution are lost, defeated. Values and morale are man's spiritual weapons. As you know, regardless of his beliefs, we don't inspire a revolutionary fighter with the idea that he'll be rewarded in the next world or will be eternally happy if he dies. Those men were ready to die—even those who were nonbelievers—because there were values for which they believed it was worth giving their lives, even though their lives were all they had. How can you get a man to do this if not on the basis of specific values, and how could you possibly stain and destroy those values?

Not a single soldier who was captured by our side was executed. That helped a great deal, because it contributed to the prestige, authority and morale of the revolutionary forces in the face of the enemy that tortured and murdered prisoners and committed all kinds of other crimes. We have maintained this tradition for more than 26 years, ever since the Revolution triumphed, because it was a firm, decisive policy, and crime is something that we have never tolerated. It doesn't matter what the enemies of the Revolution say. They go around saying terrible things but we pay no attention. Every time you read a news dispatch, you see that they're irritated, furious, because they can't point to a single case that will serve as evidence that the Revolution has committed a murder, tortured somebody or made anybody disappear. There haven't been any cases of this, and they'll never find any. This is an orderly revolution that has been developing in an orderly fashion.

We've been very radical, but never to excess. We have not found or accepted, nor will we ever find or accept, any justification for violating some of those values, for staining some of those values that constitute the pillars of our Revolution. In this regard, I can assure you that no priests, no bishops and not even our worst enemies—those who have made assassination attempts against the leaders of the Revolution (and the CIA has made dozens of these attempts)—were subjected to violence. There was a time when there were 300 counterrevolutionary organizations in Cuba. Every time five or six counterrevolutionaries got together, they founded an organization. They believed that, with the United States behind them, encouraged by the United States, inspired by the United States, egged on by the United States and supported by the United States in their struggle against the Revolution, the Revolution wouldn't be able to withstand the onslaught. There were all kinds of opportunities in those organizations. Anyone who was convicted of a serious crime could have been executed, but only on the basis of the laws in effect, with a trial and uncontestable evidence of the crime. I told you that there were 300 of these organizations, and we knew more about their activities than they did themselves. This was because our security bodies didn't resort to torture; they were very efficient institutions and always used other means for finding out what the enemy was doing, getting to know the groups and infiltrating them. There was one time, nearly at the end of this period, when our people, the revolutionaries, were heading nearly all of those counterrevolutionary organizations. That was the result of perfect, painstaking work that didn't use violence to obtain information. Let's say a counterrevolutionary had done a number of things in January 1961. Well, we had a dossier on him that told us what he had done every day of that month, where he'd gone and whom he'd met. We had all the dope on him. Let's say he was arrested in 1962, when he'd become a dangerous character. He probably couldn't remember exactly what he'd done on a specific day in January or whom he'd met, but the whole story was there in the dossier. As a general rule, they became demoralized. They didn't have deep convictions; they were selfish, with material interests, material ambitions. Since they had no morale, when they were confronted with a Revolution with tremendous morale, they generally became demoralized as soon as they were arrested, as soon as we proved to them that we knew everything. In view of this, they spilled the beans. In no case was a confession or evidence obtained by means of physical violence.

You might ask if a priest was ever executed for having engaged in counterrevolutionary activities. The answer is no. Would this have been possible from a legal standpoint? Yes, and I must say that many serious crimes were committed.

BETTO – There were three priests on the Bay of Pigs invasion.

CASTRO – I'd have to check on that, because I don't remember the exact number, but I'm quite sure there were three of them. Technically, every invader was guilty of treason, because, if you emigrate to a country that is an enemy of your country and, following the orders of that country, invade your own country, and this leads to bloodshed and loss of life for its inhabitants, from a technical standpoint, that means treason and is punishable by death, as prescribed by practically every code of law.

There were also cases of complicity with serious counterrevolutionary activities, which could have led to trial and such severe punishment as execution. In no case was this applied, however. We did our best to prevent this from happening, because, regardless of the circumstances, we didn't want to play into the hands of the forces of the reaction and the imperialists by presenting the image of the Revolution executing a priest. We always took pains to avoid this. There were some cases of serious crimes, yet the death sentence was never applied. Actually, not many priests committed serious crimes because it's one thing to engage in political opposition or give political and ideological support to the counterrevolution, and it's another thing to commit acts of sabotage or engage in other serious counterrevolutionary activities. Really, there weren't many of them. Still, in none of the cases in which the death sentence was applicable was it ever applied. Priests were always treated with special consideration. Some were given prison sentences for having engaged in counterrevolutionary activities, but they never served their full terms. They were held for very brief periods, and then we always tried to have them released. We didn't want to create an image of the Revolution throwing priests into prison, even though such punishment was justified.

The fact that the Nuncio here—Monsignor Zacchi—was a very intelligent, very capable man, a person with a lot of constructive ability and a lot of personality who realized that these conflicts between the Church and the Revolution weren't advisable and tried to avoid them, was partly responsible for this. I think he made an important contribution to keeping these conflicts from becoming more serious. And, with him as mediator, we released the few priests who were in prison.

BETTO – Were the churches closed down and priests deported?

CASTRO – No churches in Cuba were ever closed down—none of them. There was a time when the political confrontation became really fierce, and because of the militant political attitude taken by some priests—especially the Spanish ones—we requested that they be withdrawn from our country, and we revoked their authorization to remain here. That happened, and that was the measure that was taken. However, we authorized other priests to come to Cuba and replace the ones who were asked to leave. That was the only measure that was taken—and it, only once. After that, relations were normalized.

BETTO – What about the case of the cardinal who went to the Argentine Embassy at the time of the Bay of Pigs invasion?

CASTRO – That was right after the Bay of Pigs invasion. It seems that, in the second half of April 1961, at the time of the Bay of Pigs invasion, the cardinal got scared. I don't know why this was so, but the fact is that he moved to the Argentine ambassador's residence. The cardinal was quite an old man. When Argentina broke relations with Cuba in February 1962, the Holy See's chargé d'affaires convinced the cardinal to remain in Cuba. He was taken to a rest home in Marianao and remained there for the rest of his life. That's what happened.

Let me give you some examples. One of the cardinal's relatives organized an armed uprising in Oriente Province. First he lived in the Cobre Seminary in Santiago de Cuba, and then he went to the mountains and organized a counterrevolutionary guerrilla group. Naturally, the group was located, surrounded and captured. In spite of the seriousness of the crime, the man was given only a prison sentence. You can see what kind of activity he was involved in: a relative of the cardinal's taking a counterrevolutionary stand, making use of a Catholic seminary, organizing a guerrilla group and using it to fight against the Revolution. And all this was at a time when the Revolution was faced with a lot of difficulties, when it was being threatened and attacked by the United States. And even then we weren't very severe. Of course, he was given a prison sentence.

That's all I know. I really couldn't tell you why the cardinal sought refuge in the embassy; there was no reason for it. Even if he'd been involved in those things, we would never have arrested him, out of political considerations. We might have talked things over with him and warned him that what he was doing wasn't right, and we would have tried to keep him from getting involved. Even if he was in cahoots with the Bay of Pigs invaders, there was no need for him to seek asylum or security of any kind, because we would never have taken drastic measures against him.

BETTO – Was the Socialist character of the Revolution proclaimed after the 1961 Bay of Pigs attack?

CASTRO – No, not after the attack—on the day the invasion began.

BETTO – At the beginning, there was the Integrated Revolutionary Organizations (ORI), composed of the 26th of July Movement, the Revolutionary Directorate and PSP—which was what the Communist Party of Cuba was called. And, in 1965, the Integrated Revolutionary Organizations became the Communist Party of Cuba.

CASTRO – Yes.

BETTO – Is it true that Christians aren't allowed to belong to the Communist Party of Cuba?

CASTRO – That's right.

BETTO – It's true. It's a confessional party to the extent that it's an atheist party that denies the existence of God. What possibilities are there that, in the future, it may become a secular party? Also, is there any possibility that, some time in the future, a Cuban revolutionary Christian may join the ranks of the Party?

CASTRO – That's one of the most interesting, most important questions you've asked concerning religion and the Revolution.

I told you that I had not only a revolutionary attitude but also a Marxist-Leninist, Socialist concept of political struggle several years before 1951. Even that far back, I had an idea of the strategy to be followed in the struggle. I also told you that a handful of those of us who organized the 26th of July Movement had that attitude, and I told you that we had a strategy, a program, that was to be applied in stages. I told you all about that yesterday, and there's no need to repeat it now. For the first stage, we had a program that, from a technical standpoint, could be described as a program for national liberation, for national independence. It consisted of a series of advanced social reforms. It was to be followed, in a given period, by new measures that could have a Socialist character.

Of course, we're talking now in 1985. Just imagine that we're back in 1956, 1958, 1959 and 1960, when we didn't have the experience that we have now, but our basic ideas about how to do things and what could be done and when were correct. If you were to ask me if we'd programmed the day, the year and the exact time for doing each thing, I'd say, "No." We had a basic idea of what should be done to bring about a social revolution in the conditions in our country, how to carry it out in its various stages. We knew that it had to be accompanied by work to educate the people, the masses—by the dissemination of ideas, so the people could draw their own conclusions—which is what happened.

The revolutionary laws made a tremendous contribution to our people's political awareness and political education. Right from the beginning, the people realized that, at last, they had a government of their own. Never before—starting from the time of the Spaniards' conquest of Cuba—had our people had a government of their own. The Spanish government here—the government set up by Diego Velázquez, Pánfilo de Narváez and others who conquered Cuba, founded cities and ruled the various regions—wasn't the Indians' government. The Indians were the toilers, the slaves, the ones who found the gold in the rivers and worked in the mines and under the scorching sun. The colonizers wiped out 90 percent of the Indian population. When nearly all of the Indians had been exterminated, hundreds of thousands of Africans were torn from their land and turned into slaves to work in the mines, in the cane fields, and on the coffee plantations, plagued by the tropical sun, heat and humidity. The mixture of Spaniards with Indians and blacks gave rise to the *mestizos*—who, if born to slave women, were considered slaves.

Our nationality started to develop, but, while the concept of being "Cuban" was emerging among the white offspring of Spaniards, the *mestizos*, and the freed blacks and Indians, the government of the island wasn't their government; it was the Spaniards'. Later on, from 1898—at the end of the last War of Independence and the beginning of the intervention and occupation of the country by U.S. troops—to 1902 (when a U.S. government was established, headed by a man who, apart from being the U.S. candidate, had even become a U.S. citizen) and up to 1959, all the governments were governments of the landowners, of the rich, of the privileged, of the foreign enterprises and of the United States. Then, in 1959, for the first time in Cuba's history—and this always produces extraordinary effects in the history of any people—a people's government came to power. This was something new. Prior to that, the state and the people had been two different things; the government and the people had been two different things.

As soon as the United States began to threaten us and the people started to organize and arm themselves, the people realized that they had become the authority. Before this, the Army—which was a professional army—had been divorced from the people, and the people hadn't identified with that authority. If a man carried a gun, it had meant that the gun was going to be used to repress strikes, student demonstrations and farmers' struggles. Guns had always supported that kind of power. After the triumph of the Revolution, the people began to become soldiers, managers, part of the social order, part of the state, part of authority. Whereas, at the beginning of the eighteenth century, an absolute monarch of France said, "The state is myself," in 1959, after the triumph of the Revolution, when the people came to power, armed themselves and started to defend their country, the ordinary citizens in our country could also say, "The state is myself." The people's approval was assured once the first revolutionary laws were passed and measures of social justice were implemented. That was very important in terms of raising the general level of awareness, in deepening our people's awareness and developing a Socialist political awareness.

Nevertheless, right from its inception, what was later to be known as the 26th of July Movement—at the time, it was the movement that was being organized to fight against Batista—had a leadership nucleus. I promoted the creation of a nucleus composed of the most valuable and able comrades; and, within that rather broad nucleus, we selected a small executive nucleus of three comrades to carry out the most secret and delicate activities: Abel Santamaría, Raúl Martínez and I.

BETTO – Where is Mr. Martínez?

CASTRO – Raúl Martínez left the Movement after the attack on the Moncada. He'd participated in the Bayamo attack. He was very active, an organizer, but not much of an ideologue. He preferred action. In contrast, Abel was very active, very able, and also had revolutionary ideas and advanced revolutionary convictions. Within this organization, my own responsibilities and tasks were well defined. The first thing I did once I decided to create an organization for the struggle was to establish a collective leadership.

Then the war began. During the war, I was Commander in Chief of the rebel forces. At one point, I was Commander in Chief of myself and two other men. Later, I became Commander in Chief of a group of seven or eight comrades, and the first successful battle was waged by 22 armed comrades in January 1957—on January 17, if I'm not mistaken. We won our first battle a month and a half after the original group had been routed. I was the chief of those troops, and in an army in a combat situation, obedience to superior officers has to be maintained; that's a principle.

But we were also members of a movement, the 26th of July Movement, which had an active national leadership. The leadership was entirely responsible for the Movement, both in the cities and everywhere else. When I was in Mexico organizing the expedition, it was entirely responsible for the Movement in Cuba. When I was in the mountains, it headed the Movement in the rest of the country. When a very important decision had to be made, we held consultations and discussions among ourselves until we arrived at a decision, but there was always a national leadership with a great degree of authority—sometimes too much authority, in fact. We had to accept the majority's opinions and carry them out; there was no other way. Sometimes, when I analyze that period with historical perspective, I realize that the majority's opinions weren't always the best. Nevertheless, our army—or, rather, the embryo of an army that we were in the process of developing —always accepted them.

Ever since our organization was founded—even before the attack on the Moncada—we had a small, trusted, collective leadership. A political movement can't be directed in any other way. We always had a leadership nucleus and collective leadership, sharing responsibilities. That was before the Revolution triumphed on January 1, 1959. Of course, at the time of the triumph, the Rebel Army played a considerable role; at that point, we had around 3,000 men armed with combat weapons. With only 3,000 men, we had besieged 17,000 soldiers in Oriente Province and had managed to cut the island in two; the regime was in a shambles, and Batista's Army couldn't hold out any longer. In other words, the combat units of the Rebel Army played a vital role in the final stages of the war.

The people's support was, of course, a decisive factor. This was proved when the higher-ranking officers in Batista's Army tried to stage a coup, breaking an agreement we'd reached. What happened was that the enemy operations chief asked me for a meeting. In it, he admitted that they'd lost the war, and we reached an agreement. I suggested, "Let's try to find an acceptable solution and save a lot of officers." Not all the officers were murderers—though, unfortunately, many of the highest-ranking officers in the Armed Forces were very cruel. But that operations chief, who was in command during the last offensive in the Sierra Maestra—a remarkable thing, because their 10,000 men couldn't defeat our 300 men in 70 days of fighting; at the end, our initial 300 had turned into 805 armed men; they had suffered more than 1,000 casualties; and we had defeated the offensive and the best enemy troops, seized a large number of weapons and nearly tripled our forces—anyway, that operations chief was a very stable, prestigious officer, not a criminal.

We took that into consideration—plus the fact that he was the commanding officer of all the forces that were participating in combat against us—and we met nearly at the end of the war. He said, "We've lost the war," and I suggested that we stage a joint uprising, saying, "We can save a lot of able and valuable officers who haven't been involved in crimes." He agreed, but at the same time, he insisted that he had to return to Havana. I recommended that he not do this. I told him, "There are risks," but he insisted, saying that he had a lot of contacts and that he couldn't be harmed. At that point, I set three conditions: "We don't want any contact with the U.S. Embassy, we don't want a coup in Havana, and we don't want to let Batista escape." Who knows who convinced that man or what disturbed him, but after we'd agreed that all the troops participating in operations would stage an uprising on December 31, he did precisely the three things that he'd pledged not to do: he established contact with the U.S. Embassy, staged a coup in Havana and saw Batista off at the airport. The next day, I called for a general strike and instructed all the troops to keep on fighting. In 72 hours, the rest of the Army had been forced to lay down its arms.

I'm telling you this to show that the Rebel Army played a decisive role. The fundamental expression of the Movement at that point was the guerrilla army. As I put it then, "The people are like the Amazon River running through a narrow channel which can neither organize nor handle the masses of the people," because the people were as strong as the Amazon River in their support for the Revolution and for a relatively small political organization. Moreover, there were several trends within our Movement—some people were somewhat to the right, and others were somewhat to the left—so there were some contradictions.

I realized, however, that the masses of the people supported the Revolution and that those masses were much larger, much more all-encompassing, than our Movement. We couldn't be sectarian. We had such great support because of the role our Movement had played, but we rejected all hegemonistic ideas, even though, if we'd wanted to exercise total hegemony, the conditions existed for our doing so. I wonder how many people, how many political leaders, on finding themselves in the conditions in which we found ourselves in Cuba, would have rejected the idea of hegemony.

BETTO – You spoke of not being sectarian. I wonder if a component of that position was to avoid the frequent use of classical Marxist-Leninist slogans. I'd like to add a comment to this question. When you come to Cuba for the first time, you find to your surprise—because of what imperialism has impressed on you—that you never see statues of Marx or Lenin in the streets; what you always see are busts of Martí. I wonder if that nonsectarian position also involved rescuing national values and the symbols that have meaning in the people's culture while being cautious about things—however important—that people don't tend to understand easily.

CASTRO – I didn't mean that, because that depends on other factors, other criteria, other ideas. I mentioned sectarianism because our movement had played the basic role in the struggle and the victory, and it was supported by the people as a whole; in other words, we could have tried to make our organization and our Movement prevail as the key revolutionary center. We could have said, "We're stronger than all the other organizations. Let's not share responsibilities; let's take them all." That has happened over and over again, throughout history—it's what almost always happens—yet that wasn't what we did. I believe that the Revolution's successes have, in many cases, been preceded by correct, serious, intelligent solutions.

The first form of sectarianism I started to fight against was the sectarianism of those of us who'd been in the mountains, who were beginning to view things differently than those who had remained in the cities and who had fought in the underground. I said, "They fought and took risks too; often, they took more risks than we did." They may not have walked as much as we did, and they didn't climb the mountains we climbed, but they took risks every day. When we controlled a territory, planes could, of course, appear and find us at dawn or at sunset or at noon, so we were dealing with other kinds of risks that we could foresee, but the comrades who fought in the underground took many risks. Many of them died. In fact, it is probable that many more people died in the underground than in the guerrilla struggle. Of course, the guerrillas, the combatants in a military unit, became more disciplined, shared more in a collective spirit. The man who fights in the underground is a little more individualistic; he's generally more alone, more isolated. I'd say that the open struggle helps more than the underground one to promote the emergence of brotherhood, discipline and a group spirit.

The second sectarian tendency that had to be opposed was that of our organization in its relations with the other organizations, which were smaller and less powerful. This had to be avoided not only with regard to the People's Socialist Party, which had the second greatest degree of organization—second to the 26th of July Movement—and had considerable influence among the workers, but also with regard to all the others. Our Movement, our guerrilla army, had tremendous prestige among the workers, even though all the trade unions—I mean, the trade-union leaderships—were controlled by Batista. On January 1, when the coup that I mentioned took place in Havana, I called for a revolutionary general strike—which was, in fact, part of the plans we'd had five and a half years before, when we attacked the Moncada Garrison; the basic idea was the same. I ordered the troops to continue advancing and asked the workers, the people, to halt all activities. They did this, with an impressive degree of discipline; the whole country was paralyzed. TV and radio workers then started to carry the broadcasts of Radio Rebelde, the radio station of the rebel headquarters, over all the TV and radio stations in the country. The only things that weren't shut down were the TV and radio stations, and they were tuned to Radio Rebelde. I was able to speak to the people, because those were the only centers that kept functioning. We had a great deal of moral influence among the workers.

The People's Socialist Party had the most experience in party work, the highest level of political organization and the greatest number of experienced cadres. Our group, that had carried out that phase of the struggle, was smaller, but we had many young comrades who'd amassed great merits during that stage. Then there was the Revolutionary Directorate, an organization that had emerged among the students and which José Antonio Echeverría had led until his death, when Faure Chomón became its leader. Three different organizations had taken part in the struggle.

Then there were all the other parties and organizations that had opposed Batista, even though they didn't participate in the armed struggle. I talked with representatives of all the organizations and all the parties—even the old, discredited parties that had been displaced from power. We didn't want to be sectarian even with these last, and we raised the flag of unity.

If 95 percent of the population was in favor of the Revolution and 85 or 90 percent of the people supported the 26th of July Movement, while the other organizations were backed by 5 or 10 percent of the people, our policy was that that 5 percent was needed, that unity was needed. In a revolution, unity isn't just a quantitative matter; it's also a matter of quality. I wasn't thinking of whether or not the other parties amounted to 10 or 15 percent of the forces. The other parties give the Revolution a quality—unity and the principle of unity. If the principle of unity doesn't prevail, you'll be separated from the other parties, and divisions will also arise within your own organization as soon as currents, criteria and antagonisms—sometimes even class antagonisms—appear. Our Movement was very heterogeneous; a characteristic of our Movement was that it included the large masses, like an Amazon of people in a small riverbed, and you could find everything, from all sectors, in that Amazon.

We applied the principle of unity with all organizations. You can be sure that those who left the Revolution did so because they didn't want to stay—not because they didn't have an opportunity to remain. We gave everybody the opportunity, but then came the nonconformity, the ambitions and the frustrations. The United States started its divisive, subversive policy. The conflicts of interests began, and, of course, many of those parties started to support the interests of the United States and of the reaction. Basically, it was the three organizations which had the most prestige in the struggle—the 26th of July Movement, the People's Socialist Party (the old Communist Party) and the Revolutionary Directorate (the students' political organization)—that remained. We began to coordinate our efforts immediately.

This wasn't easy, because sectarianism appeared. We'd fought against sectarianism in our ranks, but the PSP hadn't fought against it, and there was sectarianism that gave rise to discussions and criticism. At one point, we had to end it. There may have been some manifestations of sectarianism in the Revolutionary Directorate too, but only in the first few days.

Unity and cooperation among these forces was forged, both in the ranks and among the leaders, so that, a few months after the triumph of the Revolution, we started to create a collective leadership in which the various forces were represented. The main cadres were in this organization, of course; Che belonged to it, and so did Raúl and I and a group of others from the Rebel Army and the 26th of July Movement, plus some comrades from other organizations.

Following tradition, the principle of collective leadership was established immediately after the triumph of the Revolution. So, even before the organizations were merged, we had a collective leadership—right from the beginning of the Revolution. We analyzed and discussed almost all measures in the leadership. That is, we created the leadership body at the very beginning of the Revolution, and that principle still prevails. Then all the forces were integrated when the various organizations merged and became a single organization. That was when the Integrated Revolutionary Organizations was created.

There were manifestations of sectarianism in that period. How did they originate? The People's Socialist Party was a more homogeneous organization than ours; it was a working-class organization with better political education. Our organization was more heterogeneous, with some difficulties and tendencies. That was when imperialism began to step up its activities. Since we had a fairly small number of cadres, we sometimes chose an experienced member of the Communist Party when we had to designate someone for a political task that required a cadre who was absolutely trustworthy. Sometimes it was safer to do this than to choose a younger comrade who had less experience.

The PSP provided cadres who were very useful—not large numbers of them, however, for, even though the Party's membership was large, it couldn't be compared to the large masses of our Movement. Its contribution was important as far as cadres were concerned, however, which was the advantage of having cadres. Remember that barely six years passed between the creation of our Movement and the triumph of the Revolution. We couldn't say that the members of our Movement had been 15, 20 or 25 years in the organization. The People's Socialist Party had been organized many, many years before; its members were well trained ideologically, and it provided cadres. Of course, our Movement provided a lot of cadres, but the PSP provided cadres, too, as did the Revolutionary Directorate.

Members of other organizations also joined the Revolution; their leaders left, but the honest rank-and-file members remained. A part of their very small number of supporters remained with the Revolution. I say "very small" because the revolutionary process, with the support of the overwhelming majority of the people, practically did away with the traditional political parties. Some could have said, "I have 100 followers," or "I have 200," but the Revolution was supported by millions. Then we applied the principle of unity—a basic principle—and collective leadership—another basic principle.

There were some problems, as I've already told you. At one point, the fact that the People's Socialist Party had cadres who could be trusted because they were experienced members of the Party led to sectarianism by the old Communist Party. This problem wasn't new; it didn't appear when unity was achieved. Rather, some of those manifestations arose within the Party when the Communists were underground, during the struggle against Batista, because of the ambitions and the incorrect methods of some people who, taking advantage of the conditions in which underground activity is carried out, had begun to exercise too much power. When the parties merged, those elements were present, but this was solved without problems, without difficulties, by fighting against sectarianism. That's what I did: first, I fought against the sectarianism of the guerrillas; then against that of our Movement; then against that of the other organizations; and then against any other manifestations of sectarianism that cropped up. The People's Socialist Party had been sectarian, and we had to prevent sectarianism elsewhere; there couldn't be any more of it. It was a constant struggle to preserve unity and fight against all forms of sectarianism. We carried on in this way until we founded the Party in 1965.

Socialism was proclaimed in 1961. When? At the time of the Bay of Pigs invasion.

By the time of the invasion, we'd already made many laws; the United States had taken some measures against Cuba, such as declaring an embargo, the economic blockade, and we replied by nationalizing U.S. industries; it cut off our sugar quota, and we nationalized some industries and all the sugar mills. We responded to its measures by taking measures of our own. All of those measures that the United States adopted against Cuba speeded the nationalization process.

Then a big anti-Communist campaign was launched. That was the first thing the United States did to play on the political ignorance of a large part of the Cuban population, the people's lack of political education and culture, in order to take advantage of all the prejudices it had instilled throughout the years.

The United States did some infamous things. For instance, as part of the campaign to promote the exodus, a completely false decree was invented one day—it was said that somebody had taken the decree out of a Ministry. It was alleged to be a decree to deprive families of legal authority over their children. How absurd! But, as you know, many absurd things instill fear, because they appeal to instinct, not reason. A reasonable person would never say that such a thing could be credible, but a mother who is told, "Hey, they're going to take your child away," may panic. Another rumor was that the children were going to be sent to the Soviet Union—things like that.

I wondered if those rumors against us were something new. Later, when I read *And Quiet Flows the Don* and some other novels of Sholokhov's—he was later awarded the Nobel Prize for Literature—I found that this tactic was as old as the Bolshevik Revolution. The same rumors that were used against us over 40 years later were spread at that time; they were old rumors, not even the result of fresh imagination. Many of those campaigns were also launched against Cuba.

BETTO – Such things were also said about Christians in the first few centuries; people also said that they ate human flesh.

CASTRO – That's right. You've chosen a good example. Every so often, I remember that—the kind of slander campaign that was launched against the Christians at that time. I guess the same rumors were spread at the time of the French Revolution too; they've been spread all over.

The United States did it, among other things, to promote the exodus. It opened its doors—something it had never done before—to all who wanted to go to that country, in order to deprive us of teachers, doctors, engineers and technicians. The exodus of skilled personnel began. The United States offered high salaries; it offered what it had never offered before.

We took up the challenge. We didn't tell those people they couldn't leave. We said, "All right, we're going to train new generations of technicians and professionals, and they'll be better than the ones who are leaving." We began to develop our universities with those who stayed in Cuba.

BETTO – How many left the country at that time?

CASTRO – To give you just one example, there were 6,000 doctors in our country; 3,000—half of all the doctors in the country—left. Now, Cuba ranks first among the Third World countries and is ahead of several developed countries in terms of public health. Our health program was started with half of the doctors who had been in the country. We already have 20,500 and a few months from now, at the end of this academic year, 2,436 more will be graduated. This number will increase in the coming years, and then, starting in 1988, we'll be graduating 3,000 doctors every year—and 3,500 after 1990. We'll have 50,000 new doctors in the next 15 years. However, there was a time when we were left with only half of the doctors who had been in the country. The United States forced us to take up the challenge. Well, we've taken up a lot of them. I think that's why we're here.

The enemy resorted to prejudice, lies and campaigns in order to mislead, confuse and wound. At that time, the people didn't have a solid political foundation, but they supported the Revolution, trusted the Revolution and knew that the Revolution had brought them a government that was on their side.

We were applying our program, step by step. All those acts of aggression speeded the revolutionary process. Did they cause it? No, it would be a mistake to say that. I'm not saying that the acts of aggression caused socialism in Cuba. That's not true. We were going to build socialism in Cuba in an orderly manner, in a reasonable period of time, with as few traumas and problems as possible. Imperialism's acts of aggression simply accelerated the revolutionary process.

The United States also spread the rumor that the Revolution had been betrayed, that we'd told the people one thing and were doing another. Anybody who reads my defense at the Moncada trial—which was later published as *History Will Absolve Me*—will see that it set forth the program we were applying. Naturally, when we drew that program up, we couldn't imagine that the United States was going to deprive us of our sugar quota, that it was going to take aggressive measures or that it would try to destroy the Revolution by force and even invade the country. At that time, I may still have idealistically believed that everybody would respect what Cuba did just because Cuba was a sovereign country and the things we did were fair.

This was a practical lesson for us; it was a good lesson, teaching us that imperialism doesn't allow social changes to take place; it doesn't accept them and tries to prevent them by force. The decision we made at that time was also essential. If we had hesitated, if we had been frightened or if we had stepped back, we'd have been lost.

That was when the invasion took place. First, a surprise attack was made on all our air bases at dawn on April 15, 1961, to destroy the few airplanes we had. I stayed up the whole night at the command post, because there were reports that an enemy force that had been detected just off the coast of Oriente Province was going to land.

Raúl was in Oriente. Whenever such situations arose, we divided up the regions: Almeida was sent to the central part of the island; Che was sent to the western part; and I stayed in Havana. Every time it seemed that the United States was going to invade Cuba, we divided up the country. Of course, we didn't have the organization we have today—not in any sense. I was told of the possible landing; I stayed on the alert, and at dawn I saw some planes flying near the command post—which was a house here in Vedado—and, a few seconds later, I saw that they were using rockets to attack the air base at Ciudad Libertad. They attacked several air bases to destroy the few planes we had. Some fighters were killed too.

A really impressive thing happened. One of the fighters who was wounded, bleeding to death, wrote my name with his blood on a door. That part of the door has been preserved; it must be in the museum. I tell you, it was a very impressive thing. It reflected the people's attitude; a young militiaman was dying, and his protest was to write a name with his blood.

The indignation was enormous. On April 16, tens of thousands of armed militiamen and units of the Rebel Army gathered in honor of the victims. The Army was still small; most of its members were workers, farmers and students. On that occasion, I gave not only a military but also a political response: I proclaimed the Socialist nature of the Revolution before the fighting at the Bay of Pigs.

The landing began that same night, at around midnight (between April 16 and 17). They tried to destroy our Air Force so as to control the skies, but we still had more airplanes than pilots: eight planes and seven pilots. Shortly after dawn on April 17, all of the ships had been sunk or were fleeing—the whole fleet—and we achieved this with the few planes we had. At dawn, they were in the air, heading for the Bay of Pigs, as soon as we realized that that was where the main attack was being made. The battle took place there, but I'm not going to talk about that. On April 16, the Socialist nature of the Revolution was proclaimed.

Therefore, our people were fighting against the invasion organized by the United States and for socialism. The people had been fighting to have the Constitution respected, to overthrow Batista and to have an advanced social—but not yet Socialist—program ever since 1956. At the Bay of Pigs, they were fighting for socialism. That was very symbolic, for tens of thousands of men were ready to face whatever might come. You shouldn't forget that the battle of the Bay of Pigs was fought while ships of the U.S. Navy—warships, cruisers and aircraft carriers—were only three miles off the coast. The U.S. warships were only three miles away from where the battle was raging, and tens of thousands of men fought with great determination. More than 100 of them were killed in that battle. The number of those who died isn't as high as the number of those who were ready to die if U.S. troops had landed in our country. The crushing, victorious counterattack didn't give the United States a chance to create the minimal political conditions it needed to justify the intervention.

From April 16 on—I told the people this on the eve of the decisive struggle—we were fighting for socialism in our country.

Now, in response to your other question, about those who are allowed to join the Party, that process was preceded by all the struggles I've already mentioned. What happened? All of the privileged social classes that had a monopoly on the Church were against the Revolution, so when, in organizing the Party, we excluded those who believed in God, we were excluding them as potential counterrevolutionaries, not Catholics. This doesn't mean that all Catholics were counterrevolutionaries.

We had to be very strict in our ideological and doctrinal requirements, very strict. We weren't exactly demanding that the person had to be an atheist; we weren't inspired by antireligious ideas. What we were demanding was complete adherence to Marxism-Leninism. It was circumstances that made us so strict, for we had to watch over the Party's ideological purity. Of course, within our conditions, it was politically possible to do so, because the great masses of the people—workers, farmers and others who supported us—weren't active Catholics. Individuals weren't required to renounce their beliefs to join the Party. It was assumed that anybody who joined the Party would accept the Party's policy and doctrine in all aspects.

Could this have happened in another country? No. If the

masses in our country—the great masses of workers, farmers and university students—had been active Christians, we couldn't have formed a revolutionary party based on those premises; we couldn't have done it. We couldn't have made a revolution, either, if the masses had been counterrevolutionary —something which, of course, would never have been the case. But, since most of the active Catholics were well-to-do, supported the counterrevolution and left the country, we could—and had to—establish a severe, orthodox rule: Marxism-Leninism had to be accepted in all aspects—politically, programmatically and philosophically. This rule was established as a result of the circumstances.

If you were to ask me, "Does this have to be so?" I'd say, "No, it doesn't. I'm sure it doesn't have to be so and that it hasn't been so historically." In some countries, the immense majority of the people are Catholic; this is the case in Poland, where many members of the Communist Party are Catholics. This restriction doesn't form part of the traditions of the revolutionary movement or even of the Communist movement; it isn't so in Latin America.

BETTO – As a member of the Communist Party of Cuba, do you think that, during the Third Congress, to be held in February 1986, the lay character of the Party will be proclaimed and Cuban revolutionary Christians will be allowed to join the Party in the future?

CASTRO – The Congress will be held very soon, and I don't think the conditions have been created in our country for that as yet. I say this very honestly. You're speaking about February, which is very close. You and I have talked a lot about many topics, and we've even talked about this.

This is a period of coexistence and mutual respect between the Party and the churches. Some years ago, we had difficulties with the Catholic Church, but they were solved, and all the problems that existed at a given moment disappeared. We never had those problems with the Protestant churches, and our relations with those institutions have always been and still are excellent. Not only Catholics but also many active members of Protestant churches who always supported us may say, "That formula that discriminates against us isn't fair." There are more Catholics than Protestants in our country, but, even so, there are a lot of Protestants, and they've always had very good relations with the Revolution.

I've said that we should do something more than coexist in peace. There ought to be closer, better relations; there should even be cooperation between the Revolution and the churches, because they can't represent the landowners, the bourgeois and the rich anymore. It was impossible to draw closer to and cooperate with them when they represented the landowners, the bourgeois and the rich. I could be self-critical in this regard, and so could the churches, for not having worked in this direction during the past years but contenting ourselves with coexistence and mutual respect.

As you know, absolute respect for the religious beliefs of citizens is established and guaranteed in our Constitution. This isn't just a political tactic. As a political principle, respect for believers is right, because we live in a world with many believers, and confrontations between revolutions and religious beliefs aren't advisable. When they take place, the opposition and imperialism may use religious beliefs as a weapon against the revolutions. Why should we make it easy for them to use the religious beliefs of a worker, a farmer or anyone else in the low-income brackets against the Revolution? It's politically wrong to do that. I'm looking at this not only from the political standpoint but also as a matter of principle. It's not just a question of political tactics. I feel that every citizen's right to his own beliefs should be respected, along with his rights to health, life and freedom and all his other rights. That is, I believe that the individual has the inalienable right to have or not to have his own philosophical ideas and religious beliefs. I believe that this is the inalienable right of every individual, along with many other rights—that is, it's not just a question of political tactics.

Now, you were asking if the conditions existed for that. I don't think they do, because we haven't worked in this direction, as we should have done. If you were to ask me, "Is this matter vital for the Revolution?" I'd say, "No, it isn't, because our Revolution has tremendous force, tremendous political and ideological force." But, if we don't achieve this climate, we can't say that our Revolution is perfect, for, as long as there are circumstances in which, because of their religious beliefs, some individuals who fulfill their social duties in exactly the same way as others don't have the same rights they have, our revolutionary work isn't complete.

BETTO – Of course, but this presupposes the elimination of the confessional nature of the Party.

CASTRO – Well, I can't accept what you say about the confessional nature of the Party, even though I can see that your way of approaching the question has some foundation. But it definitely isn't a confessional formula—I'm telling you how I feel about this problem—for that doesn't form part of our philosophy. As I explained, I believe that this arose from a historical situation, and I'm not trying to present it as a model. I too would rather see all those who have the virtues of revolutionaries closely united with the Revolution and all given the same recognition, regardless of any religious beliefs they might have.

This is why I say that it can't be confessional, for it might tend to resemble or become, as you say, a sort of religion; we really don't think that people can practice nonbelief as a philosophy, or atheism as a religion.

I'm telling you what happened. I took part in it and they were my ideas, not other people's. I take full responsibility for that rigor. I don't deny it, because I was the one who said, "Under certain circumstances, this is the correct thing to do. We have to demand absolute purity. We have to demand it because the United States is against us and is threatening us, because we need a close-knit Party in which there isn't the smallest crevice or the slightest disagreement. We need a very strong Party because we're facing a very powerful enemy that's trying to divide us, because we have an enemy that has been using religion as an ideology against our Revolution. This is why it must be this way." I was the one who said this, and I accept the responsibility for it. If anyone is historically responsible for it, I am, because I proposed it and argued for it. And, now, I'm setting forth my ideas and viewpoints and the historical reasons for all this and the real need for helping to create the conditions for advancing in this field, because 26 years have passed since the triumph of the Revolution.

I could criticize myself as much as the churches in Cuba—mainly the Catholic Church—for not having created the conditions required for ending the vestiges, the traces, of what forced us to demand this rigor in the selection of Party members in the past.

As a politician and revolutionary, I also feel that what we've done shouldn't be taken as a model and that things should be different in the rest of Latin America. I state this categorically, without the slightest doubt.

BETTO – In the Cuban domestic situation, do you believe that it's wrong for Christians who want to join the revolutionary process to be discriminated against in school, in the university or in their professional activities and be considered diversionists?

CASTRO – In principle, I can't agree with any kind of discrimination. I say this very openly. If I were asked if any subtle discrimination existed against Christians, I'd say "Yes." I'd honestly have to say "Yes." It's something that we haven't overcome as yet. It's not intentional; it's not deliberate; it's not programmed. It exists, and I believe that we have to overcome this phase; the conditions must be created and confidence must be built up even though imperialism is still threatening us and many of the people who are over there are the former bourgeois, landowners and members of the privileged classes that turned religion into a counterrevolutionary ideology. We aren't going to ask those who are over there—the imperialists and their clients —to cooperate; we aren't going to ask them to do that. But we must say that the conditions should be created so that their use of religion as a counterrevolutionary weapon will be nullified by the confidence and brotherhood that will exist among all revolutionaries in our country.

I'm telling you what I think. I'm against any form of discrimination. You've asked me if we could do this in the next Congress, and I've said, "No, not yet," because this must be explained to all the Party members and analyzed with all of them. It isn't our policy to say "This is so" from the top or in a meeting of the Political Bureau or in a meeting of the Central Committee. Until the required conditions and awareness are created, I can't even mention it or tell the people, "Let's make him a Party member." What explanation can I offer? It's necessary for Party members to know and understand the explanation, and I think you can be a great help in this regard. You can help with the talks you're giving. Many other progressive priests in our hemisphere can help, and so can that part of the Church that has joined the poor in Latin America, with the example it's setting, fighting for the poor in many countries—as it has done in your country, in Nicaragua, in El Salvador and in other countries. I think that all of you can help the Cuban churches to work in this direction.

This problem can't be solved just by your—or my—thinking about it. It's necessary for you and me to think about it; for our Party members, our cadres and the members of our Central Committee to understand it; for our people to think about it; and for the Cuban churches to think about it too. I think that we should work in this direction. These contacts and exchanges of views that you and I have had are a very important effort in this direction.

BETTO – I realize by now that things aren't imposed from the top here. Before asking my question, I emphasized that I was asking a Party member, not the First Secretary.

CASTRO – That's right, and I answered as a Party member, as a revolutionary and also as a Party leader—as the First Secretary of the Party.

It was a few minutes before 10:00 P.M. when I disconnected the tape recorder. The Commander was scheduled to attend a dinner at the home of the Argentine ambassador. Before leaving, he gave me a beautiful present: a reproduction of the first 26th of July Movement poster, with a drawing of Fidel's face and, in the foreground, the barrel of a rifle. The original was made in 1959. On the poster, he wrote, "He hasn't achieved this yet, but, if anybody can make a believer of me, it's Frei Betto. I dedicate this poster from the early years of the Revolution to him. Fraternally, Fidel Castro."

Three

O N the afternoon of Saturday, May 25, 1985, I went to the meeting that a group of around 40 young members of the University Federation of the Christian Student Movement (FUMEC) was holding in our convent in Havana to meditate on the text of St. Luke that tells of Jesus' reading a passage from the prophet Esaias in the synagogue in Nazareth (Luke 4:16–19):

> And he came to Nazareth, where he had been brought up; and, as his custom was, he went into the synagogue on the sabbath day, and stood up for to read. And there was delivered unto him the book of the prophet Esaias. And when he had opened the book, he found the place where it was written, The Spirit of the Lord is upon me, because he hath anointed me to preach the gospel to the poor; he hath sent me to heal the brokenhearted, to preach deliverance to the captives, and recovering of sight to the blind, to set at liberty them that are bruised, to preach the acceptable year of the Lord.

The "acceptable year" was, every 50 years, the year in which all the Jews should pay or cancel their debts and free their slaves. It was a symbol of God's justice and mercy.

The coordinator suggested that the young people split up in groups to analyze the meaning of the text for our lives today, in Cuban reality. I joined one of the groups and made notes about what was said.

"In Cuba, there are Christians who question social liberation from a selfish point of view. They don't know what's going on in the rest of Latin America and the world. They don't view liberation seriously. They think that the liberation announced by Christ is just the liberation of the soul, forgetting that we have the duty to free not only the soul but also the entire person. Christians' commitment is to their faith and to society. God came for all of us, poor and rich, but He demanded that the rich share their possessions, and He announced integral liberation for the poor—their development as human beings."

The group leader finished his commentary, and there was a long silence. The six young people around me seemed stuck. I observed that this wasn't the case in the other groups nearby.

"If you want, I'll leave, so you can talk," I said jokingly.

A young man broke the silence. "Christ came to announce deliverance, but why don't people listen to a prophet in his own land?"

Nobody answered, but all seemed to understand that behind the question lay some uneasiness that many young Christians in Cuba feel because they are considered "diversionists" by their schoolmates or comrades at work—as if faith, in itself, were a form of ideological deviation.

I made my modest contribution: "Yes, Jesus came to bring us integral deliverance, and, for Him, there's no division between body and soul. He couldn't consider the individual apart from society. On healing the sick, He made it clear that God is for life. God doesn't want sickness, and He doesn't rejoice over poverty. Our faith, in itself, is subversive. If we believe that there is only one God, who is the Father, then we are all brothers, and no social or racial differences are justified among us. To struggle for equality is to struggle to make a reality of the fraternity God sought, for, when we stop struggling against the obstacles that divide men, we are denying the paternity of God."

Another young man spoke up: "Now, there's a Socialist society in Cuba in which, unquestionably, we had a first moment of confrontation, which wasn't positive. But many Christians have overcome their rancor and division and entered into a dialogue with the nonbelievers. That dialogue is based on the fact that, in this country, nobody starves to death. People complain about the ration card, but, in spite of the tight blockade, nobody has ever gone hungry here. We don't have to stand in line to solve our health problems; we have polyclinics and hospitals. It isn't like other countries, where those who have money to pay the doctor are given priority. In spite of the democracy that people say exists in those countries, there's inequality, and many people live in misery. Here, in our society, we don't have those problems, but many Christians forget that. Latin America is now faced with a serious problem of the foreign debt. In the text we read, Christ spoke of the jubilee that the Jews celebrated every 50 years, when all the debts were canceled and justice was done. In his interview with *Excelsior*, Fidel repeated what Christ said when he stated that the foreign debt was unpayable. In that, he was calling for a new jubilee, and it's a Marxist who's issuing this call for justice. Sometimes we Cubans spend all our time complaining, forgetting that our worries are very trivial, compared to the problems of other nations."

I attended the plenary session, which went over the same ideas, and I listened to a short talk that a young Protestant gave on "The Cultural Renovation of the Church." I was asked to speak about the Brazilian situation, and I repeated some of the data that Joelmir Beting had given the Commander and went more deeply into some other matters. Shortly after that, I was called to the phone. It was the office of the Palace of the Revolution, telling me to get ready for the third part of the interview.

It was almost 8:00 P.M. when I went into the Cuban leader's office.

"This interview is worse than the spiritual exercises," Fidel said, in very good humor.

"The difference, Commander, is that, on the Jesuits' retreats, you just listened; now, I'm the one who's listening," I replied.

We sat down at the table and began.

BETTO – Commander, today we're beginning the third part of this conversation. Let's leave aside the history of your struggle for the Cuban Revolution and go into the internal relations between the Church, the government and the state in Cuba. I have two questions. First, how did your meeting with the U.S. bishops here last January go? Second, how are relations with the Cuban Episcopal Conference at present?

CASTRO – I think that the meeting with the U.S. bishops was good. They'd scheduled a visit to our country, and we arranged to have them visit various places on the island. They were in Santiago de Cuba and participated in several activities in a program organized by the Cuban bishops. As part of that program, one day was set aside for activities sponsored by the Cuban government— that is, for a program organized by the government. That day began early. It included a series of visits. For example, they were taken to the historic heart of Havana, which UNESCO has called a part of world heritage and where a restoration project is under way. Then they visited a modern hospital in the city. They went on to a vocational school on the outskirts of Havana, in which 4,500 students are enrolled. Later, they went to see a new kind of educational institution—one of the most important ones created by the Revolution, several years ago—a school in the countryside. We have around 600 schools in the countryside. They visited one of the oldest ones and had considerable contact with the students.

In the afternoon, we had a meeting that lasted for several hours. I had to go to a small reception I was hosting—to which they'd been invited, along with all the Cuban bishops and some nuns who were engaged in social work—and, since we hadn't finished, we broke off our conversation, went to the reception and resumed our talk afterwards.

BETTO – How long had it been since you'd met with the Cuban bishops?

CASTRO – Well, the last time I'd seen some of them was during Jesse Jackson's visit to Cuba. There was a tribute to Martin Luther King, organized by the Protestant churches, in which the Catholic Church also participated. Jackson invited me to hear a speech he was going to make there. They asked me to say a few words, which I did with pleasure. On that occasion, I greeted several church leaders, including some Catholics.

I already knew something about the U.S. Catholic Church's position, because there's a prestigious bishopric there and I think they've taken a number of correct, courageous positions on important issues of our time. I can cite, for example, their concern about peace and their opposition to the arms race. They've also drawn up certain theses of a moral nature with regard to the use of nuclear weapons—essentially as regards the use of nuclear weapons against cities and the civilian population. They have shown serious concern over and a reasonable attitude toward the poverty that still scourges millions of U.S. citizens. At the same time, they're concerned about and opposed to the interventionist policy in Latin America. In addition, they're concerned over the poverty and all the other problems of the underdeveloped world. They're aware of the terrible poverty from which billions of people in the Third World suffer. I feel that these are matters of basic importance.

I was interested in having a broad, frank conversation with them on these matters and on everything else they wanted. With regard to Cuba, they were interested in learning about the relations between the Church and the government, our opinions and our positions. In addition, they wanted to achieve a greater rapprochement and better understanding between the Church and the Revolution. I explained the origins of the conflicts that had emerged, in much the same way I explained them to you yesterday when we spoke of these problems. I also gave them some very frank historical analyses of those political-revolutionary events and made some comparisons with the historical evolution of the Catholic Church. I told them that I felt there were many things in common between Church doctrine and the Revolution.

BETTO – For example?

CASTRO – There was one time—I'm going to mention the critical things first—when I said, "We've been dogmatic at times, but you're dogmatic too, and sometimes you've been more dogmatic than we have; no other institution in history has been as dogmatic as the Catholic Church." I also told them that revolutions had sometimes been inflexible but that no other institution in history has been more rigid or inflexible than the Catholic Church. That rigidity, inflexibility and intolerance had led, over the centuries, to the creation of institutions with ideas such as burning people at the stake for holding dissident views from those of the Church. I also reminded them of the exploits of Torquemada and of the scientists and thinkers who'd been burned alive for disagreeing with the Church.

BETTO – Torquemada was a Dominican, like me. My consolation is that I'm also a brother of Giordano Bruno, Tomás de Campanella, Savonarola and other Dominicans who, like Bartolomé de las Casas, struggled for liberation.

CASTRO – I don't think that, just because Campanella happened to be a Dominican, you're going to be a utopian Communist.

BETTO – No, I don't expect to be utopian. At any rate, I think that communism has a great deal of utopia about it, and theologically, we call things that have something of utopia the Kingdom of God. As soon as there are no contradictions and the state no longer exists, I think we'll reach another sphere of spiritual qualities in human life.

CASTRO – I agree with you, because it's true that every revolution has hopes and dreams of great things. They may not all come true, due to the percentage of utopianism that every revolutionary idea may contain. I also think that Christianity has utopian elements too, just as socialism and communism have. But, from my own experience of what has happened in our country during the past 26 years, I can tell you that our realities have surpassed our dreams. We went through not a utopian phase but a less-than-utopian one. That is, our dreams fell short of utopia, yet our reality went beyond it.

I really didn't know that Torquemada had been a member of your Order, but you've mentioned some illustrious and prestigious names as well, which makes me very happy.

I talked with the bishops not in a polemic or critical spirit but in one of meditation on historical experiences and events. I told them that there were things in common, that we could follow almost all of God's Commandments perfectly, that they were very similar to ours; the Church says, "Thou shalt not steal," and we apply that principle rigorously. One of the tenets of our Revolution is to prevent theft, embezzlement and corruption. The Church says, "Love thy neighbor as thy self"; this is exactly what we preach through feelings of human solidarity, which is the essence of socialism and communism, the spirit of fraternity among men, which is one of our most valued goals. The Church says, "Thou shalt not bear false witness"; well, lying and deceit are among the things that we most severely criticize and censor. The Church says, for example, "Thou shalt not covet thy neighbour's wife"; we believe that one of the ethical elements of relations among revolutionaries is, precisely, the principle of respect for the family, and respect for your comrade's wife—your neighbor's wife, as you say. When, for example, the Church fosters the spirit of self-sacrifice and the spirit of austerity and when the Church urges humility, we have exactly the same thing in mind when we say that it is a revolutionary's duty to be self-sacrificing and live modestly and austerely.

BETTO – I like St. Theresa of the Infant Jesus' definition, which was that humility is commitment to the truth.

Now, I'd like to add that it seems to me that you also observe another important Commandment: "Thou shalt not take the name of the Lord thy God in vain." Reagan and many capitalist governments do precisely that—invoke His name in vain. I prefer fair policies applied in the name of human principles and ideology; colonialist, imperialist and Fascist policies are often applied in the name of God.

What reassures me is the biblical awareness of the fact that idolatry exists in religious phenomena—that is, many people believe in gods, and, in general, it isn't the Lord Jesus Christ. I'm convinced, for example—I've often wondered about this—that there isn't any similarity between the God in whom the Latin American workers and farmers and I believe and the God of Reagan and the murderous Chilean generals, such as Pinochet. They don't appear to be the same; they're different concepts, and one of those concepts is nothing but idolatry. The evangelical criterion for defining the concept that isn't idolatry is the commitment to love they neighbor—and, above all, the poor.

CASTRO – I think you've given some very clear examples. We could say that not only idolatry but also enormous hypocrisy is involved in all this. As I told you, I detest lies, and I've never lied—not to the people or to anyone else, because anybody who lies is degrading himself, lowering himself, prostituting himself, demoralizing himself. Nevertheless, I've observed that, in U.S. politics, not only Reagan but all the other functionaries as well systematically resort to deliberate, conscious lies every day—not just one day, but every day.

You mentioned the case of some "gentlemen" such as Pinochet. Pinochet is allegedly a devout man and yet bears on his conscience the deaths of thousands of people, thousands of murdered, tortured or missing people. The people suffer from terrible repression and are forced to make enormous sacrifices. Chile is the Latin American country with the highest unemployment rate—which is also the highest rate the country has ever had.

We may not be able to imagine all the suffering that has been inflicted on millions of people by a policy that serves the interests of wealth and imperialism. The Vietnam War, in which more bombs were dropped than in all of World War II, took the lives of millions of people. Without a doubt, it wasn't an example of Christianity. That war was also begotten in lies; the whole Tonkin Gulf incident was made out of whole cloth; all the pretexts used to launch that war were invented.

That is what we see in each and every declaration that the U.S. government makes about South America, El Salvador, Nicaragua—I'm not going to tell you about Cuba; the United States has been lying about Cuba for 26 years. There's enormous hypocrisy in all these people, who often invoke the name of God to commit these crimes.

BETTO – Excuse me, Commander.

I too deny the god whom you Marxist-Leninists deny: the god of capital; the god of exploitation; the god in whose name the Spanish and Portuguese missionaries came to Latin America and slaughtered the Indians; the god who justified and sanctified the ties between the Church and the bourgeois state; the god who today legitimizes military dictatorships such as Pinochet's. I also deny that god whom you deny and whom Marx denounced in his time. That isn't the God of the Bible, the God of Jesus.

The biblical criteria for one who really fulfills the will of God are found in Chapter 25 of the Book of St. Matthew: "For I was an hungred, and ye gave me meat: I was thirsty, and ye gave me drink." And today we can add, I was ignorant and you gave me schools; I was sick, and you gave me health; I was homeless, and you gave me shelter. Then Jesus concluded, "Inasmuch as ye have done it unto one of the least of these my brethren, ye have done it unto me."

I've just come from a meeting with a group of Cuban Christian students. They asked me to say a few words, and one of them asked me what I thought about being a Christian in a society where many people are atheists. I told him, "I don't think the problem of atheism is a problem of Marxism; it's a problem among us Christians. Atheism exists because we, the Christians, have historically been unable to give a coherent testimony of our faith. That's how it all began. When you analyze what the Church did by justifying exploitation on earth in the name of a heavenly reward, you have the basis for atheism."

I wanted to say that, from an evangelical point of view, Socialist societies that create better living conditions for the people are unconsciously carrying out what we men of faith call God's projects in history.

CASTRO – Some of the things you're telling me are very interesting. In my talks with the U.S. bishops—which is what led to this exchange of views—I based myself on the elements commonly found in Christian teachings—things that I was taught when I was a child and teen-ager. For example, the Church criticized gluttony; socialism, Marxism-Leninism, also criticizes gluttony, almost as forcefully as the Church. Selfishness is one of the things we criticize the most, and it's also something that is criticized by the Church. Avarice is another thing on which we share the same criteria.

In my talks with the bishops, I even added that, just as they send missionaries to the Amazon, for example, to live in the Indian communities or to work with lepers or the sick in many parts of the world, we have our internationalist workers. Thousands of Cubans are on internationalist missions. I mentioned the example of our teachers who went to Nicaragua: 2,000 teachers, who shared the very difficult living conditions of the Nicaraguan farmers. An interesting aspect of this was that nearly half of the Cuban teachers who went to Nicaragua were women, many of them with families and children. They left their families for two years to go to the remotest, most out-of-the-way places in the mountains and rural areas of Nicaragua, to live where their students lived, in thatched-roof huts, and eat what they ate. Sometimes the family—the married couple and their children—the teacher, and the animals all lived under the same roof.

At one time, we got worried about their health. We tried to send them some food; we were concerned about their health and nutrition, but we couldn't solve the problem. We tried, but it couldn't be done. No teacher who received a chocolate bar or some condensed or powdered milk would eat it there when the children didn't have any. Immediately, they shared whatever they received.

When we asked for volunteers to go there to teach, 29,000 teachers signed up. And, when some of them were killed, 100,000 more volunteered. I wonder what other Latin American society today could mobilize 100,000 teachers to work in those conditions. I wonder if they could mobilize 500 or even 100 to work spontaneously, voluntarily, as our teachers did. Cuba, a small country of 10 million inhabitants, had 100,000 men and women teachers who were ready and willing to work there. We also have teachers in Africa, in such countries as Angola, Mozambique and Ethiopia, and in Asia, in the People's Democratic Republic of Yemen. We have around 1,500 doctors working in isolated places in Asia and Africa—tens of thousands of Cubans carrying out different internationalist tasks.

I told the bishops, "The Church has its missionaries, but we have our internationalists. You appreciate the spirit of self-sacrifice and other moral values, and they're the same values that we praise, encourage and try to instill in our people."

I also said, "Look: if the Church were to create a state in line with those principles, it would organize a state like ours."

BETTO – Yes, but I hope the Church won't do that again—that the Christian left won't try to take the place of the Christian right.

CASTRO – Well, I wasn't exactly suggesting that the bishops organize a state. I told them that *if* they organized a state in accord with Christian precepts, they'd create one similar to ours. I told them, "You surely wouldn't permit and would do everything possible to prevent gambling in a state governed by Christian principles; we've eradicated gambling. You wouldn't have beggars; Cuba is the only country in Latin America where there are no beggars. You wouldn't allow a little child to remain abandoned or to go hungry; not a single child in our country is forsaken or goes hungry. You wouldn't leave the elderly without help or assistance; in Cuba, all old people have help and assistance. You wouldn't have a country with a high unemployment rate; there's no unemployment in Cuba. You wouldn't permit drugs; in our country, drug addiction has been eradicated. You wouldn't permit prostitution, which forces women to sell their bodies to eke out a living; in our country, prostitution has been eradicated and discrimination based on sex has been eliminated, making it possible for women to work, to live in better conditions and to play a more prominent role in society. We've fought against corruption, theft and embezzlement. All those things we've fought against, all those problems we've solved, are the same ones the Church would try to solve if it were to organize a civil state in keeping with its Christian precepts."

BETTO – The only problem is that we'd still have banks, and I don't like the idea of the Church having banks.

CASTRO – Well, the banks wouldn't belong to the Church; they'd belong to the state organized by the Church. They'd belong to the state, not the Church.

In general, our conversation ran along these lines. We went deeply into those issues.

Naturally, they were also interested in the more practical side of Church matters and concerns. They wanted to know how they could help the Church, how they could send it material supplies. I explained that, in general, we helped with the repair and maintenance work of several Catholic churches, a group of churches that we considered to be a part of our cultural heritage—that we provided that kind of cooperation but that we had no objection to their sending such materials for other religious buildings. They were particularly interested in improving the relations between the Church and state. I talked to them about things that were very similar to what I explained to you yesterday: that, at the beginning, problems had come up and had been solved but that we'd stopped there; we'd simply limited ourselves to a situation of coexistence, and it was our mutual responsibility to make further progress.

I told them that I planned to hold a meeting with the Cuban episcopacy. We spoke of this that same day at the reception, and I told them I'd meet with them at a future date. That meeting's still pending, because I've had an enormous amount of work, and I wanted to dedicate some time to the matter. Perhaps one meeting wouldn't be enough. What's more, I felt that, since I'd be meeting with the episcopacy, it would also be good to meet with the other churches. I'd offered the rest of the Christian churches a meeting and had also talked to the nuns who were there about the idea of a meeting. We have very frequent contacts with the Sisters who provide certain social services.

For example, there are religious Orders that work in hospitals and old people's homes. There's also a hospital for lepers—though leprosy is being eradicated in our country. The hospital for lepers was established a long time ago, and nuns have always worked in it. Other Sisters work in other types of health institutions. For example, there's a center for congenitally subnormal children in Havana. Nuns and Communists work shoulder to shoulder in that hospital.

I greatly admire the work those religious Sisters are doing, and I'm not just saying this to you; I've said it publicly. Sometimes, I've made comparisons. Some of the old people's homes that are run by nuns are more efficient and economical than those that are run by our own administrators. Is it because we lack people who are willing to work round the clock? No. It would be unfair if I failed to say that there are thousands of nurses, doctors, health technicians and other hospital employees who do hard, difficult work with love and dedication, exactly as a Sister of Charity does. However, in addition to working with love, the Sisters of Charity and those of other religious Orders are very strict about the use of resources; they're very thrifty, and the institutions they run are very economical. I say this because we're very glad to help those institutions.

The expenses of the institutions run by the Ministry of Public Health are paid by the state, which also pays an important part of the costs of the old people's homes that are run by nuns. One of their sources of income consists of contributions made by old people who retire and donate a part or all of their pensions to the home, but, since the triumph of the Revolution, all those old people's homes run by nuns have received full state support. They lack nothing; they need nothing. I've asked the team of comrades who work directly with me to visit the hospitals and old people's homes to find out what problems they have and help solve them. One comrade systematically visits the old people's homes that are run by the nuns, and all the things they've requested—construction materials, means of transportation and anything else—throughout all the years have been provided immediately.

Whenever a layman or a comrade who manages a state institution asks for material resources—even if he's a member of the Communist Party—I always have his request checked, discussed and analyzed, but I've never analyzed a request made by the nuns who manage those institutions. Why not? Because they never ask for more than they need. To the contrary, they've often asked for less than they need; they're very thrifty. During a session of the National Assembly, I spoke about those old people's homes and, making a comparative analysis of the costs, said that the nuns were model Communists—it was broadcast on television all over the country. I've always spoken of the nuns' attitude as a model for Communists to follow, because I think they have all the qualities we'd like our Party members to have.

In addition, they've applied their experience, which is one of the factors that explains the lower cost of an old people's home run by nuns. This doesn't mean that everybody who works there is a Sister; they have many lay workers who help in the kitchen, construction work and other areas.

At the beginning of the Revolution, one of the measures that was established almost spontaneously was the elimination of multiprofile jobs. People in some workplaces were doing several jobs at the same time. Maybe their job was wall cleaning, but they were also loading in the warehouse or helping out somewhere else. That custom disappeared, almost spontaneously. Unemployment may have had something to do with it, and the labor movement may have exerted some pressure in the sense of ending a practice that was reducing the number of jobs.

The nuns maintained the multiprofile tradition and are models of it. For example, I know one of the Mother Superiors, called Sister Fara, who's the head of an old people's home. She works as a nurse and has had all the required training. In addition to her administrative duties, she works in the wards. When something needs fixing or improving, she helps design what's needed— whether it's a machine or a bath adapted for the old people's needs. In addition, she drives the home's car.

I learned all of this when I sent a comrade to visit the home. They'd asked me for a truck, basing their request on the need to take the garbage away. They explained how much they had to pay when they hired a truck for the job.

I told the comrade, "Look into this. In view of the number of old people in the home, a truck may be too much; it may be more expensive to give them their own truck than to hire one when it's needed."

That may have been the only time we analyzed a request of theirs. We also needed to know what size truck they wanted. The comrade went and looked into it. It wasn't just for the garbage. They also needed the truck to transport building materials and other things, and it was for two homes—not just one. Well, we decided to give them the truck. The Sister immediately said, "I'm going to get a first-class license." What did she mean by that? That she was going to apply for a heavy-goods vehicle driver's license.

You see? Moreover, they apply their method of work to the rest of the workers in the old people's home. They employ fewer people; it's labor-saving.

I was very interested by that in the talks I had that day, and I'll bring it up in the extensive meeting I plan to have with them, for they gave me some interesting facts on the situation in that area. They explained that, since some institutions had only communal wards, if a man and wife came, they had to be separated; one lived in one ward, and the other in the other one. They asked me, "Why, after they've been together for so many years, do we have to separate them?" They proposed expanding one of the homes and building individual rooms so couples could remain together.

The old people's homes that the Revolution has built in recent years are based on modern designs—they're more like tourist hotels than homes—that provide all those options. Some homes are older and don't have those facilities.

They also told me there was a growing demand, due to the greater average life-span. People are living a lot longer than they did 20 or 30 years ago in our country, and, as a result, the number of old people has increased.

We've built many schools, hospitals and nursery schools, as I've explained, but we haven't built enough old people's homes to meet the need. We're aware of this and are even looking into a number of variants, because there are some cases where the person doesn't necessarily need to sleep in the home, because some old people live with their families—but their sons and daughters work and the problem is they're alone during the day with no one to cook their meals and do other things. Such people only need to go somewhere during the day where they're guaranteed care and attention. We're also thinking of solutions of this type, because a traditional old people's home is expensive. Looking after senior citizens is an expensive business, and we're trying to come up with different solutions.

In my talks with the nuns, my basic interest was to learn in detail from their experience. They've developed ways, methods and work habits that are very useful and instructive for us.

BETTO – You've talked about your conversation with the U.S. bishops. What about the meeting you're going to have with Cuban bishops?

CASTRO – I'm going to meet not just with bishops but also with representatives of the Protestant churches, so they won't think I'm ignoring them, and with the nuns from the old people's homes. That's three meetings. I haven't been able to have them in the last few weeks, but they know we're going to have these meetings, and they're very happy about the prospect. We want to have serious, deep discussions on matters of common interest.

I forgot to add that the U.S. bishops also took an interest in some cases of counterrevolutionary prisoners—some of whom, they said, had been reported to them as having problems related to age or health. They brought lists, and I promised that all those cases in which there was a real health problem would be studied. I told them why some kinds of counterrevolutionary prisoners were serving their sentences. To release them and send them to the United States would only swell the ranks of those who are working against Cuba, carrying out acts of sabotage or other crimes against our country. Or they could go and do the same thing in Nicaragua or another country—counterrevolutionaries have already been used in Nicaragua and El Salvador to commit atrocities there too. We haven't put anyone in prison for counterrevolutionary crimes simply out of vengeance. It was essential to defend the Revolution; we had a responsibility in this. Therefore, we couldn't release individuals who would later become new instruments for the United States to use against Cuba. But we were going to analyze the cases of those who really had serious health problems— who we felt couldn't be used for violent activities against the Cuban Revolution or other countries.

We also talked to them about some prisoners who, as soldiers and officers in Batista's Army, had tortured people and committed other crimes, had been sentenced and had been in jail for years. I told them, "Listen: hardly anybody's worried about them. The United States is more concerned about the counterrevolutionaries it recruited, to whom it feels morally committed." I told them we were going to examine the cases of those former army officers and make some proposals about the oldest ones and those in the poorest health, if the United States was prepared to receive them if we set them free. Later, I found that some of those Batista supporters were included in the group of men the members of the U.S. Church delegation were concerned about.

We took the lists; looked at them and studied them in line with this criterion; reviewed the cases of the Batista supporters;

and, not long ago, sent the U.S. bishops a list of all the cases we were ready to solve, including both counterrevolutionary prisoners and a large group of the old prisoners who'd been soldiers and officers under the tyranny. There were around 72 or 73 in all. We told the bishops we were prepared to release them if they got visas for them and their families to go to the United States. The problem with some of these people is that they were Batista's soldiers or officers; they murdered or tortured people; and, even after more than 26 years, the people haven't forgotten those things. There could be a problem if they appeared where their victims' children, parents, brothers, sisters and other relatives are living. They were given long prison terms; some are already old men and have been in prison for years. Vengeance has never been the reason for the Revolution's sanctions, but the crimes that caused our people so much grief and suffering shouldn't go unpunished, and we have had to defend the Revolution against its enemies. Unfortunately, many of them escaped without punishment and were welcomed with open arms by the United States.

We told the bishops, "It would be better if you got visas for the cases we propose. It would be difficult to find a solution for them here." Recently, the head of the Cuban Interests Section in the United States contacted the bishops who'd visited us and told them of the decision we'd made. It pleased them very much, because a solution for all those cases was found on the bases we'd discussed. It's now up to the U.S. Church to get the visas.

BETTO – Let's move on to other things.

Commander, the first time we met was on the evening of July 19, 1980, when the first anniversary of the Sandinista Revolution was being celebrated, in the home of Sergio Ramírez, now the Vice President of Nicaragua. We met through a mutual friend, Father Miguel D'Escoto. That evening, we had a chance to speak for two hours on religion and the Church in Latin America, and you gave me a very interesting overview of religion and the Revolution in Cuba.

My question then was, what attitude was the Cuban government thinking of taking with regard to the Church? I thought there were three options. The first would be to do away with the Church and religion, but history has shown that this not only doesn't work but helps to reinforce the imperialist campaign concerning the ontological incompatibility of Christianity and socialism.

The second would be to keep the Church and Christians marginalized. Then I thought that, in some ways, this would not only back up the imperialists' accusations about what was happening in the Socialist countries but would also favor the conditions for turning people with faith, Christians in Socialist countries, into counterrevolutionaries.

The third option would be to include the Christians in the process of building a society of justice and fraternity.

We had a chance to meet again, over the years, and you invited me—an unusual attitude, a praiseworthy attitude—to begin a series of talks on religion and the Church, because the Cuban government was interested in exploring that topic. At that point, I made a counterproposal: I would be willing to do so if I could also get closer to the Cuban Church.

I then had the opportunity to take part in the February 1983 Cuban Episcopal Conference meeting, in which I told the bishops, "I have not had and continue not to have any delegation from the Church, but I am prepared to help the process of rapprochement between the Church and state in Cuba as much as possible."

Now, you know my love of the Church, my dedication to the Church. I'm tempted by politics, but I have a pastoral interest, a calling, and I'm here and we're going to do this work because of that pastoral interest.

I'd like to ask you what interest you, the Cuban government and socialism have in having an active Church, in having a participating Christian community. Imperialism often spreads propaganda to the effect that socialism is radically opposed to each and every religious manifestation. So, I ask you: how do you view this?

CASTRO – Well, you referred to the time we met in Sergio Ramírez' house, in Nicaragua. It was the first anniversary of the triumph of the Sandinista Revolution. They invited me over; I went; and, in the middle of a very full schedule, they took me very late at night to Sergio Ramírez' house, where we talked about these things.

You knew of my meetings with the Christians for Socialism in Chile in 1971, when I visited the country during the Allende Administration and had a very pleasant, extremely interesting meeting with that group of priests and other Christians—there were around 200 of them. There were also some from other countries who were visiting there at the time. I'd already met Father Cardenal, a Sandinista, writer and poet.

BETTO – He wrote a very beautiful book about Cuba.

CASTRO – I had to see him the day before I left for Chile, and I went to pick him up. We drove around for two hours and talked about the situation in Nicaragua and some other things. It really surprised me when, weeks later, he recalled everything we'd talked about with such precision and put it down so beautifully. We were supposed to see each other in Chile too, but our visits didn't coincide. I had a long talk with the Christians for Socialism there, and I touched on these matters at that early date—that is, around 13 years ago.

Later, during a visit to Jamaica, I also met with representatives from various Christian communities there. That was in October 1977. We also had a long and serious conversation, in which I explained some of my theses. I spoke of the idea of an alliance between Christians and Marxists. They asked, "A tactical alliance?" I said, "No, a strategic alliance, to carry out the social changes our peoples need." I'd already said that in Chile.

I'd also been in contact with some important leaders of the World Council of Churches, who'd shown a lot of interest in the problems of the Third World and the struggle against discrimination and apartheid—a number of problems of this sort—on which we fully agreed.

The development of these ideas was greatly influenced by the emergence of a movement within the Church in Latin America which concerned itself with the problems of workers and farmers, the problems of the poor, and began to struggle and preach the need for justice in our countries. That was how the movement started. It had different names. In Chile, it was called Christians for Socialism. The movement appeared in different places in Latin America after the triumph of the Cuban Revolution—that is, during the last 25 years. I noticed a growing awareness within the Catholic Church and other churches concerning the seriousness of the social problems, the terrible conditions in which those people were living, and an increasing number of Christians chose to struggle for the poor.

This was also seen in the attitude of Christians in Nicaragua, in the important role they played in the struggle against Somoza and for social reforms and justice in that country.

I told you I met Father Ernesto Cardenal many years before the triumph of the Sandinista Revolution. I knew his way of thinking and admired him. I admired him as a writer and poet, but even more as a revolutionary. Later, I met such men as Fernando Cardenal, his brother; D'Escoto; and a number of other prestigious priests and outstanding personalities who identified with and struggled for the people and who, in spite of all the pressures that imperialism brought to bear, haven't wavered in their support for the Revolution, viewing it as their own cause and as a truly deep-seated matter of conscience. That was why, when I visited Nicaragua, I had a meeting with a group of religious leaders.

BETTO – I was there.

CASTRO – That meeting wasn't like the meeting in Chile or the one in Jamaica, because it was short and there wasn't any time to go deeply into any problems. It was simply a meeting at which I greeted them, though I did get to know a small group of nuns of the Maryknoll Order who were working in Nicaragua. They were extremely kind, enthusiastic, noble people, and I was very impressed. They were U.S. nuns. They were at the meeting, and I talked with them about these problems. They were very kind and friendly.

I'd say that the movement within the Church for the people, the poor and social justice has already grown very strong in Nicaragua.

At that time, the revolutionaries in El Salvador were already struggling hard—with the support of many Christians—to end the crimes and do away with the tyranny under which the country has suffered for decades. The conduct of Monsignor Romero, Archbishop of El Salvador, who courageously denounced all the crimes that were being committed, was particularly outstanding, and it even cost him his life.

Some time after that, I heard the shocking news that four churchwomen of the Maryknoll Order, including some of the ones I'd talked with that day, had been brutally murdered in El Salvador. Later, I learned how it happened and who the people responsible for the crimes were: agents of the repressive regime backed by the United States, who raped and murdered those four nuns. It was also agents linked to the CIA and imperialism who atrociously and treacherously murdered Monsignor Romero, Archbishop of El Salvador.

By then, I'd had a lot of meetings with groups of Latin American and Caribbean Christian leaders. They knew how I thought, and I greatly respected the work they were doing. It was under those conditions that we met, when you explained the work the Church was doing in Brazil. That's when the conversation you mentioned took place. You already knew, of course, what I thought, and you knew that we never had the idea of doing away with religion in our country. I spoke to you at length about this. It wasn't just a political matter. I'm a revolutionary, which means a politician in the highest and purest sense of the term. Those who aren't aware of political realities have no right to even undertake a revolutionary program, because they couldn't lead their people to victory and carry out their program. But, as far as religion is concerned, the moral element—principles—must be considered even before the political element. Deep social changes, socialism and communism, are in no way to be conceived of as something that interferes with a person's inner life or denies any human being's right to his thoughts or beliefs. I think that this is a part of man's most intimate self, and, therefore, I view the rights established in our Socialist Constitution of 1976 not as a purely political matter but as a matter of principle, of respect for a person's right to profess his beliefs. That is in the essence of socialism, the essence of communism and the essence of revolutionary ideas concerning religious beliefs, just as respect for life, a person's dignity, the right to work, well-being, health care, education and culture are an integral part of the principles of the Revolution and socialism.

In our country, of course, the Church didn't have the same influence or ascendancy it has in other Latin American countries. Here, it was the Church of the rich minority, and the rich minority left the country, emigrated. This never meant the closure of a single church in our country or any other measures against the institution, even though, as I told you, those people took a militant stand against the Revolution and many left for the United States. Some priests too adopted a militant attitude; left for the United States; and launched campaigns and even blessed the criminal mercenary invasion of the Bay of Pigs, the blockade against Cuba and all the other crimes imperialism has committed against our country—which, in my opinion, totally contradicts the principles of Christianity. But that didn't result in measures of any sort against the Church. A small number of believers remained—most of them left the country, attracted by the riches and ideology of imperialism—but they didn't constitute a quantitative force or what could be called a political one in our country. Strictly as a matter of principle, rather than for political reasons, we were consistent with revolutionary standards of respect for religious beliefs and institutions.

As I already told you, the initial difficulties were overcome in a relatively short period of time, without any trauma, partly due to the stand taken by the Papal Nuncio in Cuba. We were left with a situation of not exactly marginalization but of coexistence between the Revolution and the Church. There was complete mutual respect, but nothing more. I went into all this yesterday.

Of course, relations with the other churches, with the Protestant churches, were fine throughout those years, with no conflicts of any kind. I did mention some cases of sects that have conflicts everywhere (not just with socialism or the Cuban Revolution)—and, in the case of Cuba and the United States, the attitude of some of those sects is useful to the United States, a very powerful nation that is threatening our country, for, if a sect says, "Don't take up arms to defend your country, don't pledge allegiance to the flag and don't sing the National Anthem," it is objectively going against the integrity, security and interests of the Revolution and serving the interests of imperialism. Some of those sects have had problems in a lot of places. In a powerful country such as the United States, they cause no harm. It's better for them to stay there and oppose the Star Wars weapons program. If they did, they'd be doing the world a favor.

The idea of an opening is implicit in what I said in Chile and Jamaica. It's implicit as an idea, but no progress has been made along those lines. That is, when we met, all the conditions existed for relations of mutual understanding between Christianity and the Revolution. Let's call it that. We're not going to call it "the Church," let's call it "Christianity and socialism."

That's why that meeting took place in a friendly, harmonious atmosphere. After that, you carried out your activities here. I wasn't really informed of all that, because, after our meeting, life went on with its struggles and battles. I found out that you'd been here and what you'd done later on. We didn't meet again until recently, but I must say I was pleased and encouraged by your perseverance and by the constancy with which you followed up the conversation we'd had, meditating and working out ideas along those lines. Then, at our last meeting, when we were already deep into these matters, we decided to have this exchange of views and hold this interview, which you thought would be useful for coming to grips with the subject.

In this same spirit, we've made progress—in this spirit, because the meetings I'm going to have with the Cuban bishops aren't directly connected with the meeting I had with the U.S. bishops. In the meeting with the U.S. bishops, I explained what I thought about all this, and I told them that I planned to meet with the Cuban episcopate. I told them what was being done, in view of all the contacts I'd had. First came the ideas, which emerged from facts. We'd observed a fair attitude on the part of the church—or, if not by the Church, by many Christians, highly esteemed priests, bishops and other Church figures who'd taken a correct stand of struggling against exploitation, injustice and dependence and for liberation. That was the first thing; I think that was what really inspired my thought, as expressed in the interview we talked about. That helped those contacts. This process has been developing for nearly 15 years—13, to be more exact. And now, I think we're getting to the point when concrete steps have to be taken—which, in fact, we're beginning to do.

Facts, ideas and then new facts: that's the way it has developed so far, which is really decisive if we want to make progress.

As I said yesterday, this isn't just a question of principles or ethics anymore; in a sense, it's a matter of aesthetics. Aesthetics in what sense? I think the Revolution is a work that should be constantly improved; moreover, it's a work of art.

BETTO – A beautiful definition!

CASTRO – We can't feel satisfied if, in a revolution, we find there's a group of citizens—no matter how many; it doesn't have to be 2 million, 1 million, 500,000 or 100,000 out of 10 million; it doesn't have to be 1 percent of the citizens—who feel that, for religious reasons, they aren't understood or even that they may be the object of political discrimination (such as what we spoke about yesterday, concerning Party membership), which can be accompanied by other subtle forms of discrimination. It's enough not to be understood in a social milieu; it's enough for others not to understand—that's enough to cause suffering, for it can be expressed in subtle ways, such as mistrust.

As I told you, this had an exclusively historic origin, because the Revolution was determined to survive in a struggle against a very powerful enemy that wanted to crush it, even at the cost of millions of Cubans' lives. The identification that existed in the early days between the Church hierarchy, the counterrevolution and imperialism was what led to this mistrust—which took the form of a subtle kind of discrimination, as related, for example, to Party membership and perhaps to other politically sensitive activities—which led to the view that there might be a contradiction between a given belief and the fundamental duties of patriots and revolutionaries.

If somebody were to tell me that there were 100,000—or whatever the exact number of Christians is in Cuba—people who have this problem; people who may have all the qualities of patriots and revolutionaries; kind, hardworking disciplined people, that would necessarily be a cause for dissatisfaction. If 50,000 or 10,000 people —or even one person—were faced with this problem, the Revolution wouldn't be complete as a work of art. The same would be true if even one citizen was discriminated against for being a woman. What other country in Latin America has struggled more and made more progress than Cuba against discrimination against women? Racial discrimination also existed in Cuba prior to the Revolution. If even one person were discriminated against because of the color of his skin—just one—it would be a cause for deep concern. The Revolution wouldn't be complete as a work of art. That's what I referred to before.

To these concepts, criteria and principles, political considerations were added. If, in a revolution that embodies as much justice as the Socialist Revolution in Cuba, there were to be any form of discrimination against a person for religious reasons, it would only serve the interests of the enemies of socialism and the Revolution. It would only serve the interests of those who exploit, plunder, subjugate, attack, interfere with and threaten other peoples— those who would rather wipe out the Latin American and Caribbean peoples than lose their privileges. So, in analyzing these concepts, we also kept political considerations in mind.

I think this was the reasoning behind our thinking, and it explains our interest—in terms of both principles and politics, in the purest sense of the word—in freeing our still-unfinished Revolution from these limitations.

BETTO – Very good, Commander.

Now, I'd like to ask another question. You undoubtedly know —in fact, you've referred to this many times—that, after the Second Vatican Council, which was convened by Pope John XXIII, and the Latin American version of the Council—the 1968 meeting of the Latin American Episcopal Conference in Medellín—many changes began to be made in the Church in this part of the world. It drew closer to the poor, particularly in countries such as Brazil, which were governed by military dictatorships for many years. It wasn't so much a question of the Church's opting for the poor as of the poor's—forced by the repression of the people's and trade-union movements—opting for the Church. In other words, the poor turned to the Church in order to remain organized, articulate, conscious and active. It's no joke—I'm quoting at least two Brazilian bishops—but, to the same extent that the poor invaded the Church, Catholic priests and bishops started to be converted to Christianity. So, today, there are countless Christian Base Communities throughout Latin America. There are around 100,000 of them in Brazil: groups of Christians, workers, farmers and marginalized people, with around 3 million members.

What explains the emergence of Christian Base Communities in this part of the world?

CASTRO – How many million people did you say?

BETTO – Three million in Brazil. Around 100,000 groups, close to 3 million people

Why is this happening? There are communities in Chile. Bolivia, Peru, Ecuador, Guatemala and Nicaragua that, as you yourself have said, play an important role in the liberation process; there are communities in Mexico and even in the parts of El Salvador that have been liberated by the guerrillas. Why is this so; why?

If we were to ask a Latin American farmer, a worker or a domestic servant what concept he had of the world, he would surely couch his reply in religious terms. The most elementary concept that the oppressed Latin American people have of the world is a religious one.

I believe that one of the most serious mistakes of the Latin American left, particularly of the left within the Marxist-Leninist tradition, has been to preach atheism to the masses. It's not that they shouldn't say what they really think. It's not that at all. The thing is, they weren't being sensitive to the people's religious concepts, and, by acting in that way, they were, in fact, foreclosing the possibility of establishing a link between their political outlook and the masses.

It's not easy, for instance, to convince a worker or a farmer that he has to fight for socialism, but it's very easy to tell him, "Look: we believe that there's only one God, who is the father. If that's true, we should all live as brothers, but the brotherhood that God wants doesn't exist in our society. It's denied by racial discrimination, class inequalities and economic contradictions, by the fact that some men are very rich, while most people are very poor. So, for us, basing ourselves on the very roots of our faith, fighting for brotherhood means fighting against all those things that concretely and historically hinder social equality, justice, freedom and full dignity for everyone, no matter what his job, color or ideas." This is why this approach has been so successful in the last few years.

The line of thought that emerged from those communities, the faith that has enlightened and encouraged people to struggle for their liberation in Guatemala, Peru, Brazil, El Salvador and every other country and which has been systematized by the theologians, is what we now call Liberation Theology.

I'd like to know what you think about those communities. Liberation Theology is a very polemic issue; Reagan and the Santa Fe Document have even described it as a subversive element. What do you think about Liberation Theology?

CASTRO – You've given a rather long, very interesting explanation and added a question at the end. To answer your question, I'll have to refer to some of the points you mentioned.

You said that the political movement, the Marxist-Leninist left-wing movement, has been mistaken in its analysis of the religious question and in preaching atheism in Latin America. I'm not really in a position to know how each of the left-wing movements and each of the Communist or other left-wing parties in Latin America has approached the religious question, because my talks and discussions with these organizations are usually centered around other problems—the economic situation, poverty, the situation of the masses, etc. In other words, they're usually focused on political problems. I don't really remember if we analyzed these problems in any of the countless talks I've had with representatives and members of those parties in the course of the last 26 years, so I can't tell you what they think, but you live in one Latin American country and travel through others, so you probably know more about it than I do.

I believe, of course, that the political movement, the revolutionary movement, should base its analysis on the conditions that exist at a given moment, and its tactics and approach on more than doctrine—though, of course, you have to use doctrine as a starting point, and it has to be implemented and put into practice. If political thought is applied without a correct strategy and tactics, then, no matter how correct that political thought may be, it will become utopian, because it can't be put into practice either objectively or subjectively.

I can understand the contradictions that have emerged between political-revolutionary thought and the Church. If I'd been a Cuban Indian, a Siboney, and some foreigners came over armed with harquebuses, crossbows, swords, a royal standard and a cross; attacked my village; killed the people they thought they should kill; and captured the ones they wanted to capture—one of the first things Columbus and the Spaniards did when they went back to Spain was take a group of Indians with them in what amounted to a flagrant violation of their most basic rights, because they didn't ask anybody's permission to take them to Europe as booty, and they captured them in the same way you'd capture a wolf, a lion, an elephant or a monkey—what, then, would I think of all that? The violation of animals' rights is still more or less uncontested, but I believe that, for a long time now, human conscience has respected the rights of men—regardless of whether they're white, Indian, yellow, black, *mestizo* or whatever.

If we were to ask a Mexican Indian what he thought of all that, his answer wouldn't contain much reverence for the conquistadores and their religious beliefs. They came armed with the sword and the cross to subjugate, enslave and exploit "the heathen"—who should have been considered God's children too. That's how they conquered this part of the world, with a messianic faith that tried to impose Western Christian faith and civilization through bloodshed. Those who think they're in possession of a truth can't spread it through the murder and enslavement of the peoples.

The most objective truth that the conquered countries learned from the more advanced nations was the loss of their freedom; the imposition of abuse, exploitation and slavery; and sometimes even annihilation.

It should be noted, however, that, even during that early period, there were some priests who reacted against those outrageous crimes—as, for example, Father Bartolomé de las Casas did.

BETTO – He lived here. He was a Dominican too.

CASTRO – The Order should feel proud of him, because he was one of the most honorable priests. He denounced and opposed the horrors that followed the conquest.

For centuries, colonialism was a reality. Entire continents were divided up among the European powers: Asia, Africa and the Americas were divided up, occupied and exploited for centuries. The Europeans brought their religion with them; in a way, it was the religion of the conquerors, the enslavers, the exploiters. It's true that, by its nature and, I'd say, its human content, its noble essence of solidarity—even though that essence was in contradiction with the facts and realities to the priests—that same religion became, in the end, as in ancient Rome, the religion of the slaves. In this hemisphere, where the Spaniards remained for three centuries—for almost four in Cuba, because it was among the first to be conquered and the last to be freed—the religion of the conquerors became very widespread.

This wasn't so in Asia, because it had other religions that were very deeply rooted and ancient cultures that proved more resistant—Hinduism, Buddhism and other indigenous religions that were also very rich in content. So Christianity clashed there with the other religions and philosophies, and the result was that its control was less widespread, less universal. In the Arab world and the Middle East, Islam prevailed, in spite of the Crusades and the subsequent conquest and Western European domination. In Southeast Asia and India, Hinduism and Buddhism prevailed, even though those countries were colonized by Europe. The indigenous religions also prevailed in the East Indies and other parts of Asia, such as China, in spite of European domination.

Even in feudal Europe, where the noblemen and feudal lords owned both the land and the serfs, the Church—which comforted souls—was an ally of that system of exploitation. There was a contradiction between the social system and Church doctrine.

In the czarist empire, a close alliance existed between the empire, the noblemen, the feudal lords, the landowners and the Church. That was an indisputable historical reality that lasted for many centuries.

With the exception of only one country—Ethiopia—Africa was conquered by force of arms. The conquerors stayed longer in some places than in others, but there was less cultural assimilation; Christianity never really triumphed in Africa. In northern Africa, Islam was widespread; the rest of the religions in the continent were animistic. For centuries, Westerners went to Africa not to preach Christianity but to procure slaves. I don't know if anybody knows exactly how many tens of millions of free men the Europeans captured in Africa to enslave them and bring them to Latin America, the Caribbean and the Unites States, to sell them as merchandise. Perhaps 100 million. I think that some research has been done on the subject and that it's been established that around 50 million survived but that many—perhaps most—of them died while being captured or during the trip across the Atlantic.

BETTO – Four million reached Brazil alive.

CASTRO – Just think how many died far from their places of birth, from their families, from everything. That dreadful system lasted for almost four centuries. For centuries, Western Europe's technical, economic and military superiority prevailed over the peoples of what is now the Third World.

The Indians were wiped out in many places. In Cuba, the conquerors practically exterminated them, though they couldn't do the same thing in other places—either because there were too many Indians or because they were better cared for as a work force.

The Africans were enslaved—without distinction—for centuries. Even after the independence of the United States, slavery wasn't abolished, in spite of the solemn declaration about the inalienable rights of man "to which the Laws of Nature and of Nature's God entitle them," which truth has held to be self-evident. For almost a century, millions of African blacks and their descendants continued to be enslaved. That was their only self-evident truth and the only right granted them by the creators of slavery and capitalism.

In that same country, after the proclamation of independence, the Indians were simply wiped out; they were wiped out by European Christians and their descendants. And all of those people were very religious and considered themselves to be Christians, as did the ones who, for centuries, hunted the Indians down and scalped them in order to seize their wealth and their land. That is an undeniable historical fact.

Even in Argentina, during Rosas' time, the Christians, follow-

ing the example set in the United States, invaded the Indians' land
and exterminated them. In many places, the extermination of the
aboriginal population was the procedure that was followed.

So, in Europe, there were the feudal lords, the noblemen and
the ecclesiastical hierarchs, who, in a close alliance that lasted for
centuries, imposed their exploitation on the serfs and peasants. In
the czarist empire, the same situation prevailed up to the end of
the nineteenth century.

Analyzing it from a historical perspective, nobody can deny
that the Church—the Church of the conquerors, oppressors and
exploiters—was on the side of the conquerors, oppressors and exploiters. It never categorically denounced slavery, an institution
that is so repugnant to our consciences now. There was never a
denunciation condemning the slavery of blacks or Indians. The
Church never denounced the extermination of the aboriginal population or any of the other crimes that were committed against
those people—the fact that they were robbed of their land, their
wealth, their culture and even their lives. None of the churches
denounced those crimes, and the system lasted for centuries.

No wonder the revolutionary ideas that emerged in the struggle against those age-old injustices had an antireligious spirit. Yes,
there's an objective, historical explanation for the origin of those
ideas within the revolutionary movement. Those ideas were
present in the bourgeois French Revolution and also in the Bolshevik Revolution. They were present in liberalism, first; the philosophy of Jean-Jacques Rousseau and the French Encyclopedists also
contained this antireligious spirit. It wasn't just in socialism; those
ideas were present afterwards in Marxism-Leninism, for historical
reasons. There was never a denunciation of capitalism. Maybe, 100
or 200 years from now, when capitalism has been completely
wiped out, somebody will say bitterly, "For centuries, the capitalists' churches didn't denounce the capitalist and imperialist system," just as we say today that, for centuries, they didn't
denounce slavery, the extermination of the Indians and the colonialist system.

Now, revolutionaries are fighting against the existing system
of exploitation, which is also ruthless. So, there's an explanation
for the things that you say are mistakes and which may, in fact, be
considered mistakes. The question is how to implement an idea or
a revolutionary social program. If what you mean is that, in the

present conditions in Latin America, it's a mistake to stress philosophical differences with the Christians—who, as the majority, are massively victimized by the system—rather than to try to persuade all who share the same aspiration of justice to unite in a common struggle, I'd agree with you. I agree even more strongly, because we are witnessing an awakening in an important sector of the Christians in Latin America. If we base our analysis on this fact and on these concrete conditions, it is absolutely correct and fair to say that the revolutionary movement should have a correct approach to the subject and that it should, at all costs, avoid doctrinal rhetoric that goes against the religious feelings of the population—the workers, farmers and middle strata—for to engage in such rhetoric would only serve the interests of the system of exploitation.

I'd say that, faced with a new reality, the left should change the way it has dealt with the problem and its approach to the subject. I fully agree with you on that point. I have no doubts about it. But, for a long period of history, faith was used as a tool of domination and oppression, so it is only logical that the men who wanted to change that unjust system entered into contradiction with religious beliefs, with those tools and with that faith.

I think that the enormous historic importance of Liberation Theology, or the Liberation Church—whatever you want to call it—lies precisely in its profound impact on the political views of its followers. It constitutes a point of contact between today's believers and those of the past—that distant past of the first few centuries after the emergence of Christianity, after Christ. I could define the Liberation Church, or Liberation Theology, as Christianity's going back to its roots, its most beautiful, attractive, heroic and glorious history. It's so important that it forces all of the Latin American left to take notice of it as one of the most important events of our time. We can describe it as such because it can deprive the exploiters, the conquerors, the oppressors, the interventionists, the plunderers of our peoples, and those who keep us in ignorance, illness and poverty of the most important tool they have for confusing, deceiving and alienating the masses and continuing to exploit them.

Throughout the long period of history I've mentioned, people in the Christian, mercantilist West even went so far as to discuss whether or not American Indians, Negroes, Indians of India and other Asians had souls. Virtually the only thing they were granted throughout centuries of horror, exploitation and crimes of all kinds was that, in effect, they did have souls. But this didn't imply any rights other than the right to slavery, exploitation, plunder and death.

Even the bourgeois revolutions, which spoke of the inalienable rights of men in France, the United States and everywhere else, didn't recognize those rights for Indians, Negroes, Asians and *mestizos*. They were inalienable rights for whites only. The right to life, liberty and security—and to health, education, culture and decent employment—was recognized by the great bourgeois revolutions as valid only for white Europeans. There you have history's bitter and unappealable testimony. None of those rights were for the peoples of the Third World. Of course, Latin America is in the Third World. And, so far, the only concession granted to the tens of millions—hundreds of millions—of poor farmers and workers who eke out an existence on very low wages and to the slum dwellers in every Latin American capital is to admit that they have souls.

But, if we accept this, if we admit that they have souls, then I think that the position adopted by Christians like yourself, of proclaiming and demanding these same rights for everyone, constitutes a historic event of great importance.

BETTO – Body and soul, Commander; a unit: a human being.

CASTRO – And, if you begin to admit that there is spiritual equality between the poor and the rich, blacks and whites, and landless farmers and landlords, then you have to begin to acknowledge that all those men and women, human beings, who have bodies and souls just like the whites, just like the rich, should have the same rights the others have.

That's how I see the struggle that you've been waging. It's not surprising that the empire, its government, its theoreticians and its spokesmen are beginning to take or to recommend a firmer stand against Liberation Theology as something subversive. In practice, they have to maintain the principle that we don't even have souls —because, if we have souls and bodies, they'll have to admit that we also have a right to live, to eat, to be healthy, to receive an education, to have a roof over our heads, to have jobs and to live with dignity. They'll have to admit that the wives and daughters of workers have the right not to become prostitutes and that families have the right not to live off gambling, drugs, theft or charity in shantytowns.

Logically, a religious position or theory that seeks out the best in the history of Christianity completely contradicts the interests of imperialism. I still think that even though, theoretically, they admit that we have souls, deep down, the theoreticians of imperialism, the gentlemen who drafted the Santa Fe Document, don't believe it about blacks, Indians and *mestizos*—people who live in the Third World. And they call themselves the Santa Fe (Holy Faith) group! That's what lies behind their discriminatory approach, and I can understand their rabid position, just as I can appreciate the historic significance of the decision made by an important part of the Latin American Church to side with the poor.

Your description of how the poor invaded the Church was very beautiful. I believe that the pain of the poor invaded the Church; the indescribable tragedy of those masses invaded the Church. I believe that the cry of pain reached the Church—above all, reached those pastors closest to their flocks, who could hear their cries and note their pain and their suffering more clearly.

The echo went a little farther: it reached bishops, cardinals, even Pope John XXIII. The Third World and Third World revolutionaries felt the impact of John XXIII's profound statements. Everyone in our countries, including the Marxist-Leninists, remembers him with respect and fellow feeling. I believe that John XXIII's preaching undoubtedly had a great deal to do with this choice and the attitude adopted by many priests and bishops toward the poor in the Third World—especially in Latin America.

BETTO – John XXIII was a farmer who became a pope.

CASTRO – That factor may have had a great influence on his thinking. We can't talk about the Church movement in Latin America, this coming together with the people, without mentioning John XXIII. I myself wasn't aware of these changes, because you're speaking about from 1968 on. I've seen the influence which John XXIII's thinking has had on the evolution of the Catholic Church and the emergence of this movement. I think that the influence was mutual, reciprocal: the poor influenced and invaded the Church, and the Church, in turn, as a reflection or as an echo of that suffering, also reached the poor. I can assure you that never before has the Church had as much influence and prestige in this hemisphere as it has had since many priests and bishops began to identify themselves with the cause of the poor.

BETTO – You know that many people, including Church people, in Europe today think that Liberation Theology is merely a Marxist manipulation of the Church.

I'm fully identified with Liberation Theology, and I'd also say, Commander, that I consider my Christian faith to be deeper today, thanks to Liberation Theology.

For many centuries, the European Church, like European society, was the center of the world. And the Church grew accustomed to exporting not only its model of the Church but also its theology to the rest of the world. I believe in theology. Theology is the reflection born from the faith of the Christian community. In this sense, every Christian is theologizing when he reflects on his faith, but not every Christian is a theologian. Theologians are those who have a scientific basis, the scientific knowledge necessary to theology, and, at the same time, contact with the community and who are capable of practicing and systematizing the reflections of the Christian people.

We are aware that Europe has produced a theology that we call Liberal Theology, which has its value. However, like every other theology, it reflects the problems of a specific reality—in this case, that of Europe. And what were the most important European events of this century? The two World Wars. This fact has caused all European culture to raise anguishing questions about the value of human beings and the meaning of life. When we look at the philosophy of Heidegger and Sartre, the films of Fellini and Buñuel, the paintings of Picasso, and the literature of Camus, Thomas Mann and James Joyce, we see that all of them try to answer the disturbing question of what value human beings have. And, along these lines, in individualistic philosophy, European theology found the means it needed for relating to reality.

Now, what is the most important event in Latin America's history in this century? A war? No. We've had local wars but no continental ones. The most important problem or fact in Latin America's history is the massive number of poverty-stricken people. Therefore, our problem isn't a philosophical problem of the human being. The anguishing question that we must ask is why, when the world has such advanced technology at its disposal, there is such an overwhelming majority of nonpersons, people without rights or hope, in Latin America. Most Latin Americans have no rights. That is, in many cases, they live in worse conditions than animals. Cattle in Brazil live better than most of the Brazilian population. And theology needs more than philosophy to analyze this. You have to seek the causes of the situation and turn to the social sciences for help, and the social sciences can't ignore Marxism's contribution.

As soon as—out of a sense of justice toward the people and of respect for the truth, as required by scientific analysis—Liberation Theology was articulated in this way, it triggered a very strong reaction from a sector of the Church, which led to sanctions being applied against some of our comrades, such as Leonardo Boff, a Brazilian theologian. He has been punished for exercising his most basic right as a Church theologian: that of reflecting on faith on the basis of the history and reality of his people.

I'd like you, who keeps close tabs on world events, things as they happen, to give an opinion. What impact has all this polemic on Liberation Theology had on you? How have you reacted? Has it sparked any special interest in you, any personal reaction as a man and politician? I'd like you to talk about this.

CASTRO –You've asked a very difficult—and a very delicate—question. Once again, I must refer to some of the points in your explanation—first, the question of manipulation.

We've already spoken about this. We went into it the other day before we began the interview. I said that manipulators have never deserved anybody's respect or been successful anywhere. Manipulators are like little sailboats that go with the wind and the waves. Manipulation is synonymous with opportunism. Manipulation doesn't have substance; it doesn't have roots. I don't think you'd have any respect for me if you thought I was a manipulator, and, by the same token, no revolutionary would have any respect for you or for others like you if they thought you were being manipulated. I think that everything—respect, relationships, serious analysis and understanding—is possible among people who are honest with themselves and with others. If you weren't a profound believer, your ideas wouldn't have had any impact on us.

Personally, what most inspired my respect for you was my perception of your deep conviction and religious belief. I'm sure that the other men of the Church who have concerned themselves with these problems are just like you. If we revolutionaries thought you weren't honest, nothing we've said would make any sense—neither the ideas discussed nor the idea of an alliance or even unity (as I already said in Nicaragua) between Christians and Marxists—because a true Marxist wouldn't trust a false Christian, and a true Christian wouldn't trust a false Marxist. Only this conviction can be the basis of a solid, lasting relationship.

Let's leave it at that. As the saying goes, "It's easier to discover a liar than a cripple." The faith of a Christian and the faith of a revolutionary can't be simulated, and a lie can't be dissimulated.

I can understand why those who are worried by the existence of so much faith resort to simplistic arguments. This holds true for both sides.

I can see that you've given it a great deal of thought. This was evident as you spoke about Europe, Liberal Theology, the historic factors and the great events that have influenced the ideas of Europe's most important thinkers. I was very impressed by what you said concerning the difference between European reality and that of our hemisphere, where the massive nature of poverty is the basic, determining factor. This has been true for the past 40 or 50 years, and this has become more and more evident. The economic crisis of the 1930s was one of Latin America's most serious economic and social tragedies, but the current crisis is even more serious. Then, Latin America had a population of about 100 million inhabitants; today, it has around 400 million. Its subsistence resources and even its natural resources have been depleted.

I don't know how primitive men lived, though a number of theories have been formulated on this subject. It's said that they hunted, fished and gathered fruit to survive. There was an abundance of wild animals, and many fish in the rivers and lakes. There was no pollution. They had plenty of wood, so they could build fires for warmth. There were roots and fruit for them to eat. These natural resources have dwindled and become increasingly scarce. They are polluted or are zealously guarded by their owners. Meanwhile, the number of human beings has multiplied many times over.

Today, people can't survive by hunting and gathering. They must use intensive farming, fish breeding, deep-sea fishing with modern technology, and industry. Modern men can't live without education and health care. The law of natural selection insured that only the fittest primitive men survived. Modern men must get the most from the land, for life can no longer be dependent on nature and the environment. Hundreds of millions of people in this hemisphere lack means of livelihood—and, as a result, there is large-scale poverty. I fully agree with what you said about non-persons.

Joelmir Beting told me that in Brazil, a country with a population of around 135 million, 32 million form a consumers' market similar to that of Belgium, 30 million are just below that level, 40 million are at the minimum subsistence level and the 30 million that are left are below the minimum subsistence level. In what category should we place the people who live in shantytowns, don't have jobs, can't go to school and have no means of livelihood? Clearly, in that of nonpersons. More than half the people in most Latin American countries belong to the nonperson category, while perhaps 15 percent—possibly 20 percent; let's say between 10 and 20 percent—live on a par with Belgium, with similar opportunities and patterns of consumption. In other words, we could say that between 250 million and 300 million people in this hemisphere—about three fourths of the total population—could be considered nonpersons.

I entirely agree with what you said, and I'm also very interested in your explanation. It's a long one, but history shows that all these things are closely related to colonialism and slavery. The wealth extracted from this hemisphere served to finance the development of the industrial powers in Europe and the United States. As I said before, slavery didn't disappear in the United States until nearly 100 years after independence.

All this is based on underdevelopment; neocolonialism; various forms of plunder through unequal terms of trade, protectionist policies, dumping, the ruthless exploitation of the natural and human resources of this hemisphere, high interest rates, monetary policies and a whole series of other methods of exploitation that have kept the Third World countries dependent, underdeveloped and impoverished. Latin America is particularly sensitive to this, because of its higher social, political, educational and cultural levels and the extent of its information about Western consumer societies, which are so highly touted in this hemisphere. As a result, its awareness of inequality and poverty is much greater than that of the other Third World regions, such as Africa and Asia. All this makes the situation potentially more dangerous and explosive from a political and social standpoint.

I share your view that Marxism is an important contribution to the development of the social sciences. I understand why those who are concerned about these questions from a religious standpoint are interested in finding an explanation and doing research and have used Marxism as a tool for analysis, because research must have a scientific foundation and a scientific method of analysis. They haven't used Marxism to explain theological, metaphysical or philosophical problems. They've used it to explain economic, social and political phenomena. It's like doctors diagnosing a disease. They use scientific methods and equipment and couldn't care less whether the equipment was made in the United States, France, the Soviet Union, Japan or some other country. Science per se has no ideology. That is, a scientific instrument, a medicine, any kind of medical or industrial equipment or a machine—any of those things—has no ideology in itself. A scientific explanation may lead to a political ideology. I'm not talking about religious beliefs.

I understand this. Now, who uses Marxism as a tool? All Liberation Theologians, or only some of them? I'm not in a position to state that Liberation Theologians have used Marxism as a method or tool for research on social problems, but I do know that it's used by practically all scientists.

For example, I read a lot of scientific books and research works that aren't about social problems. Countless scientists are studying biology, the stars, the planets, life itself, botany and mineralogy. It's clear that they're all engaging in scientific research independently of their religious convictions. The theory of evolution was rejected for quite some time; some scientists were strongly censured for accepting it. In fact, there was a time when the theory that the Earth was round was rejected, as was the idea that the Earth turned on its axis and orbited around the sun. In the course of man's scientific advance, many scientific truths were rejected at first.

Today, any scientist—Catholic, Protestant, Muslim, Hindu or Buddhist; from the United States, Japan, China or any other country—regardless of his religious beliefs, will approach a problem from a scientific standpoint without the slightest hesitation. That's precisely why science has made such tremendous progress, discovering the laws of genetics and achieving the amazing feat of changing cellular structures—in other words, creating new species. It was a monk, in fact—Mendel (I'm not sure, but I think he was a Benedictine)—who discovered the laws of genetics. Others delved deeper and discovered mutations and their causes. Still others studied the cells, their nuclei and their chromosomes; analyzed DNA; and discovered what is known as the cell's genetic programming. They've probed even further and have succeeded in transferring genes from one kind of cell to another.

The same thing happened with those who discovered the fabulous power of the atom through mathematical calculations and physical research, those who explored space and made its conquest possible, and those who developed modern pharmacology and can even design molecules that aren't found in nature and produce them in laboratories. For example, whereas, 30 years ago, a certain antibiotic was produced by means of a fungus culture, it's now produced through chemical synthesis, and scientists can develop medicines that are better or more effective than the ones existing in natural forms.

I'm giving this long explanation because the study of any social problem requires the application of scientific methods. Many scientists have used methods that are closely related to Marxist concepts. They've used scientific methods for interpreting natural, physical and chemical phenomena—but not for interpreting philosophical or theological ones. They're using the theories of natural evolution, the laws discovered by astronomers and the laws of physics, from the law of gravity to those that govern the existence of galaxies. Many of those who work in this field, in genetic engineering and biology, are world famous, and many of them are Protestants, Catholics, Muslims, Jews, Hindus and Buddhists, or belong to some other religion. Others are atheists, nonbelievers or agnostics. Therefore, Liberation Theologians aren't the only ones who use science in research; it's used by every researcher in every field of human knowledge, and it's evident that the use of scientific methods hasn't entered into contradiction with their religious faith.

As I already told you, I wish I'd had more time for this interview, because I wanted to have more information and more knowledge on the way the Liberation Theologians think and on Liberation Theology itself. I wanted to know all about Leonard Boff and Gutiérrez. I've collected literature on them, a large number of the main works by Boff, Gutiérrez and others. In spite of my heavy work load, I'm very interested in learning about them, in really knowing what they think.

We'd concluded that the chances of your visiting Cuba again in the near future weren't good and that I didn't have much time for going into the subject now. I intend to learn more about it, but I already have some general ideas and information, because the first thing I do in the morning is read a lot of dispatches from the international wire services, choosing the ones with important information on politics, economics, medicine and the other sciences—and, of course, the ones on Liberation Theology and the problems and debates that have sprung up around it. It's not easy for me to give an opinion on these issues. It's easier for me to express an opinion on matters that are related to the revolutionary or Communist movement, the international economic situation or political issues in general, since that's the field in which I carry out my activities. It's my field, the one in which I feel more entitled to express my views.

Now, since we're dealing with the Church, the Church's internal policy and discussions within the Church itself, I feel that I should be very cautious and not give opinions that might contribute to argument or division within a religious trend or take sides on such issues. It's much easier for you and other Christians and Catholics to do that. Reading the news dispatches has given me a great deal of information on what is being said in Europe, Latin America and elsewhere. In view of the nature of the subject, I've avoided making any analyses, drawing conclusions or meddling in the problem. This, of course, doesn't keep me from evaluating everything that's done and the views that are expressed.

The Church is a very old institution. It's almost 2,000 years old.

BETTO – The oldest one in existence.

CASTRO – Well, I think Buddhism and Hinduism are older.

BETTO – Yes, but they're not institutions.

CASTRO – You're right; if it's a question of institutions, that's possible.

The Church may be the oldest institution, and it has gone through some very difficult trials—schisms and divisions of all kinds. Other churches—the Orthodox Church, for example— were created as a result of schisms. Then came the Reformation, which led to the appearance of many other churches.

It's true that the rock of St. Peter, on which the Catholic Church was built, is solid and lasting. Throughout history, that institution has demonstrated its experience, its wisdom and its capacity to adapt to reality. It must have had some very difficult trials, from the time Galileo was condemned, to the nuclear age and space flights, theories on the origin of the galaxies, the laws of evolution and the advances made in modern biology, some of whose great feats I've already mentioned, but the theologians always came up with explanations; new religious concepts were developed, and steps were taken to adapt the institution to the major political, economic and social changes and scientific discoveries that have taken place in the world.

Now too the Church is going through some very difficult trials and must make some important changes. I wouldn't say that I fully agree with the positions that the Church as an institution has taken regarding a series of problems. For example, I'd say that it's necessary to go more deeply into the very serious problem of uncontrolled population growth. As I understand it, the Church is taking more interest in this problem now. The ideas that are being expressed on this issue now are completely different from the ones that were held when I was in the fifth or sixth grade. Major changes have been made in some of those ideas since then.

I'm not promoting ideas or standards that depart from the principles or the theological ideas of the Church, but I do feel that it's necessary to approach the important problems of our times realistically, and one of them is how to handle the need for birth control, which in some countries has led to serious political conflicts and disputes.

I discussed this problem once with an African cardinal—he was from Benin and lived in Rome. I told him, "Listen: it's a good thing the Catholic Church isn't very influential in China and India," because both countries—one has more than a billion inhabitants, and the other, around 700 million and very limited resources—must be seriously concerned over the problems of birth control. These matters are so vital that they shouldn't enter into contradiction with religious beliefs. The Church should solve complex problems, and one of them is that of avoiding traumatic contradictions between Catholics' beliefs and their reality.

BETTO – One small clarification, Commander.

As a matter of principle, the Church now limits birth control to the concept of responsible parenthood—that is, parents should decide on the number of children they want to have, and they are duty-bound to promote the fullest development of their lives. The discussion in the Church concerns the methods of birth control. There's a political concern (which I think is very important and very fair) that birth control shouldn't be promoted without a thorough discussion, because the one who'll have the last word—this is what's happening in our capitalist countries—is the World Bank, with the U.S. policy of sterilizing poor women in health centers. If a woman goes there with a headache or pregnancy problems, she's immediately sterilized. So, in view of its importance, this problem should be dealt with very carefully.

CASTRO – Naturally, I'll never side with imperialism's practices and methods for maintaining its domination over our countries. I also think that compulsory sterilization is one of the most brutal violations of human rights. I'm in complete disagreement with that. I'm not suggesting solutions; I'm simply pointing to a real problem of our times.

I'm not informed about the time when this analysis, this criterion, this idea of responsible parenthood appeared. Could you tell me when the discussion began?

BETTO – After Vatican II, which ended in 1965. The serious analysis began at that time.

CASTRO – And when was a decision reached?

BETTO – During the pontificate of Pope Paul VI, with the encyclical *Humanae Vitae*.

CASTRO – What year was that?

BETTO – I can't remember exactly, because he was pope for around 15 years; I don't remember the exact date.

CASTRO – More than ten years ago?

BETTO – Yes, I think so.

CASTRO – Then that idea already existed when I talked with the cardinal from Benin.

BETTO – Yes. Just when was that conversation?

CASTRO – A little over ten years ago. He didn't mention the idea of responsible parenthood, even though I told him about my concern.

I referred to the real problems I saw in the Third World and possible conflicts of conscience between the need to plan population growth—for, if this isn't done, there will be terrible consequences in those countries, sooner or later—and the Church's traditional position on the use of contraceptives. No developing country can sustain a population growth rate of 2–3 percent a year and pull itself out of the abyss of poverty and suffering accumulated over the centuries. I think that the Church should take a realistic, rational, reasonable position on problems that have so many political, economic, social and even moral implications.

The number of children who die in the Third World each year for lack of food must be taken into consideration. Tens of millions of children die before reaching 15, and hundreds of millions of the survivors are physically or mentally harmed by malnutrition. This is inhuman, cruel and tragic. You can't imagine a worse fate, and we can't afford to wait for centuries for people with no access to schools or even a humble teacher to acquire sophisticated moral notions such as sexual abstinence and to follow them with the inflexibility and discipline of a convent. It isn't realistic. No theology, religion or church can ignore this tragedy. If the Church doesn't have a political theory on how—technically, scientifically and socially—to solve the problem of providing all those people with food, education and health and guaranteeing their lives—if it lacks that theory—it should at least have a rational moral theory on how Christian families should handle the problem.

That is, there are points of discrepancy on these subjects, if the traditional criteria I was taught haven't been modified and made more rational and feasible—which would be extremely valuable and important for our peoples. I'm not referring to religious or theological questions; I'm talking about real political and social problems that are of tremendous importance to all the Third World countries—and especially the Latin American countries, where the Catholic Church is so influential.

I'd like to see the Church meditating on these problems—and, what's more, I'd like to hear clear, profound ideas on the economic and social problems of the Latin American and other Third World countries; on the immense tragedy of what is going on; on the deep economic crisis and the Third World's debt; and on the exploitation and plunder to which our peoples are subjected through a ruthlessly selfish, unfair system of international economic relations. I'd like to see the Church take a constructive, supportive position regarding the problems from which our peoples suffer. It would be an extremely valuable contribution to world peace and well-being. As things now stand, the economic resources wrenched from our peoples are being used for military purposes.

We don't want—nor can we want—divisions within the Church. We'd like to see a united Church supporting the legitimate claims of the peoples of the Third World and of all mankind—especially the claims of Latin America, where, very soon, at the present rate of growth, most of the Catholics in the world (the poorest ones) will be living. I don't think it right to try to reform or improve the Church from outside; nor do I think it right to promote division from outside. I do think, however, that solidarity with mankind's most deeply felt aspirations for a united Church is politically better for us both, and I sincerely hope that these problems may be solved rationally.

BETTO – And, as a Christian, I would add "and democratically."

CASTRO – I think that concept is implicit in a rational solution, because, if the solution isn't democratic, it won't be entirely rational.

I'd find it a little strange for the pope to speak, for example, about how we should organize parties, whether we should or shouldn't apply democratic centralism and how we should interpret Marxism-Leninism. You can do so if you want to, and I can speak about those topics all you want.

I hope that the Church's problems will be solved rationally and that it will understand the serious, tragic problems with which our countries are faced and give them its support. You don't have to be very perspicacious to realize that we fully support—and this is absolutely consistent with everything I've said—the Church's siding with the poor. This is consistent with the historical analysis I made, in which I said that, throughout centuries of feudalism and colonialism, centuries during which men were enslaved, exploited and exterminated, the Church didn't take a stand against those great historical injustices. Nobody can be more earnestly in favor of the Church's taking a correct position on the most serious social problems of our times. Nobody wants to hear again that, for centuries, the Church didn't deal with those problems. I've already told you about the admiration and pleasure I felt when I saw that many priests and bishops were drawing closer to the poor in Latin America and identifying with their problems. And, of course, Liberation Theologians have been the standard-bearers of the Church in drawing close to the poor and to the people as a whole. In this sense, it's hardly necessary to say that I was very glad to see the efforts that these men—whom we might call enlightened—have made in this regard.

That's why I don't want to criticize the measures that have been taken against some of them or to interfere in this problem. I simply want to study their works in depth.

I've been trying to gather material. I now have almost all of Boff's and Gutiérrez' works, and I also asked for and obtained copies of the speeches that the pope gave on his last Latin American tour, including his speeches in Guyana, the Indian communities in Ecuador and the Peruvian shantytowns. As a politician and revolutionary, I read the reports on his statements with great interest—especially when he said that the farmers should have land, that everyone should have three meals a day, that all heads of families should have jobs and that all children should be healthy. I also read a dispatch that told of a poor resident in Lima who approached the pope and, voicing the general feeling, told him that they had no jobs, their children were hungry, they were sick, they had no medicine and their wives became pregnant while suffering from tuberculosis. Very dramatically, with great faith, he appealed to the pope, asking for his support.

I'm convinced that, on his tour through Latin America, the pope must have understood the differences that exist between the abundance and squandering of material goods that can be seen in the rich, developed European consumer societies—in such splendid cities as Rome, Paris, London, Amsterdam and Madrid—and the frightful, massive poverty that you spoke of, that he found in the Latin American cities and countryside, where hundreds of millions of people lack even the most basic means of livelihood. I was interested in those statements, and I sent for all of his speeches, because I wanted to know what the head of the Church thought about these problems, which I believe are of tremendous importance. I admit that the concern expressed by the pope pleased me.

I mean to study all that material, and I'll be able to talk about all those topics more fully in political terms in the future. I don't want to make a superficial judgment. In any case, when I approach those problems, I'll do so from a political point of view. Naturally, I wouldn't think of doing this theologically.

• • •

It was nearly 11:00 P.M. when we finished our work. The Commander accepted an invitation to come over to the house where we were staying and share our dinner of corn *canjiquinha* with pork chops and loin of pork, which my mother made, and shrimp *bobó*, that I prepared. Some other friends were there too—around 15 people in all: Cubans, Brazilians, Argentines and Chileans. During the relaxed conversation, especially on the similarities between cooking in Cuba and Minas Gerais, Fidel Castro chose, among other drinks, to keep a small glass of Velho Barreiro—that I'd brought from Brazil—by him. When dessert time came, Dona Stella's "husband-catcher," that some call ambrosia, was highly praised. The Commander asked for the recipe, and she sent him a plate of the dessert the next day.

Four

T HE fourth and last part of the interview took place on Sunday, May 26, 1985. I got to the office a little before 7:00 P.M. The Cuban leader gave me a memento, a photocopy of the page on which his picture appeared in the yearbook the year he was graduated from the Jesuits' Colegio de Belén. Under the photo of the beardless 18-year-old was the following commentary:

FIDEL CASTRO RUZ
(1942–45)
He distinguished himself in all subjects related to Letters. A top student and member of the congregation, he was also an outstanding athlete, always courageously and proudly defending the School's colors. He has won the admiration and affection of all. We are sure that, after his law studies, he will make a brilliant name for himself. Fidel has what it takes and will make something of his life.

I asked the first question in our last work session.

BETTO – Commander, we're beginning our fourth talk on religion now, on a bright, sunny Sunday evening in Havana.

Yesterday, at the end of our talk, you said that you were interested in learning in depth, in detail, about the speeches that Pope John Paul II gave on his last trip to South America.

In recent months, the world press has speculated on the possi-

261

bility of a meeting between John Paul II and yourself. *Trenta Giorni* magazine, the unofficial organ of the new right wing within the Church in Italy, has even published a photo of you and another of the pope on its cover and speculated a bit on that possibility.

I'd like to ask you, first, if there's anything concrete regarding an invitation for the pope to visit Cuba, and, second, if the possibility of the meeting arises, what you'd like to tell John Paul II.

CASTRO – It's true that, for some time, there has been talk about the possibility of the pope's visiting Cuba. Pope John Paul II is known to be a very active man, one who's traveled a lot and visited many countries. I think that the pope's many trips to different countries and his contacts with the crowds are something new and unusual.

The pope has a dual function; he's the head of the Church and also the head of the Vatican City state. In a way, his activities are also political, not only pastoral. As a politician, I'd say that I'm especially interested in observing his capacity for political action— that is, his capacity to travel around the world and get in contact with the people. From the political point of view, I think that that's one of this pope's virtues. I also think that, from the religious point of view and from the point of view of the Church as a doctrine, as a religious creed, the pope's activities and contacts with the people must unquestionably be very important. But, as I already told you, I don't want to pass judgment in this field.

Limiting myself to strictly political considerations, I must acknowledge that this pope is an outstanding politician, because of his activities, trips and contacts with the masses. We revolutionaries meet with the masses, speak with the masses and convey messages to them, but it's a new thing for the head of the Catholic Church to do this.

Within this context, there has been talk of the possibility of the pope's visiting Cuba, but there's absolutely nothing concrete in this regard. I recall that, when the pope visited Mexico one time—

BETTO – On the occasion of the Episcopal Conference that was held in Puebla, in early 1979.

CASTRO – Yes, I think it was around that date. On going back to Rome, he had to make a stopover. We asked him to stop over in Cuba, but the Cuban-born émigrés in Miami also asked him to stop over there. And, in that situation, the pope decided not to stop over in either Havana or Miami; he went to the Bahamas, where there must be very few Catholics, because, since it is a former British colony, the main religion there is probably Protestant.

The possibility of a contact with us existed at that time. I must say that I didn't feel entirely satisfied with that decision, since I consider that this is the Cuban nation, that the Cuban nation is here and that the people in Miami abandoned the Cuban nation to become U.S. citizens, most of them. I thought—logically, I believe —that a visit to Miami wouldn't be a visit to Cuba; it would be a visit to the United States and to those who think and feel as U.S. citizens. That's where all those people are—the ones who engaged in torture and perpetrated other horrible crimes during Batista's time and managed to escape; all the embezzlers and thieves who stole from our country; the overwhelming majority of the ones who exploited this country or deserted their country. I'm not saying that all of the émigrés in Miami are former landowners, henchmen from the time of Batista or thieves and embezzlers; but all of the henchmen, embezzlers and thieves who were able to escape are there.

There's also a mass of the middle strata—doctors, teachers, administrators, engineers and even some skilled workers who opted for the real or illusory material benefits that they could get there, in the United States. You can't fail to recognize that it's the richest, most developed country in the world—and, logically, is much richer than Cuba. Its wealth is badly distributed, but there's more of it. Our wealth is more evenly distributed, but there's less of it.

There are some very important social aspects: citizens in this country are safe in their homes; there's no danger of their being thrown into the street; the help they can get from society is guaranteed—their pensions and all that—and their children's education and their own and their families' health is guaranteed. They can't get all that there, but many people think about how much money they'll make, about buying a cheap secondhand car and about some of the other material advantages they can get.

Some people actually decided to go to the United States for reasons of that kind. I already told you that there were even mothers who were deceived; they were told that we were going to take away their parental authority, etc., and they left or sent their children ahead and then went to join them in the United States.

Unfortunately, in all too many cases, those sons and daughters ended up as criminals, prostitutes, gamblers and drug addicts.

Also, when we took steps against gambling, many of the people who made a living from that activity went to the United States, which welcomed them with open arms. Others who lived off the exploitation of women, who ran brothels, also decided to go there, and the United States welcomed them too with open arms. Still other people who engaged in the drug traffic and other activities that were eradicated by the Revolution also went to the United States.

Also (and I must say this with the same honesty) a large number of *lumpen* elements went to the United States: people who weren't working and didn't want to work, people who were sworn enemies of work and who, posing as dissidents—not that they were political dissidents; they simply took cover behind that very profitable, well-paid label; and, logically, they were definitely out of step with the Revolution, that dignified work and in which work became an essential part of life—went to the United States to live as parasites. Some were put to work for the CIA; others were recruited for other activities. Of course, we don't classify all the people who are there under the same heading, but, in essence, they didn't represent the Cuban nation; the Cuban nation is represented by those who stayed here, struggled, fought, defended their country and worked for its development and to solve the material and social problems that had accumulated for centuries.

Frankly, I didn't like it when, on that occasion, the pope didn't make even a modest stopover in our country, but it didn't prejudice me against repeating the invitation that he visit Cuba.

Those days have been left behind, though, and these are new circumstances. From some of the recent questions the pope has been asked and from his answers, some interest in having contact with our people may be inferred.

What do I think about this? Because of what the pope and Cuba stand for, such a visit shouldn't be improvised. I don't believe it should be just another visit to another country, since Cuba is a state that's struggling for social justice; a state that's struggling against imperialism; a revolutionary, Socialist country that is faced with very different circumstances than the rest of the Latin American countries.

Of course, I should begin by telling you that we feel honored by any interest the pope may have in visiting our country—that's beyond question. I would also consider it a courageous action, because you shouldn't think that all heads of state or all politicians dare to visit Cuba; they have to take the opinion of the United States into account, and many of them do. They fear economic and political reprisals; they fear the displeasure of the United States, either because they need some of its assistance or credit from the World Bank or the Inter-American Development Bank or because they have to negotiate with the International Monetary Fund, etc. I know that there are many people who, while morally supporting Cuba's activities, have to take all those interests into consideration before making the near-heroic decision of coming to Cuba. In fact, visiting Cuba has become an expression of independence. Undoubtedly, the Vatican is an institution or state with a high concept of independence; this doesn't mean, however, that we fail to appreciate the courage implied by a visit to our country.

Nevertheless, we feel that such a visit should take place in the most favorable conditions so it may be useful, both for the Church and what it stands for and for our country and what it stands for. I'm sure that a visit by the pope would be useful and positive for the Church and for Cuba, and I also think it would be useful for the Third World in general. It would be useful for all countries in many fields, but the conditions for that meeting must be appropriate and favorable.

We keep in contact with the Vatican—in fact, we have very good diplomatic relations. I already told you about how, in the early years of the Revolution, a papal Nuncio helped to sort out the difficulties that had arisen with the Catholic Church. I usually send a lot of documents that are important in economic and social terms and deal with Third World problems to other governments, to the heads of state of the other Third World and industrialized countries—with some exceptions in both cases, since, for instance, I don't generally send documents to the apartheid government in South Africa, to Pinochet's government or to a few others of that type. I do send them to the rest of the governments, though—for instance, the documents related to my speech at the United Nations after the Sixth Summit Conference of Non-Aligned Countries, the report on the international economic crisis and its impact on the Third World that was presented in New Delhi in 1983, and some other documents in which I analyzed the foreign debt and the economic and social tragedy of the Latin American and other Third World countries. Of course, I've always sent them to the Holy See, and now I do so with greater interest after having examined the pope's statements that I talked to you about.

Thus, I believe—and I think the Vatican will agree on this— that the pope's visit to Cuba shouldn't take place until the minimal conditions are guaranteed for it to be a useful and fruitful meeting, both for the Church and for our country, since this is a very important period.

A visit by the pope shouldn't be just a matter of protocol. Undoubtedly, we would discuss everything that the pope is interested in regarding the Church in Cuba, the Catholics in Cuba. I'm sure he'd be interested in this topic. He'd also be interested in having contacts with our revolutionary people and getting to know them. On our part, I'd say that our country's main interest would be related to an analysis of the issues that are of great importance for the underdeveloped nations of Latin America, Asia and Africa —all the issues that affect our poor world, that is exploited and plundered by the industrialized capitalist nations—issues that affect billions of people. Of course, a meeting with the pope in our country would also take up matters that are of great interest to all mankind, such as the ones related to the arms race and peace.

Cuba is a Third World country, a developing country, a revolutionary country and also a Socialist country.

BETTO – And a country subjected to a blockade.

CASTRO – I indicated just those four categories—two of which are quite similar, since revolutionary countries and Socialist countries have a common connotation—because I didn't want to get involved in other aspects and introduce the fact that Cuba is resolutely fighting for its independence, its liberation and its very survival against the blockade and a few other things.

So, in view of all these things—especially peace—I think that a dialogue with the pope could be very useful, fruitful, interesting and serious. Also, in view of my respect for the Vatican, the Holy See and the Catholic Church—for I don't underestimate it at all—I believe that, under such circumstances, a visit by the pope to our country would have maximum implications, and such a visit is something I consider possible. Naturally, I'm analyzing and offering opinions about what I think may also be the view of the Vatican. I believe that its leaders may have thought about this, and that, in due time, they too will analyze and express their points of view on this matter.

Nothing concrete has been decided so far, though I can reiterate my belief that such an exchange, under those circumstances, would be useful. For instance, I think that the topic of peace is important, not because we are of importance with regard to peace, but rather because we have very clear ideas about how important it is for the world to seek peace. I believe it is also very important for the Church, since, if the catastrophe of a world war is unleashed again, the Church will most probably lose its flock and the flock will lose its shepherds, and this is valid not only for one church but for all churches in the world, since what is really being discussed now is whether or not mankind can survive a thermonuclear war.

I think we can all contribute in one way or another to prevent that catastrophe. I believe the Church can exert a lot of influence to prevent it, and I believe that we, with our knowledge, our information, our experience, our concepts and our points of view, could make a modest contribution toward preventing it too.

With this, I think I've answered both aspects of your question about whether anything concrete had been decided about the visit and the topics that might be discussed. The pope would also have to be asked what he'd like to discuss, though I imagine that he would be interested in all of these matters and would be especially interested in issues related to the relations between the Church and state in a country where a thoroughgoing revolution has taken place—something that may take place in many other Third World countries as well.

BETTO – Now, I'd like to hear your views on somebody else, somebody much more important, much more universal and also much more discussed and much more loved than the pope. What are your views on Jesus Christ the person?

CASTRO – Well, I've already told you the story of my education and my contacts with religion, with the Church. Jesus Christ was one of the most familiar names to me, practically ever since I can remember—at home, at school and throughout my childhood and adolescence. Since then, in my revolutionary life—even though, as I told you, I never really acquired religious faith—all my efforts, my attention and my life were devoted to the development of a political faith, which I reached through my own convictions. I couldn't really develop a religious concept on my own, but I did develop political and revolutionary convictions in that way, and I never saw any contradiction in the political and revolutionary sphere between the ideas I upheld and the idea of that symbol, that extraordinary figure that had been so familiar to me ever since I could remember. Rather, I concentrated on the revolutionary aspects of Christian doctrine and Christ's thinking. Throughout the years, I have had several opportunities to express the coherence that exists between Christian and revolutionary thought.

I've cited many examples; sometimes I've used Christ's words: "It is easier for a camel to go through the eye of a needle, than for a rich man to enter into the kingdom of God." I've heard various people, including a priest, say that Christ wasn't referring to the small needle we know now, because it's impossible for a camel to go through the eye of that kind of a needle. Rather, it meant something else; it had to be interpreted differently.

BETTO – Some Biblical scholars take it to mean the narrow corners in Jerusalem, Palestine and the heart of Beirut, for it was very difficult for the camels to turn those corners. Why doesn't anybody question how difficult it is for a rich man to enter the kingdom of heaven? That's unquestionable. Commander, from the theological point of view, it doesn't mean that Jesus discriminated against the rich; it means that Jesus opted for the poor. That is, in a society characterized by social inequalities, God decided to assume the likeness of Jesus; He could have been born in Rome, to a family of emperors; He could have been born to a Jewish landowners' family; He could have been born to the middle strata of parishioners. Instead, He chose to be born among the poor, as the son of a carpenter—one who certainly worked on the construction of the Brasília of his time, the city of Tiberias, built as a tribute to Emperor Tiberius Caesar, in whose reign Jesus lived. It's interesting that Tiberias is on the banks of the Lake of Gennesaret, where Jesus spent most of his life and carried out most of his activities. In the Gospels, he doesn't visit that city even once.

So, what do we say? We say that Jesus unconditionally opted for the poor. He spoke to everyone, both rich and poor, but from a specific social stand, from the social stand of the interests of the poor. He didn't speak in a neutral, universalist, abstract way; rather, He reflected the interests of the oppressed strata of the times. If a rich man wanted to have a place next to Jesus, he had to opt for the poor. There isn't a single example in all the Gospels of Jesus' welcoming a rich man beside Him without first making him commit himself to help the poor.

I can cite three examples: first, that of a rich young man who was a saint because he observed all the Commandments, but, in the end, Jesus said that the man had to do one more thing: go and sell what he had, and give to the poor before he could follow Him. I believe that many priests today would say, "Look: if you observe all the Commandments, come with us; stay here next to us; and, in time, you'll improve." But, since Jesus was a little more radical than we are, He told the man, "You go honor your commitment to the poor and then come."

The second example is that of the rich man whose home Jesus visited. Jesus had no prejudices, but he was consistent; so he went to Zacchaeus' home not to praise his ceramics, which may have come from Persia, or his Egyptian figurines, but rather to tell him that he was a thief because he'd stolen from the poor. And Zacchaeus, who wanted to be at peace with Him, said, "Behold, Lord, the half of my goods I give to the poor; and if I have taken any thing from any man by false accusation, I restore him fourfold." That is, the practice of justice was the basic requirement for following Jesus.

The third example is the preaching of John the Baptist, who prepared for Jesus' coming. His preaching began with the practice of justice. The people who wanted to be converted didn't ask what they should believe; they asked what they should do, and John replied, "He that hath two coats, let him impart to him that hath none; and he that hath meat, let him do likewise."

The universality of Jesus' preaching must also be explained; it is a universality that derives from an option and a very specific social and political stand: the cause of the poor.

CASTRO – I've been listening to you with great interest, because there's a lot of substance in what you've said. However, I could make a mathematical objection: a rich man could never give back four times what he'd stolen, because everything a rich man has must have been stolen. If he didn't steal it himself, it must have been stolen by his parents or grandparents, so it's impossible —if everything he has is stolen—for him to return fourfold what he's stolen, for he'd probably have to steal four times as much again to keep that promise.

BETTO – You're repeating something that St. Ambrose said in the early centuries.

CASTRO – I'm glad to have concurred with him.

So, what do I think? It may be a bad translation of the Bible; maybe the translators are to blame, because they didn't take into account the meaning of the eye of a needle. I realize that many of the phrases in the Bible are related to that environment, to the society and customs of the times; but I don't know how this could be proved in this case. Anyway, somebody well versed in religion, somebody well versed in languages, must have interpreted, with quite some grounds, that it was the eye of the needle that everybody knows about in our language, because we don't know of any other, for the people in Spanish-speaking countries don't know the first thing about camels, even though we do have an idea of what camels are.

In any case, I liked the interpretation that the translators gave to that phrase, as I understood it, and I also believe that that interpretation is absolutely in keeping and is consistent with all the other things that Christ preached. First of all, as you said, Christ didn't choose the rich to preach the doctrine; He chose 12 poor and ignorant workers—that is, He chose the proletariat of the times or modest self-employed workers, some of whom were fishermen. They were poor people, very poor, without exception, as you said.

At times, I've referred to Christ's miracles and have said, "Well, Christ multiplied the fish and the loaves to feed the people. That is precisely what we want to do with the Revolution and socialism: multiply the fish and the loaves to feed the people; multiply the schools, teachers, hospitals and doctors; multiply the factories, the fields under cultivation and the jobs; multiply industrial and agricultural productivity; and multiply the research centers and the number of scientific research projects, for the same purpose."

At times, I've referred to the parable of the rich man who employed several workers: he paid some of them one denarius for a full day's work; to others, he paid one denarius for half a day's work; and, to yet others, he paid one denarius for half an afternoon's work. The parable implies a criticism of those who didn't agree with that distribution. I believe that it is, precisely, a Communist formula; it goes beyond what we say in socialism, because, in socialism, each should be paid according to his capacity and work, while the Communist formula is to give to each according to his needs. To pay a denarius to each one who worked that day implies a distribution more in keeping with needs, a typically Communist formula.

Also, I believe that many of the passages of the preachings of Christ, such as the Sermon on the Mount, cannot be given any interpretation other than what you call the option for the poor. When Christ says, "Blessed are the poor in spirit: for theirs is the kingdom of heaven. Blessed are they that mourn: for they shall be comforted. Blessed are the meek: for they shall inherit the earth. Blessed are they which do hunger and thirst after righteousness: for they shall be filled," it is obvious that Christ didn't offer the kingdom of heaven to the rich; He really offered it to the poor, and I don't think that the preaching of Christ is also a case of mistaken translation or interpretation. I believe that Karl Marx could have subscribed to the Sermon on the Mount.

BETTO – In St. Luke's version, not only are the poor blessed, but the rich are damned.

CASTRO – I don't know if the phrase is in any of the versions of that preaching. You say that it's St. Luke's version. The one I recall doesn't damn the rich.

BETTO – That's St. Matthew's which is better known.

CASTRO – Maybe that's the one that was more convenient at the time, to bring us up in a more conservative spirit. You said something profound: that the difficulty lies in understanding how a rich man can enter the kingdom of heaven, if you consider many of the things that go with the mentality of the rich: insensitivity, selfishness, lack of solidarity and even the sins of the rich in all spheres. I really believe that what a rich man had to do to be a good Christian and reach the kingdom of heaven was expressed clearly. It was stated repeatedly in Christ's preachings.

You should also take into consideration that we read many books of history and literature—some written by laymen, and others, by clergymen—that reflected the martyrdom of the Christians in the early centuries. Everybody's had the opportunity to learn about those events, and I think that one of the things the Church felt most proud of during the years when I was a student —I remember this clearly—was the martyrology of the early years and throughout the history of the Church.

I think that there is no doubt—it's not just a matter of interpretation—that Christianity was the religion of the slaves, of the oppressed and of the poor, who lived in the catacombs, were subjected to the most terrible punishments, were taken to the circus to be fed to the lions and other animals, and were subjected to all kinds of persecution and repression for centuries. The Roman Empire considered that doctrine to be revolutionary and subjected its adherents to the most savage harassment—which I always related, later on, to the history of the Communists, because, ever since communism was established as a political and revolutionary doctrine, the Communists have also been subjected to savage harassment, torture and other crimes. The great historic truth is that the Communist movement also has its martyrology in its struggles to change an unfair social system. Like the early Christians, the Communists too were savagely slandered and cruelly repressed everywhere.

We know from history—quite recent history—what happened after the Paris Commune, the French workers' attempt to establish socialism in their homeland at the end of the last century. Thick volumes have been written, with exact data, about the heroism of those people and of the thousands of Communards who were tortured and murdered by the bourgeoisie and the oppressing classes with the support of the German Empire, which had just invaded France.

History also records the many Communists, Socialists, fighters and other members of the left wing who were shot in Spain after the Civil War and what happened in Nazi Germany and in all the European countries that were occupied by the Nazis —who, applying unfair, despicable criteria regarding their allegedly superior race; accusations; and irrational hatred (which I believe stemmed from shameful prejudices nurtured throughout history), murdered millions of Jews and had anybody who was at all "tainted" with communism imprisoned, tortured and shot. Very few of the Communists who fell into the Nazis' hands survived— very few—and they fought and died with great heroism.

The Nazis murdered millions of people—including old people, women and children—in the Soviet Union, simply because they were citizens of a Socialist country. And the Nazis weren't the only ones who killed Communists in Europe; the capitalists' henchmen have tortured and killed Communists, and left-wing men and women have been murdered in South Africa, South

Korea, Vietnam, Chile, Argentina, Paraguay, Guatemala, El Salvador, the Sudan, Indonesia and Cuba itself before the Revolution— in dozens of countries, wherever, in the past 150 years, the ruling and exploiting classes feared they would lose their privileges, just as they murdered Christians in the early centuries of our era.

I believe a comparison can be made between the persecution of religious ideas (that were also, essentially, the political ideas of the slaves, the oppressed in Rome) and the systematic, brutal persecution in modern times of those who are the bearers of political ideas—the workers and farmers, embodied by the Communists. If there was ever a name that the reactionaries hated more than "Communist," it was "Christian," in another time.

BETTO – I lost a comrade of the Dominican Order, Frei Tito, who died in exile as a result of the terrible torture he had been subjected to in Brazil and is now considered a symbol of the victims of torture, because the torturers affected his mind, and in France he saw torturers everywhere, until he hanged himself, after going through agonies, especially because he remained silent under the torture. The torturers told him, "We're not going to kill you; as long as you live, you'll pay the price of your silence."

I wanted to give you a piece of information: martyrologies have been published about the martyrs in Central America and Latin America under the military dictatorships. They are our popular saints. In Brazil, there was even a worker whose name—by coincidence—was Santo (St.) Díaz. He was murdered while organizing a strike, and there are images of him in many churches.

CASTRO – You'd already told me about the Dominican friar who was tortured and withstood all his sufferings with tremendous courage.

These things happen not only in the countries of Europe, Latin America and the Third World but also in the United States itself; we shouldn't forget the McCarthy period, with its harassment of Communists, who couldn't find work; were excluded from nearly all jobs and all kinds of other activities; were arrested, repressed, persecuted and slandered; and, in some cases, were even sent to the electric chair—just because they were Communists. We shouldn't forget that May Day was established in response to the assassination of workers in Chicago who went on strike to defend their class interests. In more recent years, all the politically aware were shaken by the murder of the Rosenbergs.

In that regard, I have always noted great similarities between the repression to which modern revolutionaries are subjected and that of the primitive Christians. I see no difference between the actions of the oppressors in that stage of history and in this one; they're just different moments in the development of human society, one during slavery and the other during capitalism. I can't find any contradiction between those preachings, which became so strongly rooted at that time, and our present preachings. Therefore, I feel great fellow feeling for those ideas, those preachings, and admiration for the actions and history of those Christians, in which I've observed similarities with the actions of the Communists of our times. I saw it, I see it, and I will continue to see it. On observing the efforts of your confreres, your own work, struggles and lectures, and those of many others like you in the Americas, I am even more convinced of this.

BETTO – You once said that he who becomes estranged from the poor becomes estranged from Christ. I don't know if you were aware that that statement not only is very famous but, I would say, is the basis of Liberation Theology. Moreover, in that statement, you agreed with John Paul II in his encyclical *Laborem Exercens*, which deals with human work, in which he reaffirmed that loyalty to the Church of Christ was borne out by a commitment to the poor.

CASTRO – I said that around 25, maybe 26, years ago. I remember that, in the early years of the Revolution, when the difficulties I told you about arose—when the privileged classes wanted to use the Church against the Revolution—I referred to these problems and to Christian preachings several times. The speeches are there somewhere. On one occasion, I made a statement that I can repeat and ratify today. It's the one you mentioned: "He who betrays the poor betrays Christ."

BETTO – Well, Commander, now I'd like to move on to another question.

Within the Communist movement, some people have traditionally used Marx's statement—contained in his *Contribution to the Critique of Hegel's Philosophy of Right*—that "religion is the opiate of the people" and turned that phrase into a definitive, absolute, metaphysical dogma, above and beyond any dialectics.

In October 1980, for the first time in history, a revolutionary party in power—the Sandinista National Liberation Front—issued a document on religion in which that affirmation is criticized as an absolute principle. The Sandinistas' statement reads, "Some authors have asserted that religion is a mechanism for the alienation of man which serves to justify the exploitation of one class by another. Undoubtedly, this affirmation is of historic value, to the extent to which, in different historical eras, religion has served as a theoretical prop for political domination. Suffice it to recall the role played by missionaries in the process of the domination and colonization of the Indians in our country. We Sandinistas, however, state that our experience shows that, when Christians, relying on their faith, can respond to the needs of the people and history, their belief stimulates their revolutionary militancy. Our experience shows us that a person can be both a believer and, at the same time, a consistent revolutionary and that there is no insurmountable contradiction between the two."

Commander, I ask you: do you think that religion is the opiate of the people?

CASTRO – Yesterday, I talked with you at length about the historic circumstances in which socialism, the Socialist movement and the ideology of scientific socialism, of Marxism-Leninism, emerged and how, in that society that was divided in classes—a society of cruel and inhuman exploitation, in which the Church and religion had been used as a tool for domination, exploitation and oppression for centuries—tendencies had emerged and severe criticism, justified criticism, had been leveled at the Church and even at religion itself. Place yourself in the position of a revolutionary who becomes aware of that world and wants to change it. Then imagine the civil institutions, the landowners, the nobles, the bourgeoisie, the rich, the big businessmen and the Church itself, all of them bound and determined to prevent social change. The most logical thing, ever since religion also began to be used as a tool for domination, was for the revolutionaries to have an anticlerical reaction and even an antireligious reaction, and I can fully understand the circumstances in which that statement was made.

I believe, however, that, when Marx established the International Workingmen's Association, there were many Christians in that First International; I believe that there were many Christians among those who fought and died in the Paris Commune, and nowhere does Marx make any statements excluding those Christians from the historic mission of advancing the social revolution.

If we go a little farther ahead and recall all the discussions that took place after the program of the Bolshevik Party, which Lenin founded, was drawn up, there isn't a single word that excluded Christians from the Party; the main prerequisite for joining was acceptance of the Party program. That is, it is a phrase, a motto, a statement of historic value that was entirely justified at a given moment.

There may even be circumstances in the present situation in which it's an expression of reality. Wherever the Catholic hierarchy or the hierarchy of any other church is closely associated with imperialism, neocolonialism, the exploitation of nations and of men, and repression, it shouldn't astonish you if, in that specific country, somebody were to repeat the phrase that religion is the opiate of the people, just as it's perfectly understandable that the Nicaraguans, basing themselves on their experience and on the position taken by the Nicaraguan religious people, have reached the conclusion—which, in my opinion, is also justified—that, basing themselves on their faith, believers can take a revolutionary stand and that there need not be any contradiction between their being believers and revolutionaries. As I see it, that phrase cannot be, nor is it, a dogma or an absolute truth; it is a truth in specific historical conditions. Moreover, I believe that this conclusion is perfectly in keeping with dialectics and Marxism.

I believe that, from the political point of view, religion is not, in itself, an opiate or a miraculous remedy. It may become an opiate or a wonderful cure if it is used or applied to defend oppressors and exploiters or the oppressed and the exploited, depending on the approach adopted toward the political, social or material problems of the human beings who, aside from theology or religious belief, are born and must live in this world.

From a strictly political point of view—and I think I know something about politics—I believe that it is possible for Christians to be Marxists as well, and to work together with Marxist Communists to transform the world. The important thing is that, in both cases, they be honest revolutionaries who want to end the exploitation of man by man and to struggle for a fair distribution of social wealth, equality, fraternity and the dignity of all human beings—that is, that they be the standard-bearers of the most advanced political, economic and social ideas, even though, in the case of the Christians, their starting point is a religious concept.

BETTO – Commander, is love a revolutionary requirement?

CASTRO – Of course, in the broadest sense of the term. Socially speaking, what is solidarity? What is the spirit of fraternity?

If we go back to the first great social revolution—not the first Socialist revolution, but the first great social revolution in the last few centuries: the French Revolution—it had a three-word slogan: Liberty, equality, fraternity. Liberty—as I told you—was interpreted in a restricted way. It meant liberty for the bourgeoisie, for the whites; it didn't mean liberty for the black slaves. After they'd spread their ideas throughout the world, the French revolutionaries even sent armies to Haiti to crush the rebellion of the slaves who wanted liberty. After the independence of the United States, which had taken place before that, the slavery of blacks continued, as did the extermination of the Indians and all the other atrocities. Therefore, the French Revolution confined itself to liberty for the bourgeoisie and whites, and there was no equality at all, no matter how much philosophizing or talk there was about alleged equality in a society that was divided in classes. The presumed equality between a multimillionaire and a beggar in New York or in any other place in the United States or between a millionaire and a person who doesn't have a job in the United States could be defined as a metaphysical equality. I can't see it any other way, and I don't think there's any fraternity between the U.S. millionaires and beggars, blacks who are discriminated against, the unemployed and waifs. That is sheer fantasy. I believe that only now, with socialism, can the concept of true liberty—full liberty— equality and fraternity exist. I think that the precept of loving thy neighbor, of which the Church speaks, is very concretely applied and implemented in the human equality, fraternity and solidarity upheld by socialism and in the internationalist spirit.

I believe that the fact that Cubans go to work in other lands as teachers, doctors, engineers, technicians and skilled workers and that tens of thousands—hundreds of thousands—are ready to do this, under the most difficult conditions and, at times, at the cost of their lives, thus showing a supreme spirit of solidarity in loyalty to their principles, expresses the practical application of their respect, consideration and love for their fellow human beings.

Thus, I believe that the Socialist revolution has developed this concept to its highest point and that a Communist society will develop it still more. Socialism doesn't yet uphold full equality—

we've already discussed this, in connection with remuneration. It offers many more real possibilities than capitalism does. In Cuba, for instance, the only ones who used to study were the children of the rich; now, every child—even in the most isolated parts of the country, the children of farmers and workers—has the opportunity to go to the best schools. Every child has a teacher and the opportunity to go to excellent educational institutions and on to the university—to go as far as his talent will take him—and this is a real, objective possibility, not a theoretical or metaphysical one. We have created genuine equal opportunities in our society.

Our system of remuneration for work can't be considered fully equitable, however, for some men are physically stronger than others, some are more talented than others and some are better intellectually endowed than others. In the Socialist system, the Socialist form of distribution—to each according to the amount and quality of his work—isn't yet a form of Communist distribution; that is why, in his *Critique of the Gotha Program,* Marx said that this form didn't transcend the narrow limits of bourgeois law and that Communist society would be even more equitable.

BETTO – Socialist and Communist society also seek the development of man's spiritual life.

CASTRO – Yes, of course; we seek man's broadest material and spiritual development. That is exactly how I've put it when I've spoken about education and culture. You might also add "and man's spiritual development in the religious sense." We make it a principle that all individuals are to have that freedom and opportunity.

Now, let's take fraternity. I think that our society is really fraternal. When we free men from oppression, exploitation and slavery in specific social conditions, we guarantee them not only their freedom but also their honor, dignity and morale—in short, their human condition.

You can't speak of liberty in a society that is divided in classes, where there are terrible inequalities and where the people aren't guaranteed even their human condition. Go ask anybody who lives in a shantytown in Latin America, any black in the United States or any poor person anywhere in the capitalist societies in the world today.

These are my deepest convictions. As I see it, loving thy neighbor means practicing solidarity.

BETTO – Commander, there are two concepts which cause some Christians some difficulty: first, the Marxist concept of class hatred; second, the concept of class struggle. I'd like you to speak a little about this.

CASTRO – The existence of social classes has been a historic reality ever since primitive communism, when men began to accumulate wealth, land and the means for exploiting the work of others. Social classes, which didn't exist in the era of primitive communism, when practically everything was owned in common, emerged as a result of the development of society. After class distinctions came about, we arrived at the societies about which we have the most historical records: Greece and Rome, which have erroneously been taken as the prototypes of democracy.

I remember that we used to be told about Athenian democracy, with the people meeting in the public agora to discuss political problems in a plenary assembly. And we all said, "How marvelous; what a beautiful thing that exemplary direct democracy was that existed in Greece!"

Later came history, historical research; and, when that society was studied in greater depth, it was discovered that only an insignificant minority of the citizens met in the public square. I used to wonder how all the people could meet in the public square if there weren't any microphones or loudspeakers. How could all those people meet to talk things over?

I remember that, when I was a boy, there was a bookkeeper who used to come to my house. He was a cultured man who knew several languages: Spanish, French, Latin, a smattering of Greek, German and English. He was what you might call a scholar. He was friendly to me, and he liked to talk when I came back from school for my vacations. He used to tell me about Demosthenes and Cicero, the great orators of Greece and Rome. He always had an anecdote to tell.

I don't know if it was he or somebody else who told me once that Demosthenes had a speech difficulty—he stammered. As a test of willpower and discipline, he put a small pebble under his tongue when he spoke, and he overcame the problem. He told me stories about the ancient politicians. I was in junior high school and was interested in literature; I even got a collection of Demosthenes' speeches. Some of the speeches survived the Alexandria library fire and the invasions of the "barbarians"—all those historic vicissitudes—and were preserved, or perhaps somebody reconstructed them. I had the speeches of Demosthenes, Cicero and other orators and writers of antiquity. I think that Alvarez—that worker, that Spaniard (he was a Spaniard from Asturias)—aroused my interest in these matters. I remember that I read books about those historic figures very early in my life.

Analyzing it now, I'd say that I don't like that oratory, because it was too rhetorical and grandiloquent. It depended too much on plays on words. Later, I came in contact with the works of many other orators. There must be few great orators in history whose books I haven't read. It was a topic that really interested me. As a result of all my reading, I went on to do exactly the opposite of what those great and famous orators had done. I remember that, later on, I came across Castelar and his wonderful parliamentary speeches. They were marvelous, but Castelar would be a total disaster in any parliament today.

Demosthenes and Cicero too would have enormous problems if they had to come to grips with specifics, to explain the real problems of that society today. But, anyhow, at the time, I admired Athenian democracy and even Rome's, with its Capitol, its senators and all those other figures from the Roman institutions, who seemed models. And, as I told you, later on I discovered that it was just a little group of aristocrats who met in the public square in Greece to make decisions. Under them was a huge mass of citizens who had no rights—I think they were called foreigners—and below them was an even larger mass of slaves. That was Athenian "democracy," which reminds me of today's capitalist "democracy." There were classes, and they were involved in struggle: aristocrats, foreigners and slaves.

Then we studied Rome, which was also a model. Rome really reminds me of the U.S. empire today; they're very alike in all regards—even their Capitols. The United States has a Capitol that's very similar to the one the Romans had. It was copied. It also has its senators, powerful gentlemen who discuss things; and, from time to time, its Caesars are even assassinated. It has military bases, squadrons and forces of intervention all over the world.

BETTO – It even has its Nero, who had a bonfire started in Philadelphia.

CASTRO – Well, if you're referring to what the police did there recently, I'd say they were mini-Neros with official backing.

In other words, there are the armies, the military bases, the squadrons and the legions—of course, they're much more sophisticated—all over the world; the acts of intervention; the aggressive wars; the arms buildup; all the problems that exist in our world today; multimillionaires, beggars and masses of blacks who've been deprived of their rights; and alliances with all the other reactionary governments in the world.

What was there in Rome? The same classes—the patricians, the plebeians and the slaves—and class struggle. Later on, in the Middle Ages, it was the same: the nobles, the bourgeoisie and the serfs. Who can deny that? There was a struggle because there were classes. The bourgeoisie didn't resign themselves to spending their lives stimulating the development of production yet having no rights.

After the French Revolution, we had the bourgeoisie and the proletarians—the ones who owned the means of production and those who simply contributed their labor power—and the middle strata.

Slavery existed during a long period of history. It continued to exist as an official institution up until very recently. When did slavery end in Cuba? If I'm not mistaken, slavery was abolished in Cuba in 1886.

BETTO – The same decade as in Brazil.

CASTRO – In the United States, it was abolished in the last century, in the 1860s, as a result of the Civil War. There are other countries in which it lasted even longer and where people became slaves if they couldn't pay their debts. That was the case in Rome and in Greece, for example. All those things happened.

Neither Marx nor the other Marxists invented the existence of classes and class struggles. They simply analyzed, studied and demonstrated the existence of classes very clearly and went deeply into this phenomenon, into historic reality. They discovered the laws that rule these struggles and the evolution of human society. They didn't invent classes or class struggle, so those things can't be attributed to Marxism. If you were to accuse anyone, you'd have to accuse history, as it is mainly responsible for the problem.

Now, on class hatred. Marxism-Leninism doesn't cause or preach class hatred; it simply says that classes and class struggle exist and that struggles give rise to hatred. It isn't Marxism-Leninism but the existence of classes and class struggle that causes hatred.

What really caused hatred? Man's exploitation, oppression, marginalization and social injustice. That, objectively, is what causes hatred—not Marxism. Marxism has said, "Well, classes exist; class struggle exists, and this causes hatred." It's a question not of preaching class hatred but of explaining a social reality, something that has occurred throughout history. It isn't a call to hatred; rather, it is an explanation of the hatred that exists when people become aware that they are being exploited. I told you my personal history, and I told you that I don't hate those people for the things I went through, even when I went hungry as a child. I'm even glad about it, because it taught me a lesson and prepared me for life. I really don't hate them.

For example, if you analyze revolutionary ideology in Cuba, the ideology of our own Revolution, not one word of hatred was expressed. Moreover, we had a superior thinker, a really superior thinker: Martí. In his *El Presidio Político en Cuba* (Political Prison in Cuba), a document he wrote at the age of 17, in which he told of the hardships he'd endured, and in his allegations against the Spanish republic—a republic that had emerged in Spain and provided rights for the Spaniards but denied them to Cubans; which postulated liberty and democracy in Spain but denied them in Cuba, as was always the case—Martí has some fabulous statements, such as, "Neither the blow of the whip nor the voice of insult nor the clanking of my chains has taught me to hate," "Let me despise you, since I cannot hate anyone." Throughout his life, Martí preached the struggle for independence, for liberation, but he didn't preach hatred of the Spaniards.

Martí's experience shows that it is possible to preach the spirit of struggle and the struggle for independence without preaching hatred of those whom he called his Spanish parents. I assure you that our Revolution is permeated with Martí's ideas. We who are revolutionaries, Socialists and Marxist-Leninists don't preach hatred as a philosophy, the philosophy of hatred. This doesn't mean that we feel any fellow feeling for the oppressive system or that we haven't struggled as hard as we can against it, but I think we have one supreme test, which is that we waged a battle against imperialism; we've suffered from all kinds of acts of aggression and wrongs from imperialism, yet, when a U.S. citizen visits this country, everyone treats him with respect, everyone is considerate, because we don't hate U.S. citizens. What we repudiate and hate is the system. My interpretation—which I think is shared by all other revolutionary Marxists—is that it's a matter not of hating individuals but of hating an iniquitous system of exploitation; it's not hatred of the people.

Martí hated the Spanish system. He encouraged the people to fight against the colonial Spanish system, and many Cubans fought and died on the battlefield with great courage and boldness. However, he didn't speak of hatred of the Spaniards.

What we're preaching is the repudiation, rejection and hatred of the system—hatred of injustice. We're not preaching hatred among men, because, in the final analysis, men are victims of the system. If we have to fight the system, we'll fight the system. If we have to fight the men who represent the system we hate, we'll do so.

I don't think there is any contradiction with Christian teachings, because, if somebody says, "I hate crime" or "I hate injustice, abuses and exploitation," I don't think that would be against Christian teachings. I don't think that denouncing and fighting against crime, injustice, exploitation, abuses and inequalities among men goes against Christian teachings or is in contradiction with religion. Fighting for rights wouldn't be against religion either. Within the logic that I know of religion, defending a just cause wouldn't be in conflict with it. Besides, a few days ago, we talked about biblical history, in which I was told that there were struggles—even in heaven, among the angels—and, if there were struggles in heaven, can we fail to understand that there may be struggles on Earth?

BETTO – Jesus made some very strong charges against the Pharisees and called Herod a fox. What's more, Jesus tells us we must love our enemies—He doesn't say we mustn't have enemies—and there is no greater love for an oppressor than to prevent him from oppressing another.

CASTRO – As you may imagine, I'm not at all against your interpretation of the problem. I was taught that there was a constant struggle between good and evil, and evil had to be punished. Well, I'm not going to say I share that belief. I was taught that those who committed crimes and were responsible for injustice, evil and all those other things that we are fighting against would be punished in hell. Could that be interpreted as an expression of hatred? I'll tell you what I think. I've never felt personal hatred for individuals. It's not that I love my enemies. I don't; I haven't gotten that far. I understand why they are enemies and the extent to which this is due to history, to the laws of history, to the social status of individuals. I understand how many factors predetermined their becoming enemies. There may even be genetic, or biological, explanations. Some individuals are born with hereditary defects or with illnesses. That, too, is a fact. I believe that many criminals are psychopaths. Hitler must have been sick; I can't think of him as sane. I imagine that all those people who sent millions of human beings to the crematories were mentally deranged.

Yes, I hate fascism. I hate Nazism. I hate those despicable methods. I'd even say that it was correct to punish those who were responsible. They had to be punished. They had to be imprisoned or sent before a firing squad, because they inflicted terrible harm on mankind. But I've also said that, when we punish a person who has blood on his hands, or even when we punish a counter-revolutionary, a traitor to the Revolution, we don't do it for the sake of revenge. I've said this many times. There's no sense to revenge. On whom are you taking revenge? History? The society that engendered those monsters? The illness that must have induced those individuals to do terrible things? What are you avenging? So we haven't taken revenge on anybody. I've fought and struggled a lot throughout the years, yet I can't say that there was a feeling of hatred or revenge against individuals here. We've seen that the individual was often the result of a series of situations and circumstances and that a large proportion of his conduct was predetermined.

I remember that, when I was in high school, I was taught the basics of philosophy, and one of the things we debated was whether the individual was predetermined to do certain things or whether he was fully aware of the seriousness of his actions and the harm he was doing—and, consequently, was entirely responsible for his deeds. There was a lot of discussion about individual responsibility. I think that, in those days, the teachers at the Jesuit school favored the theory that nothing was predetermined in the individual and that everything was his personal responsibility. I believe that often it's a combination of the two: an important factor predetermines people's conduct, and there are also factors of responsibility and guilt in men—except for some cases of mental illness, for some people who are mentally ill kill. It's very difficult to hold such people responsible for their actions. Some individuals are taught an ideology that makes them act in a certain way, and their attitude has been predetermined to a certain extent.

For us—or, at least, for me—in the case of any counterrevolutionary, reactionary activity by individuals who are sound of mind or whom we suppose to be sound of mind, when it has become necessary to punish a saboteur, a traitor or a murderer, we have done so not in a spirit of hatred or revenge but out of the need to defend our society, to insure the survival of the Revolution, because of all the justice, well-being and benefits for the people it entails. That's how I view this problem.

Then, if you refer to these concepts; to Martí's concepts, for example; to his teachings and his history—and he was a fighter, a great fighter, a brilliant and noble fighter—you'll see he never spoke of hatred. He never said, "Let's hate the Spaniards who oppress us"; instead, he always said, "Let's fight the Spaniards with all our might, but let's not hate them. The struggle isn't against the Spaniards but against the system." This lies at the heart of our political thinking. Moreover, I believe that Marx didn't hate individuals and that Lenin didn't hate any either—not even the czar. I think that Lenin hated the imperial czarist system, the system of exploitation by the landowners and the bourgeois; and I think that Engels hated the system. They didn't preach hatred of men; they preached hatred of the system. That is what the criteria and principles of class struggle mean—and also what "class hatred" means: not the hatred of men but the hatred of a class system, which isn't the same thing.

BETTO – Commander, the people in some Christian environments admire the Cuban Revolution's social and economic achievements, its achievements in education and health care, but say there's no democracy in Cuba—as there is in the United States and Western Europe, where people can vote in an election and change their government. What would you say to this? Is there or isn't there democracy in Cuba?

CASTRO – We could talk about this for a long time, and I think our interview is rather long already. I don't want to take too much of your time or try the patience of the people who will read this interview. I think that all that alleged democracy is nothing but a fraud, and I mean this literally.

I was asked that question not long ago.

BETTO – By whom?

CASTRO – A fellow from the United States—rather, there were two interviewers, a congressman and a professor, who wanted to publish some articles and a book. He said that some people thought I was a cruel dictator. He said some other things too.

Just imagine! What could I say? I had to resort to logic. I analyzed what a dictator was. In the first place, I said, "It's somebody who makes one-man decisions, who governs by decree." And I said, "Then you could accuse Reagan of being a dictator." With all due respect, I went on and said, "You could even accuse the pope of being a dictator, because the pope governs by decree; he makes decisions concerning the appointment of ambassadors, cardinals and bishops; they're all the pope's unilateral decisions, and nobody has thought of saying that the pope's a dictator." I've heard criticism of the Church's inner system, its inner workings, but I've never heard anybody say the pope is a dictator.

I explained about Cuba, that I didn't appoint Ministers, ambassadors or anybody else—not even the least important employee in this country—didn't make unilateral, individualistic decisions; and didn't govern by decree. I explained that we had a collective leadership—I've spoken to you about this. We've always discussed all basic problems collectively, right from the beginning, ever since our Movement was founded. And I added, "What I do have is the right to speak and to present my arguments in the Central Committee, the Political Bureau, the Executive Committee of the Council of Ministers and the National Assembly, and I really don't want any other rights." I didn't deny that I had authority and prestige, just as many other comrades have authority and prestige in the Party and among the people, and their views carry weight in our country. Other people listen to them, and I'm the first to do so. I like to listen to others and take their views into consideration.

After explaining all this, I said, "Well, then, and what is cruelty?" I told them that men who have devoted their lives to the struggle against injustice, crime, abuse, inequality, hunger and poverty and to the struggle to save the lives of children and the sick, to find jobs for all the workers and to provide food for every family—men who have devoted their lives to this couldn't be cruel. I asked, "What is it that's cruel? The capitalist system, that's responsible for so much poverty and calamity; capitalist selfishness; and capitalist exploitation."

Imperialism is cruel; it has caused the deaths of millions of people. How many were killed in World War I? Somebody said 14, 18 or 20 million. How many were killed in World War II? Over 50 million. And who promoted those deaths and those catastrophes? In addition to the dead, there are the maimed, the blinded, the crippled and countless other victims. How many were orphaned, how much property was destroyed and how much human labor was wiped off the face of the Earth? Who was to blame for that? The imperialist system, the capitalist system, and the struggle for markets and colonies in World Wars I and II. They were responsible for those tens of millions of deaths.

Who is cruel, then? Those who struggle for peace? Those who struggle to put an end to so much misery, so much poverty and so much exploitation? Those who struggle against the system? Or is it the system and those who support and uphold it? Who are the cruel ones? The U.S. troops killed millions of human beings in Vietnam and—as I said before—dropped more bombs on that small country, which was fighting for its independence, than were used in World War II. Isn't that cruel? Can that system be called democratic?

I also explained that Reagan won an election in which barely half of the U.S. population voted. He was elected by 30 percent of the voters in that alleged democracy. And Reagan has powers that not even the Roman emperors had, because a Roman emperor, a madman like Nero, could cause Rome to be set on fire—I don't know if Suetonius told the truth or not, if it's a historic fact or if it was a fable made up by a historian who said that Nero set Rome on fire and then played the lyre. It seems to be true that all of the emperors joined in those games at the circus, where—according to all the historians—they made gladiators kill each other or had Christians devoured by the lions. These modern emperors have more power than the earlier ones; Reagan could set off a nuclear conflagration that would be much worse than what may have happened in Rome under Nero.

A nuclear holocaust may incinerate Catholics, Buddhists, Muslims and Hindus; the followers of Confucius, Deng Xiaoping and Mao Zedong in China; Christians, Protestants and Catholics; the rich and the poor, multimillionaires and beggars; the young and the old, children and the elderly; men and women; farmers and landowners; workers and industrialists; businessmen and proletarians; and intellectuals and professionals. The whole world may disappear in a nuclear holocaust, though I don't believe that Reagan would have time to play the lyre while the world was going up in smoke, for scientists have already determined that all life would be wiped off the face of the Earth in a matter of minutes, hours, days or even months—with the possible sole exception of certain insects that can withstand nuclear radiation better. They say that cockroaches have great resistance. So, Reagan could turn this world into a world of cockroaches. He has a locked briefcase in which he keeps nuclear codes, and it's said that, if he issues a coded order, a nuclear war would start. So the emperors of our times have much more power than did the emperors of the past. And that's what they call a democracy, and it isn't considered cruel. All those countries that you've mentioned—England, West Germany, Italy, Spain and all the others—which praise democracy so highly are also members of NATO and share in that unbelievable notion. And they're called democracies. It's democracy characterized by unemployment: Spain has 3 million unemployed; France has 3 million; England, 3 million; and Germany, 2.5 million. There's unemployment in all those countries.

But I don't want to go into details. I admit that progress has been made and that Europe isn't the same now as it was during the Middle Ages—it's not the Europe of the Conquests, the Europe that burned religious dissenters alive; it's no longer the Europe of colonial times. It's the Europe of neocolonialism, of course; it's the Europe of the imperialist system. But I'm ready to admit there's been some progress. I don't know what they're so proud of, though; I don't know if they take pride in the progress that was made some years ago, when they emerged from fascism and the massacres that took place during the two World Wars they unleashed. What I still haven't seen is a clear, unambiguous admission and criticism of the long centuries of slavery, exploitation and atrocities they imposed on the world. I see that they're still subjecting the world to great exploitation, because, in the first place, their development was financed by the Third World. They financed everything with the gold they wrested from their old colonies, plus the sweat and blood of men, women and children that went into the establishment of capitalist society—which, as Marx said, came into the world dripping blood from every pore.

I don't see what they can feel so proud of or how they can possibly consider themselves more democratic than we, the former slaves, the formerly colonized, the formerly exploited; we, the survivors of the peoples they nearly exterminated; we who live in the lands that the big U.S. companies and those of other imperial powers had forcibly seized, just as they took away our countries' mines and other resources. Those who, like us in Cuba, have struggled hard against and freed ourselves from this situation; we who now own our wealth and the fruits of our labor; we who not only enjoy what we have but are willing to share it with other countries; we who are no longer the slaves or the colonized or the illiterate or the sick or the beggars of the past; we who, through a genuine social revolution, have united the people, all the people—workers, farmers, manual and intellectual workers, students, the old and the young, men and women—we have always had the resolute support and the confidence of the vast majority of our fellow citizens, because we have dedicated our lives to serving the people's interests.

It cannot be said of the so highly praised Western governments that they are generally backed by the majority of the people. At times, they have that majority for a few days after the election, but, for the most part, they win with a minority vote. Let's take Reagan, for example. In his first election, only about 50 percent of the voters cast their votes. There were three candidates, and with the votes of less than 30 percent of the total number of U.S. voters, Reagan won the election. Half the people didn't even vote. They don't believe in it. Half of the U.S. voters didn't vote. He may have gotten a few more votes, but when he won his second presidential election, Reagan wasn't supported by much more than 30 percent of the U.S. people with the right to vote.

Others get a majority of 50 percent plus one of the votes, which is far from being the total of the voting population, and, as a rule, that backing lasts for a few months, or maybe one or two years at the most. The people's support immediately starts to decline. It doesn't matter whether it's the Prime Minister of Great Britain, the President of France, the Prime Minister of Italy, the Chancellor of West Germany, the Prime Minister of Spain or the head of state of any other Western country—models that are referred to constantly—after a few months in office, they're backed by a minority of the people.

An election every four years! The people who elected Reagan four years ago had no other say in U.S. policy, simply because Reagan could draw up a military budget, concoct the Star Wars weapons program, produce any kind of missile or other weapon, make complications of all kinds, invade or intervene in the internal affairs of other countries and send Marines anywhere without having to consult anybody. He could cause a world war without consulting with the people who voted for him, just by making one-man decisions.

In this country, one-man decisions are never made on important basic issues. We have a collective leadership that analyzes and discusses all those things. More than 95 percent of the voters take part in our elections. The candidates who run for office at the grass-roots level, to be delegates of the voting districts (in which every 1,500 citizens in the case of the big cities—in some cases, 1,000 or fewer citizens—in rural areas or in special voting districts, depending on the territory—elect a delegate), are nominated by their neighbors. There are around 11,000 voting districts in the country, so there's a delegate for every 910 citizens. Those delegates aren't nominated by the Party; they are nominated directly in the neighborhood assemblies. Each voting district may have from two to eight candidates. If none of them receives at least half the votes plus one, then a runoff election is held between the two who got the most votes in the first round. Then, those delegates are the ones who elect those who exercise state power in Cuba; they elect the members of the municipal bodies of People's Power—who, in turn, elect the members of the provincial bodies of People's Power, who elect the members of the National Assembly. More than half the members of our country's National Assembly are delegates who were elected at the grass-roots level and nominated by the people. For example, I'm not a delegate at the grass-roots level. I'm a member of the National Assembly who was nominated and elected by the delegates of a municipality—Santiago de Cuba, where we began our revolutionary struggle.

The delegates who are elected at the grass-roots level are practically slaves of the people, because they have to work long, hard hours without receiving any pay except the wages they get from their regular jobs. Every six months, they have to report back to their voters on what they've done during that period. Any official in the country may be removed from office at any time by the people who elected him. All this implies having the backing of most of the people. If the Revolution didn't have the support of most of the people, revolutionary power couldn't endure.

Our entire electoral system presupposes the support of most of the people, and our revolutionary concepts are also based on the premise that those who struggle and work for the people, those who carry out the work of the Revolution, will always have the support of the vast majority of the people, because, no matter what is said, nobody is more grateful than the people; nobody appreciates the efforts that are made better than the people. In many countries, people vote for a lot of individuals who don't deserve their votes, but, when there's a revolution that identifies itself with the people, a power that identifies itself with the people —a power that is their power—they always give it their whole-hearted support. As I already explained, any Cuban citizen can truly say "I am the state," because he's the one in charge, he's the one with authority, he is the army, he is the one who has the weapons, who has the power. When you have this kind of a situation, it's impossible for a revolution not to have most of the people behind it, regardless of the mistakes the revolutionaries may make, as long as they correct them quickly and are honest men and women and as long as it's a real revolution.

That's why I say that everything that's being said is nothing but a big lie, because there can be no democracy and no liberty without equality and fraternity. Everything else is fiction; everything else is metaphysical, as are many of the so-called democratic rights. For example, when you speak of freedom of the press, you're really talking about the freedom to own the mass media; a true dissenter from the system won't be allowed to write on the most renowned U.S. newspapers—*The Washington Post, The New York Times* or whatever. Look at the two parties that take turns governing the United States, that run candidates for all the government posts and monopolize them. You won't see a single Communist in their midst, nor will you find him writing for *The Washington Post, The New York Times* or any other important U.S. newspapers or magazines. Nor will you hear him on the radio or see him on coast-to-coast television programs. Those who really dissent from the capitalist system will never have access to those mass media. That freedom exists only for those who agree with the capitalist system. They're the ones who shape public opinion; they create opinion; they even create the people's political convictions and beliefs. Yet they're called democracies.

We're a little more honest. There's no private ownership of the mass media here. The students', workers', farmers', women's and other mass organizations; the Party; and the state—each has its own publication. We develop democracy through our own methods of election to positions of power and, above all, through constant criticism and self-criticism, collective leadership, and constant participation and support by the masses of the people.

As I already explained, I don't appoint any ambassadors here —though I can give my opinion when one is proposed—or even any low-ranking civil servants, because we have a system of promotion to higher posts and responsibilities that's based on capacity and merit. I don't appoint anybody. I can't, I don't want to, and I really don't need to make any one-man decisions to appoint even a low-ranking civil servant.

In other words, I believe—I'm being perfectly frank with you —that our system is a thousand times more democratic than the capitalist, imperialist system of the developed capitalist countries —including the NATO countries, which plunder our world and ruthlessly exploit us. I believe that our system is really much fairer and much more democratic. I'm sorry if I've offended anybody, but you force me to speak clearly and sincerely.

BETTO – That's very good; those are Christian virtues, Commander.

CASTRO – Wonderful, I'm all for them. I fully endorse them.

BETTO – Commander, another question: Does Cuba export revolution?

CASTRO – I've already talked about this many times, but I'll try to summarize what I've said.

It's impossible to export the conditions that foster a revolution. How can you export a $360 billion foreign debt? How can you export a dollar that's overvalued by 30 to 50 percent? How can you export interest spreads that amount to more than $10 billion? How can you export the International Monetary Fund's measures? How can you export protectionism? How can you export dumping? How can you export unequal terms of trade? How can you export the privations and poverty that exist in the Third World countries? Those are the factors that bring about revolutions. They can't be exported—at least, not by a revolutionary country.

I say that the United States', Reagan's and the International Monetary Fund's policies and the present unfair system of international economic relations are basic factors in the "subversion" in Latin America and the rest of the Third World.

I think it would be simplistic, superficial and idealistic to talk about exporting revolution. You can generate ideas, criteria and opinions, and you can spread them throughout the world. Almost all of the ideas that exist in the world have been generated in one place and then spread elsewhere.

You talked about democracies. The concept of bourgeois democracy was born in Europe with the French Encyclopedists and then spread to the rest of the world. They weren't the ideas of the Aztecs, the Incas or the Cuban Siboneyes. Christianity itself wasn't the religion of the Aztecs, the Incas or the Siboneyes, and today it's the religion of many people in this hemisphere. Not even the language we use originated here, and I'd even say it was a pity that the richness of the Indian languages has been almost entirely lost. It would only be fair to say this. Yet, one of the few good things about the colonization was that we were given a language that enables us to communicate from Mexico to Patagonia. There may be a little confusion at times among Brazilians, Cubans, Argentines, Venezuelans, Mexicans and other Latin Americans, but generally speaking, we understand each other perfectly well. But did Spanish, Portuguese and English (that's spoken on the Caribbean islands) originate here? No, they were imported. And the same is true of all the ideas that have spread throughout the world: philosophical ideas, political ideas, religious ideas and literary ideas. And this happens not only with ideas; even our coffee came from another hemisphere, and cacao—which is from this hemisphere—tomatoes, corn and deadly tobacco have been spread throughout the world. The horses, cows and pigs in Latin America—plus other items of food that constitute an important part of our diet—have all come from other continents.

I admit that ideas grow and spread; that is a historical fact that no one can deny. But it is childish—ridiculous—to talk about propagating exotic ideas. I warn you that the reactionaries are terribly afraid of ideas. If this weren't so, there wouldn't be so many anti-Socialist, anti-Marxist, anti-Communist campaigns. You can spread ideas, but you can't export revolution. Crises generate ideas; ideas don't generate crises. It's impossible to export a revolution, and it's childish—ridiculous—to affirm the contrary. That simply shows ignorance.

You can express fellow feeling and solidarity with or political and moral support for a revolution. You can sometimes provide economic assistance—as was the case of Cuba when the Revolution triumphed—but did anybody export the Revolution to Cuba? Nobody! Nobody sent us a single cent to make the Revolution; nobody sent us a single weapon to make it, with the sole exception of a few rifles in the final stages, when the war was practically over, which were sent to us by a democratic Latin American government that had just come to power. We fought the war entirely on our own, which shows that a revolution can only be carried out from within; it can't be imported. We can speak of the growth and spread of revolutionary ideas, but—I repeat—they don't generate crises; rather, they are the result of those crises.

This is what I have stated and continue to state. I have to laugh when I hear somebody talking about exporting a revolution.

BETTO – Commander, I'd like you to comment briefly on your proposals regarding the problem of the foreign debt and on the first part of this book, the one related to your discussions with Joelmir Beting on this problem.

CASTRO – You were present during my talks with Joelmir. We talked a lot, exchanging opinions and points of view.

As you know, I invited him here because I'd been told that Joelmir was one of the most brilliant journalists and economic analysts in Brazil. As a rule, I avoid giving my opinion on problems and processes I'm not well informed about. I'm very careful in that regard. Even when I quote figures, I always use the most conservative ones; when there are several figures, I always take the most modest, the most conservative one; and even the lowest figures prove that we're faced with an incredible catastrophe.

Joelmir was able to come—I don't believe it was difficult for him, after the democratic opening—and I met with him. We exchanged views on these problems. I attach a lot of importance to Brazil, because it carries tremendous weight in this hemisphere due to its production figures, its natural resources, its economic development and a number of other circumstances. As I've explained in other interviews, I wasn't too well informed about the Brazilian situation; from afar, I'd noticed that the Brazilian military hadn't followed the same procedures as the Chileans, Argentines and Uruguayans—all of whom had really bound their countries over hand and foot: they eliminated tariff barriers, implemented the doctrines of the Chicago School and really ruined their countries, in addition to incurring an enormous debt. I noticed that, in contrast, the Brazilian military had tried to protect their industry against foreign competition; what they did was open the door wide to transnational investments, which isn't exactly the same thing. Joelmir explained some ideas that were implemented in the Brazilian development process that gave rise to the debt. For a certain period of time, big investments were made in various areas, such as energy. Some of those investments—70 percent of them, I believe, according to what he told me—were made through state-owned enterprises, but it was the big hydroelectric power projects, the big energy projects, that originated the debt.

He also explained that this was greatly influenced by the syndrome of the hike in oil prices, because of the belief that, in one to ten years, the price of oil would reach $80 a barrel. That led to some theories propounded by the Pentagon and some U.S. specialists that the Brazilian military governments believed. Anyway, he explained the factors that originated those lines of investment —which, in turn, contributed to the debt's mushrooming. He told me that, at one time, as much as 30 percent of the Gross National Product was being invested—around 20 percent from the Gross Domestic Product and the remaining 10 percent evenly distributed between foreign loans and currency issues. He explained the mechanisms they'd used. That's how inflation and all the other problems came about.

We analyzed the international factors that have had an influence on this, particularly the deterioration of export prices, unequal terms of trade, protectionist measures and dumping. We analyzed those problems, not so much as Cubans and Brazilians but as men of the Third World who wanted to identify our problems, to assess our situations and to find possible solutions.

It was very interesting. As you know, I called in a group of the main government leaders, so Joelmir gave a kind of lecture, and we held lengthy discussions on those subjects.

This is a crucial matter for Latin America. I believe that we are faced with a tragic situation; as I told you before, this crisis is worse than the one of the thirties. Though greatly depressed, our exports' prices in the thirties were higher; our countries' purchasing power was greater then than it is now. There were only a fourth as many people then as there are now; the population has quadrupled. Moreover, our accumulated problems have multiplied.

Now, we have the phenomena of enormous cities, such as Mexico City, with 18 million inhabitants and incredible problems. Mexican ecologists have explained them to us. They say, for example, that the city has 2 million unemployed and half a million criminals and that 600–700 people pour into the capital from the countryside every day. They, who are Mexican patriots, are pointing to these problems. They say that the forests have disappeared and that the air has become more and more contaminated—500 tons of chemical particles from the exhausts of cars, buses and factories are spewed into the air every hour. They say that there is much less oxygen at an altitude of 2,200 meters and that, within 14½ years, there will be 34 million inhabitants and no oxygen to breathe in the Mexican capital. Not long ago, they said that 6 million of the city's 18 million inhabitants defecated in their yards. They've even estimated the amount of human excrement there is in Mexico City yards—20,000 tons, according to their analyses—which irritates people's eyes and respiratory mucous membranes when the north and the northeast winds blow over the city in the summer. In short, they've made thorough studies on this. The same problem pops up all over: in São Paulo, Rio de Janeiro, Bogotá and Caracas; in short, those unbearable headaches have continued to develop.

This problem didn't exist in the thirties. Above all, in the thirties we didn't owe $360 billion.

I've explained that, at the time of the Alliance for Progress, Kennedy spoke of a $20 billion investment program over a period of 10 to 15 years in an attempt to prevent social outbreaks and revolutions. Now, however, we have twice as many people and three or four times as many social problems as we had then, and we are handing over enormous sums each year. We'll have to hand over $40 billion each year for the next ten years in interest payments alone, and $10 billion is lost through the flight of capital —$50 billion in all.

On top of this, we're paying for the overvaluation of the dollar. We also have to add what the deterioration of our prices entails—the trend, the phenomenon or law of unequal terms of trade, which hit the $20 billion mark in 1984. Arithmetic, mathematics, shows that this underdeveloped part of the world, with almost 400 million inhabitants and so many accumulated problems, is handing over $70 billion to the wealthy industrialized countries every year, while its investment and credit income is only around $10 billion. Thus, our net loss is equal to $60 billion a year.

This is totally untenable: materially, politically and morally untenable. We say—and have mathematically demonstrated—that the debt is unpayable; it cannot be paid; it is absolutely unpayable. We say that it is economically, politically and morally impossible to pay it. And, therefore, I advocate the total cancellation of the debt—both capital and interest.

I've also analyzed the historical causes of the debt and consider the moral factor to be very important as well, because everything that has been done to the Third World countries for centuries has been morally untenable. Our countries have been and continue to be plundered. Hundreds of millions of people have died working in the mines here to finance the development of the industrialized world—the same world that is robbing us now—and what it has stolen from us far surpasses the debt.

There's also a moral aspect. But, leaving the moral aspect aside and just considering the economic aspect, paying the debt is mathematically impossible. Politically speaking, it is just as impossible, because it would mean having the Army and the police fire on the people, kill the people. Nobody can tell how much bloodshed the debt would cost us. I think it is morally indefensible to kill the people, to shed the people's blood, to pay the debt to the big exploiters.

How were these debts contracted? Whom did they benefit? A large part of this money once again fled to the industrialized countries or was invested in weapons or squandered or embezzled or stolen, though I admit that some of it was used for development, for infrastructure projects. That's my position on this situation.

Therefore, I say, Now is the time to struggle, not only to have the debt canceled but also to solve the problems that gave rise to the debt and to wipe out the unfair system of international economic relations—unequal terms of trade, protectionism, dumping, interest spreads and monetary manipulation, all that—with which all Latin American politicans, statesmen and economists are so familiar. Therefore, now is the time to struggle to implement the New International Economic Order, which the United Nations adopted practically unanimously ten years ago. That is the position I'm defending.

Mathematics shows that it can't be paid. I've talked with a lot of people and have said it's unpayable. I haven't met anybody who isn't convinced of that.

How can this be approached? Some people have suggested a formula consisting of a ten-year moratorium, interest included. The more or less diplomatic, more or less pleasant, more or less elegant terms in which this is couched aren't the main point. I think that, if a ten-year moratorium that included the interest were really obtained, it would, in practice, be tantamount to the cancellation of the debt because the figure that would then be amassed would be even more astronomical, more unpayable. Thus, the form the solution will take has yet to be defined.

I'm stating the need for unity. This is very important. We've been speaking about class struggle and a whole series of problems. I've posed the need for unity, both inside these countries and in their relations with one another, to fight this battle. Of course, this is as a general principle; you'd have to see how it could be applied in each specific case. I think it would be impossible to promote domestic unity in Chile, so I'm leaving Chile out. There are some countries that are out of it, where it's impossible to achieve domestic unity, but I think that, in those cases, the opposition parties, the various forces, can struggle to achieve a goal of the cancellation— that is, the annulment—of the debt.

I think that, even if the debt is canceled, Pinochet's regime can't be saved. It's too isolated; too much hatred has been built up against it; and it has too great a share of the responsibility for this problem for it to be saved. And it will be impossible—absolutely impossible—in the democratic process that will ensue, for the people of Chile to pay the enormous debt that Pinochet has run up.

I'm postulating domestic unity as a prerequisite for waging this battle; it seems to me that this is the basic question. This also applies to unity among the Latin American countries and unity among the Third World countries, because all of them have been seriously hit by the same problem.

We are proposing formulas for unity: domestic unity in order to have the strength required to wage the battle, unity in order to present economic problems in correct terms, and unity to propose sacrifices for each country's development and to create the necessary wealth for solving our countries' abysmal social problems. We are proposing sacrifices for development, not underdevelopment; sacrifices so investments can be made inside the country, not sterile sacrifices to try to pay the unpayable debt. We are proposing unity among all the Latin American and other Third World countries for waging the struggle to cancel the foreign debt and implement the New International Economic Order approved by the United Nations, without which the cancellation of the debt would bring some respite but wouldn't solve the basic cause of the problem.

I'm not going to go into a full explanation of all this. You should refer to the materials that have already been published. Basically, what we are proposing is domestic unity and unity among the Latin American countries to confront this problem, to achieve the cancellation of the debt or the equivalent of the cancellation of the debt, to struggle to implement the New International Economic Order and to create the conditions for our countries' development. We aren't proposing that the creditor banks or the international financial system go bankrupt. An essential aspect of our thesis is that the creditor states, the rich and powerful creditor states, assume responsibility for the debt to their own banks, allocating 12 percent of their military spending—which now amounts to $1 trillion a year—for this purpose. With just 12 percent, they could tackle the problem of the debt. I think that, if we manage to win the battle—and we have to win it, since it's a matter of survival—and if we establish the New International Economic Order, then military spending might have to be cut by 30 percent to solve the problem of the debt and the New International Economic Order. The rich and powerful states would still have around $700 billion to spend on weapons—which, unfortunately, is enough to wipe out the Earth's population several times over.

Now, then, we are proposing that the economic problems be solved in this way, but this doesn't mean that the taxpayers in the creditor states would have to pay more; it doesn't mean that bank depositors in those countries would lose their money. Moreover, I think that this will help the world to come out of the economic crisis, for, if the Third World had an additional $300 billion purchasing power each year as a result of the cancellation of the foreign debt and the establishment of a system of fair international economic relations, this would increase employment opportunities in the industrialized countries. The industrialized countries' current problem isn't, essentially, a financial one; it's unemployment. A formula of this kind would increase the number of jobs—that is, it would reduce the number of the unemployed, increase the developed capitalist countries' industrial capacity, increase the exporters' profits and increase the export industries' profits. It would even benefit industries that produce for the domestic market, since it would create more jobs and promote consumption. This would even increase the profits that are derived from investments abroad. The banks wouldn't go under, and the world financial system wouldn't go bankrupt.

I've examined this problem from every angle. I've figured it this way and that, and I don't see any other solution. If we don't implement this solution, the economic crisis will continue to worsen; the industrialized world won't emerge from its crisis; and there will be uncontrollable social explosions in Latin America which, in one way or another, will assume a revolutionary character. That is, there will be social upheavals; the processes of democratic opening in Argentina, Uruguay, Brazil and other countries will be wiped out; and these convulsions will have unforeseeable consequences. But the trend will be of revolutionary social upheavals by civilians, the military or both, since this is a problem that has to be solved, one way or another. Somebody has to help deliver the baby in this situation, or there will be extremely painful, tragic problems. Somebody—either the civilians or the military, or the civilians *and* the military—must assist at this inevitable delivery, for it isn't a matter of interpretation or of finding a solution through technical formulas. It's a matter of applying real remedies that call for a course of action and a solution. That's what we've been proposing.

Somebody asked me what, as a revolutionary, I'd rather have, I said, "I'd rather have an orderly way out of this crisis, a delivery that is the least traumatic possible. I'd rather have this chain reaction—in a situation which brings us closer and closer to the critical mass—occur as a controlled reaction in a nuclear reactor, not as an uncontrollable explosion." I've also said, "Even more important than one, two, three, four or five revolutions, at this point, is to come out of this crisis, to establish the New International Economic Order and to create the conditions for development. This would provide us, in the future, with the resources for solving our social problems and with independence for carrying out the short- and medium-term social changes that are both essential and inevitable.

I have said that each country must make its own decisions. The united stand I'm proposing doesn't include domestic measures. We have no intention of dictating the domestic measures that should be taken to solve this crisis; that would be meddling. What it does is up to each country; each one must determine what domestic measures it will take. But, in essence, what we propound is unity. This is just the opposite of what could be considered subversion; it is the Reagan Administration in the United States— with its selfish, absurd policy—and the International Monetary Fund—with the plunder to which we are being subjected—that are rapidly promoting subversion. What they are doing is going to set off a chain reaction and a possible disorderly explosion. I am stating the advisability of an orderly chain reaction. That's what I'm proposing. I think this is the key problem of our time, and I don't think anybody is justified in calling himself a politician—in any sense of the word—if he doesn't have a clear understanding of this situation; if he doesn't take these facts into account; and if he isn't aware that they must, inevitably, be faced.

We are serene. Our position is the result of reflection; it is a conscious, constructive position. Now, we will simply await events. The leaders must decide. If they take the most intelligent, wisest course, progress can be made—which is what I'd rather have. If they don't do this, there will be upheavals with unforeseeable consequences. The problem will be solved one way or another, but nobody can assess what the consequences of the uncontrolled social upheavals in Latin American societies will be.

Do you have any other questions?

BETTO – Commander, I've taken up a lot of your time, but, with your permission, I'd like to ask you two more questions. First, would the Cuban government like to reestablish relations with the Brazilian government?

CASTRO – Well, we weren't the ones who broke off the relations between Cuba and Brazil. That happened as soon as the military coup took place. We are aware that, in spite of our different political, social and economic systems, Brazil and Cuba, like many other Third World countries, have many shared interests. Most Latin American countries' lack of relations with Cuba has been dictated by U.S. policy, influence and pressure. In one way or another, the United States forced all of the Latin American countries except Mexico to break off relations with us.

We can feel proud that we have withstood that test and that, practically alone and isolated in this hemisphere, we have held out. I think that our people have set a magnificent example of unity, firmness and courage. We have survived, have advanced and have developed and continue to develop on solid social and economic bases—which is more than some of the other Latin American countries can say.

In our relations with the other Socialist countries, we have attained what could be described as the New International Economic Order. In effect, we are proposing that the same formula be applied to the Third World countries in their relations with the industrialized countries: long-term credits; low interest rates; refinancing of the debt for 10, 15 or 20 years without interest; and fair prices for our products—conditions that have enabled us to attain our social and economic achievements.

You mentioned some of these conditions, and we've referred to a few of them in this interview. Undoubtedly, our country ranks first in health care in the Third World and even surpasses many industrialized countries. We also rank first in education among the underdeveloped countries and outrank many industrialized countries, including the United States. The United States has 26 million illiterates and about 47 million semi-illiterates—that is, people with poor reading and writing skills. The United States is in forty-eighth place in terms of education, and Cuba is well above that level. In health care, we are more or less the same. Our life expectancy equals that of the United States, and its infant mortality rate is three points better than ours: in Cuba, the rate is 15 out of every 1,000 live births; in the United States, it's 12. We are sure to equal and surpass it, even though its resources, productivity and gross national product are much higher than ours.

We have a great deal in common with the other Third World

countries, including Brazil. As a rule, the Latin American governments are used to being submissive, to obeying U.S. orders, but many Asian and African countries with social regimes that are very different from ours have excellent relations with Cuba. For example, Indonesia has normal relations with Cuba, and so does Pakistan, yet their political systems and ideologies are quite different from ours. The difference in social and political systems between Brazil and Cuba wouldn't hinder our relations. Our shared interests far outweigh our differences.

I believe that Brazil's future lies basically in strengthening its relations with the rest of the Third World. I think that its lack of relations with and policy of isolation regarding Cuba go counter to Brazil's national interests, because, even though our country doesn't have Brazil's size and resources, it does have a lot of experience in many fields and participates actively on the international scene in the struggle to promote the Third World's interests. These factors shouldn't be underestimated.

I'm not saying we supported the former Brazilian government; we couldn't. But that wasn't an insurmountable obstacle to having relations. Now there is a democratic opening, and we have a greater shared interest, for we're faced with an enormous crisis and must unite to find a way out. Brazil can count on our solidarity in its efforts to overcome its difficulties. I think that Brazil needs to unite with the rest of Latin America, and the rest of Latin America needs to have Brazil join in this struggle. Brazil owes more than $100 billion, and this debt is unpayable. No matter what is said or claimed, it's unpayable. Brazil would have to pay $12 billion a year just for interest. If you counted Brazil's foreign debt dollar by dollar, at a second per dollar, it would take you around 3,343 years to count it, and 3,858 years to count the interest payments for just ten years. If 100 people counted that same amount, working 24 hours a day, it would take them 38½ years. Brazil, the biggest country in Latin America and one of the largest in the world, with its 8,512,000 square kilometers, owes $12,218 per square kilometer, or $122.18 per hectare. In ten years it has to pay $14,098 per square kilometer, or $140.98 per hectare, just for interest. Even if the interest rates were lowered, even if the dollar were to be devaluated somewhat, a developing country such as Brazil wouldn't be able to hold up under such a burden, just as the rest of Latin America can't pay the $260 billion that is its share of the debt. Brazil's balance of trade will be less this year than it was last year; it's estimated that its trade surplus, which was $12 billion in 1984, will drop to less than $10 billion this year. The same thing is true of Mexico and Argentina, the Latin American countries with the next largest debts, after Brazil.

You can't ask the people to make enormous sacrifices just to pay interest. Tancredo clearly and courageously stated that he wasn't willing to sacrifice the people to pay the debt, nor was he willing to sacrifice development or to adopt a recessive policy. Everybody has stated this: the President of Uruguay, the President of Argentina and also the President of Brazil. I can clearly see— with mathematical clarity, for, in this, I'm resorting to mathematics—that we need a formula, and I think that we're proposing the most rational, coherent, consistent, fair and moral formula, which is to cancel the Third World countries' debts altogether.

How will this cancellation begin? Possibly by not paying a year's interest or by asking for a loan to pay it and then extending this period to two years and then to three, five and ten, through long and agonizing negotiations. The creditors may agree to that, or the debtors may impose it on them. It may come about through a consensus of Latin American countries, or, what's more probable, one country or a group of countries, out of desperation, may decide unilaterally to suspend the payment of the debt, and the rest may follow suit.

Just canceling the debt wouldn't solve the Third World's problems, however. Under the present circumstances, in which we aren't asking for money but are giving it, in which we put our hands out not to request anything but to take money out of our pockets and hand it over to the industrialized countries, we are in a position to take the initiative. We have a pressing need to unite. I think that the correct strategy is to unite; take the initiative; and try to solve not only the debt but also the problems of protectionism, dumping and unequal terms of trade—in short, demand the establishment of the New International Economic Order, which has already been approved by the United Nations. This is a unique opportunity in history. The political leaders who fail to see this will have to answer to history for it. I hope they will accept their responsibility, understand the problem, state it in correct terms, and struggle for the cancellation of the debt and the implementation of the New International Economic Order. We must choose concrete, realistic and definitive solutions—not take the path of agony. We must choose a clear, intelligent, effective solution—not head toward Calvary.

I think we've been struggling uphill for long enough. We have suffered not only the torment of Calvary but also that of Sisyphus, who had to keep pushing a boulder up a hill, and every time he was about to reach the top, it would roll back down and he'd have to start all over again. Our situation is worse than Calvary, because Calvary was climbed quickly; we've been climbing our hill for a long time, and we keep on having to start over. Calvary is preferable to Sisyphus' torment, and, if we've had our Calvary, we should also have a resurrection.

What we want is to find a real solution for the problem, but what will happen is that imperialism and the industrialized capitalist countries will try to prevent the implementation of these solutions and divide the people; they will give a little aid here and there so that each will remain with his own Calvary—and not even a Calvary, but with the agonizing torture of pushing the boulder up a never-ending hill. But, one day, the peoples are going to demand, "How much longer do we have to put up with these conditions?" and then they'll find solutions. I repeat: I prefer an orderly solution; internal and external unity; and a real, definitive solution for the problems of dependence and underdevelopment.

That's why I believe that Brazil and Cuba have some important interests in common. We don't insist on diplomatic relations. We say the same thing to Brazilians that we say to Uruguayans and others: "When it comes to formal relations, do whatever suits your immediate economic interests." We know that, right now, all of you are engaged in negotiating and rescheduling your debts, and the United States—which is the main creditor—gets frantic at the idea of such relations. We don't want anybody to have any difficulties on account of Cuba. Cuba doesn't have that kind of problem, and the United States has run out of ways to make things more difficult for us. We can take our time and wait until those countries decide that the right time has come for renewing relations. I think that this is the best way to show our country's sincere and selfless policy. It won't do us any harm to wait. Each country should handle the issue of its relations with Cuba in the way that best suits its democratic process and the solution of its most pressing economic problems. That is our position.

BETTO – Thank you, Commander.

My last question is related to Brazil's young people. Brazil has 133 million inhabitants, and around 80 million of them are under 25. Many of these young people greatly admire two of your comrades: Camilo Cienfuegos and Ernesto ("Che") Guevara. I'd like to hear your personal impressions of those revolutionaries.

CASTRO – It isn't easy to do this in just a few words, but Che had tremendous personal and political integrity, tremendous moral integrity.

BETTO – How old were you when you met him?

CASTRO – I met Che after I was released from prison and went to Mexico; that was in 1955. He'd already contacted some of our comrades there. He'd come from Guatemala, where he'd witnessed the intervention by the CIA and the United States, the overthrow of Arbenz and the crimes that were committed there. I don't know whether it was through an embassy or not, but somehow he managed to leave. He'd been graduated as a doctor not long before that, and he'd left Argentina a few times to tour Bolivia and some other countries. An Argentine comrade who accompanied him now lives in Cuba. His name is Granado. He's a scientific researcher and works here in Cuba. He accompanied Che on one of the tours. They went as far as the Amazon and were at a hospital for lepers. The two of them, who'd both been graduated as doctors, were something like missionaries.

BETTO – Was he younger than you?

CASTRO – I think so—perhaps two years younger. I think he was born in 1928.

He'd been graduated as a doctor, and he studied Marxism-Leninism on his own. He liked to learn; he had convictions. Life, his experience, the things he saw everywhere, taught him step by step. When I met Che, he was already a true revolutionary. Moreover, he was a man of outstanding talent and great intelligence, with a great capacity for theorizing. It is a great tragedy that his untimely death kept him from putting his revolutionary thinking down in writing. He was a very good writer. His style was realistic and expressive—like Hemingway's. He was sparing of words, but the ones he used were the precise, exact ones. In addition, he had exceptional human qualities: comradeship, selflessness, altruism and personal courage. Of course, I didn't know this when I first met him. I liked the Argentine—he was called "Che" because he was from Argentina—who talked about what had happened in Guatemala. As he himself said, we talked for a short time and quickly agreed that he should join our expedition.

BETTO – Did you call him "Che," or did he call himself that?

CASTRO – The Cubans there called him "Che." If he'd been any other Argentine, they'd have called him the same, since that's what Argentines usually call each other. What happened is that Che's reputation and prestige grew so much that the nickname became his. That's what his comrades called him, and that's the name I knew him by.

He was a doctor, and that was the capacity in which he came on our expedition. He didn't come as a soldier. Of course, he was trained in guerrilla warfare. He was disciplined, and he was a very good shot. He liked to shoot, and he also liked sports. Almost every week, he tried to climb Popocatepetl; he never made it, but he always kept trying. He suffered from asthma. His physical efforts and feats deserve special credit because he suffered from asthma.

BETTO – Was he as good a cook as you are?

CASTRO – Well, I think I'm a better cook. I'm not going to say I'm a better revolutionary, but I'm definitely a better cook than Che was.

BETTO – In Mexico, he used to prepare good meat dishes.

CASTRO – He had a knack for Argentine roasts, but you can only do them in the middle of the countryside. In the Mexican prisons we were in because of our revolutionary activities, we ate rice, dry beans and spaghetti in various forms, and they were my affair. I was quite an expert cook, though he knew a little about it. I have to defend my professional prestige, as you'd defend yours, or as your mother would defend hers—she's a marvelous cook.

Well, anyway, Che began to stand out because of his human and intellectual characteristics—and, later, during the war, for his military characteristics as well: his leadership ability and courage. Sometimes he was so daring that I had to hold him back. I had to curtail some of the operations he planned, and I even had to forbid some of them. When the fighting started, he threw himself wholeheartedly into combat. Besides, he was persevering and tenacious. Since I was aware of his worth and capacity, I did what I'd done with other cadres: as they became experienced, I looked for new cadres for tactical missions and reserved the boldest ones for strategic operations—that is, sometimes I assigned outstanding new fighters to simple though dangerous operations so they would acquire experience commanding small units and saved the more experienced ones for strategic missions.

In addition, Che had great moral integrity. He proved to be a man of profound ideas, an untiring worker, rigorous and methodical in the fulfillment of his duties. Above all, he set an example for all. He was first in everything; he observed all the rules he laid down; and he had great prestige and great influence among his comrades. He was one of the greatest figures of his generation in Latin America, and nobody can tell how much he would have accomplished if he'd survived.

In Mexico, after he joined our Movement, he made me promise him that, after the triumph of the Revolution in Cuba, I would allow him to return to fight for his homeland or for Latin America. He remained in Cuba for several years, carrying out important responsibilities, but he always had that in mind. And, when the time came, I kept my word. I didn't hold him back or hamper his return; rather, I helped him do what he believed was his duty. At the time, I didn't stop to think if my doing so could harm me. I faithfully kept the promise I'd made, and, when he said, "I want to go on a revolutionary mission now," I said, "All right, I'll keep my promise."

Everything was done in great accord. The things that were said about alleged discrepancies with the Cuban Revolution were infamous calumnies. He had his own personality and criteria. We used to argue fraternally on various topics, but there was always harmony, communication, complete unity on everything and excellent relations, because he also had a great sense of discipline.

For a long time after he left, rumors circulated to the effect that there had been problems between us and that he'd disappeared. In fact, Che was in Africa, carrying out an internationalist mission, fighting together with a group of Cuban internationalists and Lumumba's followers (after the death of that prestigious African leader) in the former Belgian Congo, later known as Zaire. Che spent several months there. He tried to help as much as possible, because he felt great solidarity for the African countries, and he acquired more experience there for his future struggles. After that internationalist mission, while waiting for the minimum conditions to be created in South America, he spent some time in Tanzania and then returned to Cuba.

When he left for the Congo, he wrote me the farewell letter that everyone knows. For months, I didn't want to make it public, for the simple reason that Che had to leave Africa. In fact, he did leave Africa; returned to Cuba; stayed here for a while; asked that a group of volunteers from the Sierra Maestra—whom I authorized to accompany him—be given rigorous training, along with him; and then left for South America. He intended to fight not only in Bolivia but also in other countries, including his own. That's why he chose that place. Of course, many insidious campaigns were launched against Cuba during that period, but I held out and didn't publish the letter; I published it only when I was sure that Che had arrived in the area he'd chosen in Bolivia. That was when I published it. A slander campaign was launched about that.

In short, I'd say that, if Che had been a Catholic, if Che had belonged to the Church, he would probably have been made a saint, for he had all the virtues.

You also spoke of another comrade—Camilo. Camilo too was a man of the people. He was a typical Cuban—intelligent, enthusiastic and courageous—who started on his revolutionary mission while still very young. He'd made contact with the university students in the early years of the struggle against Batista. He'd participated in some demonstrations and been wounded. When I was in Mexico, organizing the expedition, he got in contact with our Movement, joined us and came over as a soldier. He was one of the survivors and was an outstanding fighter because of his bravery and initiative. Even in our first victorious battle, on January 17, 1957—when, with 22 men, we attacked a combined unit of soldiers and sailors who resisted until all were killed or wounded— Camilo was outstanding. Also on that occasion, we gave our wounded adversaries our medicine; we looked after them and gave them medical attention.

Camilo began to show his qualities as a great soldier in that first battle. His character was different from Che's; he was always in the best of humors, more informal, more *criollo* and less intellectual than Che; he was a man of action. He was very intelligent, very politically minded, and, though less rigorously ascetic than

Che, he also set an example. As an officer, he was outstanding for his initiative, capacity and courage in many battles. In the final stage of the war, I assigned him a strategic mission: the invasion of Las Villas Province.

Camilo also had charisma. If you look at Camilo's picture, you'd see that his bearded face is similar to those of the Apostles. At the same time, he was a typical Cuban—very communicative and brave. I wouldn't say that he was a daredevil. He was capable of attempting any feat and was very daring, but he wasn't a daredevil. Che may have been more aware of the possibility of death; he had a kind of fatalism. Camilo didn't feel that way; he would do anything, no matter how audacious and risky, but he didn't give the enemy a chance. He was an excellent guerrilla, a born guerrilla. He was the first to leave the Sierra Maestra for the plains with a small guerrilla troop.

In the first few months after the triumph of the Revolution, Camilo did what we all did: go in any car, plane or helicopter without taking any security measures. Camilo had flown with me to Camagüey just after Hubert Matos' act of treason. (Hubert Matos had started to connive with imperialism; he let the reactionary classes confuse him and tried to promote a counterrevolutionary conspiracy—which we put down with the people, without firing a single shot.) Camilo went with me. After we got to Camagüey, I walked unarmed toward the garrison, followed by the entire population to disarm the conspirators. They were demoralized, and I was sure they wouldn't shoot, but Camilo didn't want me to take any risks, so, without saying anything to me, he went ahead with his bodyguard, entered the regiment's garrison—Hubert Matos was there—disarmed the officers and took command. He was already there when I arrived.

Camilo was the head of the Army. As a result of the situation created by Hubert Matos' treason, he had to make another trip to Camagüey later on. He started flying back to Havana in a small plane in the evening. It was autumn, a very stormy season, and nobody should have been flying—even in better airplanes—in weather like that.

BETTO – What year was it?

CASTRO – That was in October 1959, the first year of the Revolution.

BETTO – How old was he?

CASTRO – He was younger than I. He was 27 when he died.

Now, we have executive planes equipped with radar. Every flight is efficiently organized, and security measures are taken. The pilots know where the cumulus clouds are. Every executive flight is tracked from the ground. Camilo was flying back in a small plane over the northern part of the island in the evening. The next day, we learned that his plane had taken off but hadn't arrived. All of us had airplane or helicopter accidents in the early years of the Revolution. I had some accidents, and so did Raúl and several other leaders. At that time, we didn't have the organization or security measures we now have for all such flights. The news that Camilo was missing didn't come in until the next day. This caused all of us and the entire population great distress, pain and sorrow. I myself flew over the cays around Cuba; we searched for him by air, sea and land. He never appeared. This was used as a pretext for infamous slander and intrigues against the Revolution. It was said that we'd murdered Camilo because of rivalries and envy. The people know the truth. Nobody has ever cheated the people; the people know all of us and also know about our ethics, rules, lives and principles.

I told you what Che would probably have become if he'd belonged to the Church. With regard to Camilo, I can tell you what I said when we learned of his death. I spoke of his humble origins and his outstanding activities during his short life as a revolutionary and said that he was an example of the enormous, unlimited possibilities of the people. In a message of encouragement and comfort to the people, I said, "There are many Camilos in the people." I think that the history of this Revolution and the past 26 years have shown that this is so. I am ever more convinced that there are many Camilos in the people, just as I think that there are many Ches in the Argentine people—and that there are tens of thousands, maybe hundreds of thousands, of men like Camilo and Che in Latin America as a whole.

Our 82-man expedition arrived in Cuba on December 2, 1956. After the first, hard setbacks, around 15 men regrouped, and those 14, 15 or 16 men included outstanding leaders. Camilo and Che were among them. Where 100 or 1,000 men join together to advance a noble, correct idea, you can be sure that there will be many Camilos and many Ches.

BETTO – Before concluding this interview, I would like to thank you for your tremendous generosity in sparing me so much of your precious time, especially in view of all the work you have. In addition, I'd like to express a personal opinion: I'm convinced that your words, opinions, ideas and experience will encourage believers in their political participation and give them strength in their lives as Christians.

Thank you, Commander.

CASTRO – Thank *you*.

The sun was already up when we finished our long interview. The knowledge that I had unusual material of great international and historic interest in my hands made me feel very insignificant. I was swept by a wave of fraternal admiration for Fidel and offered up a silent prayer of thanks to the Almighty Father.

Main Topics Discussed by Commander in Chief Fidel Castro in His Talks with Frei Betto